The ANDERSONVILLE Diary & Memoirs of CHARLES HOPKINS

1st New Jersey Infantry

EDITED BY
WILLIAM B. STYPLE
AND JOHN J. FITZPATRICK

FOREWORD BY ROGER LONG

*Best Regards,
Will B. Styple*

Published By
Belle Grove Publishing Co.
Kearny, New Jersey

ISBN 0-9622053-0-3

Library of Congress
Catalog Card Number 89-112980

Copyright © 1988 by Belle Grove Publishing Co., P.O. Box 483 Kearny, New Jersey 07032.
All Rights Reserved. No part of this book may be reproduced in any form or by any electronic or mechanical means including information storage and retrieval systems without permission in writing from the publisher. Except by a reviewer who may quote brief passages in a review. Printed in the United States of America.

Portions of this book have appeared in *American Heritage*.

Second Edition

TABLE OF CONTENTS

ACKNOWLEDGEMENTS 11

FOREWORD 13

INTRODUCTION 17

PREFACE 23

CHAPTER ONE 28
TO WAR!

CHAPTER TWO 51
INTO THE WILDERNESS

CHAPTER THREE 67
THE HELL OF HELLS

CHAPTER FOUR 116
ESCAPE

CHAPTER FIVE 143
FLORENCE PRISON

CHAPTER SIX 180
THE POST-WAR YEARS

Dedicated to all the descendants of Charles F. Hopkins.

ACKNOWLEDGEMENTS

This book is the result of the love and dedication of a few 20th Century Americans who work to preserve the memory of our 19th Century forefathers. We feel that we are performing a duty for our descendants, the Americans of the 21st Century. We are passing the torch of American Civil War history to the next generation.

The primary sources for this book were the descendants of Corporal Charles Hopkins; Thomas Hopkins of Boonton, N.J., Gerald Hopkins of Saddle River, N.J., and Betty Ann Voswinkle of East Hanover, N.J. These grandchildren of a great Civil War hero must feel a sense of satisfaction that their grandfather's memoirs, which they carefully preserved, are finally being published.

Grateful thanks go to my close friend and comrade John J. Fitzpatrick whose skill in transcribing the diary made my job much easier. Also, it was Jack Fitzpatrick who traveled to Andersonville, Georgia to photograph several landmarks in the National Cemetery. It was Mr. Fitzpatrick's dedicated perseverance that pushed me to finish this book.

I am forever grateful to the many friends who lent their support to me along the way. Thank you Mrs. Henry C. deRham for your reminiscences of Charles Hopkins. Sincere thanks to my friends: Steve and Edna Berger, Larry and Carol Sangee, Bill and Karen Mapes, John and Kathleen Cimino, Jim Madden, John Carroll, Bill Dekker, Buddy Kruk, Brian Pohanka, John Kuhl, Peggy Sheppard, Jim Callahan, Howard Wiseman, Rob Stefans, Gerry Mason, Ron and Rick Veen, Bob and Dennis Meehan and especially my comrades in Company E, 15th New Jersey Volunteer Infantry, with all their interest in the American Civil War.

I must not forget my brothers; Buddy, Ken and Rob Styple for their assistance. Special thanks to Miss Nancy Blazejewski for her endless encouragement and enthusiasm which kept me going when the trials of this endeavor seemed to get the best of me.

I owe a debt of gratitude to Roger Long for writing the foreword to this book. Along with his friendly advice and help, Roger was an invaluable source of Andersonville knowledge. Thank you Roger.

Final tribute goes to the staff of Belle Grove Publishing Company, especially Miss Diana Stefan and Miss Denise Kraus for all their efforts in preparing this book and supporting this dream.

William B. Styple
Kearny, New Jersey
August 1988

FOREWORD

Andersonville!

Before the Civil War, Andersonville was a tiny, insignificant village in southwest Georgia, but when the struggle ended, the word was synonymous with terror and would become a political "bloody shirt" for decades. Near this hamlet Confederates hastily built a stockade prison in early 1864, when raids were feared on Libby and Belle Isle prisons in Richmond. Shortly, thousands of Federal prisoners were hauled to the new pen, a rectangle of clay surrounded by tall pine logs. With no prisoners being exchanged and battle action increased, the new prison was soon crammed and had to be expanded. And still prisoners poured in, despite the fact there was scarcely room to move, filthy water and little food. Eventually 50,000 men would trudge through those gates of doom. 13,000 would die--of starvation, disease, suicide, murder--in a word, of neglect.

Days after the war ended, Henry Wirz, the commandant, was arrested, tried for war crimes, and hanged. The man most responsible for Andersonville, General John H. Winder, in charge of Confederate prisons, escaped the noose by dying of natural causes. Survivors of the terror crept home, living skeletons, some without limbs, all forever scarred. A few would write memoirs and publish diaries. Books by Andersonville prisoners sold well in coming years. What they said, plus the testimony at the Wirz trial, outraged Northerners. Where was this chivalry so loudly proclaimed for the glorious Confederacy? Who were these self-styled Lochinvars and Percivals?

Placing blame for Andersonville has been cause for debate since the Civil War. Northerners blamed Wirz, certainly, and Winder, definitely, but also President Jefferson Davis and the entire Confederate hierarchy. The accusations became vicious and did not quickly abate. Stung by the vitriol, Southerners struck back, claiming gross irregularities in the Wirz trial (which there were); claiming Andersonville was the fault of Federals who declined to exchange prisoners (which they did); claiming the South lacked the wherewithal (which to some degree it did). But the defense most employed was a tu quoque fallacy, i.e., Northern prisons were just as bad as Andersonville--and worse. Statistics were presented to prove the point.

No rational person denies that Andersonville was a disgusting place or that 13,000 died there. Photographs and rows of grave stones are mute but undeniable evidence. Few deny the site was a poor choice for a prison, with only a walk-over stream to supply drinking water and carry out sewage for 30,000 men at one time. The Andersonville debate focuses on the following:

(A) Shelter. There was none, except "shebangs" erected by prisoners and holes men crawled into, to escape storms and the scorching sun. Photographs taken while the prison was full show ample trees in the background, trees that could have become barracks. Indeed, there was wood for building a second stockade around the first and for other projects not beneficial to prisoners. One conclusion is that lack of shelter was intentional on the part of Wirz or Winder or the Confederate government.

(B) Food. How could men starve in a location untouched by battle, amid fields of plenty? A logical conclusion is that food was withheld intentionally. When General Sherman's foragers rampaged across Georgia in late 1864, they found smokehouses and corncribs full. A plantation owner very near Andersonville testified that 1864 was a bountiful year in agriculture. Georgians were not starving. The blockade of Southern ports cannot be blamed for a shortage of bacon, yams and corn. Georgia's principle industry was agriculture, and there was no need to import food. Georgia exported food. Andersonville apologists contend that prisoners ate exactly the same food as guards. This is patently absurd, unless guards had a perverse craving for rancid pork, wormy beans and cornmeal with the cob ground in with the grain.

(C) Medicine. The prison hospital was a filthy place to die, crawling with maggots, putrid with sewage, stifling, without medicine, without comfort, without water. True, the problems were overwhelming: too many patients and too few doctors. Granted, medicine was scarce because of the blockade. But the lack of cleanliness and simple human decency were inexcusable, as Confederate inspectors pointed out to Richmond, time and again, to no avail.

(D) Exchange. Confederates contended (and some scholars still contend) that conditions at Andersonville should be blamed on General Grant or Secretary of War Stanton for refusing to exchange prisoners in 1864. Many prisoners also cursed their own government for this policy, with some justification. But this does not explain why Confederates polluted the only stream before it entered the prison. Nor does it explain the lack of shelter. Or lack of food. Or the hospital.

(E) Elmira. Near this upstate New York town was a prison for Confederates, with a death rate comparable with Andersonville. Elmira was (and is) used to deflect accusations leveled at those responsible for Andersonville. Elmira was certainly horrible, and conditions there were likewise inexcusable. But many deaths at Elmira can be attributed to the ill health of Confederates when they arrived. It must be admitted, however, that Federals did exact punishment at Elmira and elsewhere, because of reported conditions at Southern prisons, especially Andersonville. In 1864 testimony was taken and widely published about starvation and cruelty in Confederate prisons. As a result, rations were cut in Federal prisons, along with heating fuel, blanket supplies, etc. The hope, perhaps, was that Confederate authorities would ameliorate conditions for Federals held prisoner in the South. But the effect, predictably, was the opposite. Retribution begot retribution. No defense can be offered for the retaliation at Elmira, Camp Chase, Fort Delaware, Johnson's Island, etc.--but this still does not excuse the crimes of Andersonville.

Even today it is impossible to remain impartial about Andersonville. One either believes it was an intentionally constructed hell on earth with Henry Wirz as the devil--or one believes that Federals were culpable and that Wirz was truly a martyr to a Lost Cause, deserving of the monument to him in the village of Andersonville and worthy of the medal struck for him, bearing the word HONOR upon it. There is apparently no in-between--after 125 years. Readers who come upon Andersonville for the first time will have to decide for themselves. No honest judgment can be made from one book or one visit to the haunted earth of Andersonville.

At Andersonville today are monuments to prisoners (and of course to Wirz), row upon row of graves, Providence Spring, mounds where forts bristled with guns, and the acreage of the prison site, marked neatly with stakes. It is quiet, but it is not peaceful. If you have read the diaries and memoirs, there is an eerie shiver to the soil where so many thousands suffered and died. Perhaps it is the imagination. Perhaps it is the same at Elmira and Johnson's Island.

The war is long over and most wounds have healed. It has taken an inordinate time for the most vicious recriminations to fade. The Civil War is now a pleasant hobby for reenactors, historians and casual tourists. So why bring out a new diary and memoir of Andersonville, more accusations tucked away these many years? Why pick at healed wounds and make them bleed again? Why not let Andersonville remain a tourist stop (which it is) where visitors can stroll for an hour or so and say, "My, my," and "Is there anything cold to drink in the van?"

There are two basic reasons for this new book. First of all, there is truth. This diary-memoir provides new information and a new viewpoint by a man who was there. Somehow first person narratives have an immediacy and style no historian can attain, even celebrated writers with Pulitzer Prizes. Second, this is an excellent piece of work on its own merits, by a bona fide hero, a man with a legitimate Medal of Honor. The author did not capture a battle flag to earn his Medal, nor did he ever lobby for it. He was awarded the Medal because he had earned every grain of it. And he deserves to be heard.

Prepare then for a descent into a living hell. Once the gates slam shut, you cannot escape. Readers who like their history pure and pasteurized and tidy--beware! Choose some more placid volume from your shelf tonight. This one will make you squirm and unsettle your thoughts for nights on end.

Roger Long
Catawba Island, OH
August 25, 1988

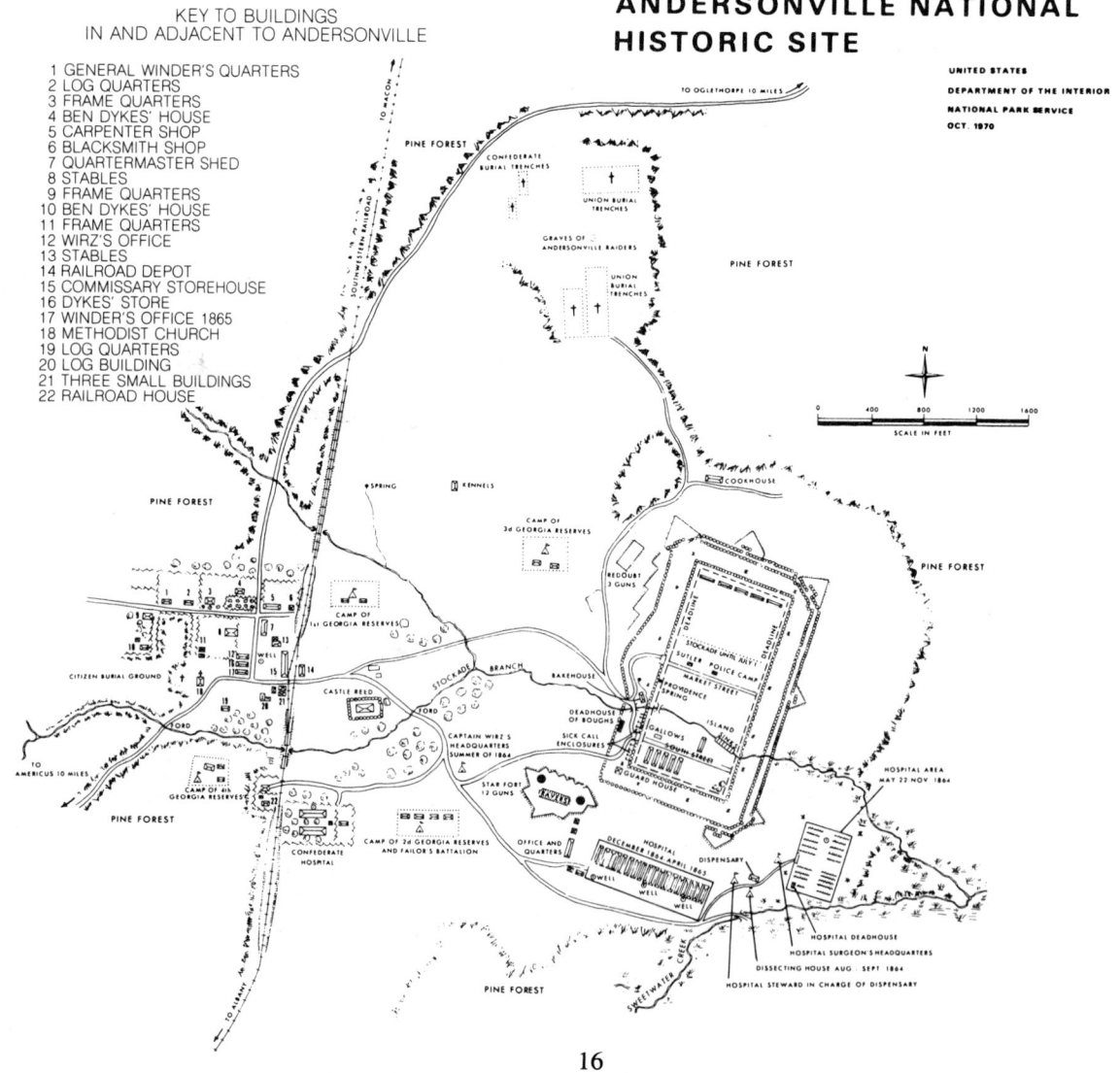

INTRODUCTION

By William B. Styple

    Among the thousands of books dealing with our great national conflict, the American Civil War of 1861-1865, it is very exciting to find an unpublished account from that war, especially a firsthand account from a common soldier. *The Andersonville Diary and Memoirs of Charles Hopkins* is perhaps one of the finest unpublished memoirs to appear in years.

    Around the year 1890, a veteran from the Grand Army of the Republic of the United States, a Medal of Honor recipient, and former prisoner of war, decided to record his memories. Using his old 1864 diary as an aid, he completed a document of his war experiences nearly 280 handwritten pages long. Corporal Charles Hopkins of the First New Jersey Infantry never had his memoirs published. Except for a few family members, no one ever read about his remarkable experiences during the Civil War because Charles Hopkins was a very modest man.

    Once in a terrible battle during the war while the fighting raged around Hopkins, though twice wounded, he rescued his wounded sergeant from capture and possible death by carrying him through a crossfire nearly a mile to safety. The man whose life Hopkins saved, after the war, decided to see personally that the proper honor was bestowed upon the man he owed so much. Sergeant Richard Donnely decided to take matters into his own hands and petitioned Congress to present Charles Hopkins the Congressional Medal of Honor, our nation's highest military award. A very grateful Richard Donnely stated to Congress in 1892, that Hopkins would never receive the medal if Congress waited for Hopkins to apply for it in person. Congress awarded Charles Hopkins the Medal of Honor on July 27, 1892 for "distinguished gallantry under fire" at Gaines's Mill, Va. June 27, 1862.

Perhaps the other trials that Charles Hopkins experienced during the Civil War, quite likely his months as a prisoner in the infamous southern military prison at Andersonville, Georgia, overshadowed his battle honors. I feel Hopkins recorded these memoirs for himself and for the future generations of Hopkins. To show his descendants that through any adversity, one with the will to live can survive. Upon examining the memoirs I found an interesting scrap of paper. It seemed to be a poem of sorts, though it was not signed. When I read the line, "What others have done, I too, can do!", I concluded that it was the work of Charles Hopkins. It resembled a certain moment during his desperate decision to survive at Andersonville when he thought, "Where others can live, we will not die!".

*If I were in school once more,
I think that I should know how to
make better use of the abilities
I have. I should not care about
measuring my achievements by my
capacity. I might not excel in quantity
of work--I would excel in my zeal
and in my joy in my work. What others
have done, I too, can do! More, what
others have not done I may yet do if I
work to my full strength.*

There was only one man the Civil War Veteran Charles Hopkins would forever dedicate his post-war years to. For nearly 70 years, Hopkins worked with the utmost dedication to the memory of his old New Jersey Brigade Commander, General Philip Kearny. It was not uncommon for veteran soldiers to hold their old leaders in high esteem. As strong as the soldiers' religious beliefs, they revered and honored the memories of Generals such as Lee, Jackson and Grant. There was none who revered the memory of Philip Kearny more than Charles Hopkins. He once wrote, "If I should live a thousand years, my love and admiration for Phil Kearny will never flag for an instant. His picture looks down upon me as I sleep and will until I sleep with him in the sleep of death." Hopkins took personal charge of the General's memory, culminating in achieving the great honor of having his beloved General removed from an obscure, unmarked grave in New York City, to a hero's plot in Arlington National Cemetery.

With all the love that Hopkins had for his old commander, he would not forget his old comrades - the common soldiers, who like himself, shouldered their muskets in 1861 to put down the rebellion in the Southern states. Scattered throughout northern New Jersey are monuments to the local soldiers who fought at Bull Run, Antietam, Chancellorsville and Gettysburg. Hopkins was instrumental in erecting these monuments. But Hopkins would not let himself forget the memory of his fellow New Jerseymen who did not return from their captivity in the hells of Confederate prisons. Charles Hopkins led the movement to have the State of New Jersey erect the first state monument at the Andersonville National Cemetery in Georgia. The Cemetery, with its 13,000 victims of the Confederate States' venomous cruelty to its Union prisoners, had yet to dedicate any monuments in their memory. Survivor Charles Hopkins addressed the New Jersey State Assembly for such a monument:

Assemblyman Hopkins Addresses the House.

When the bill providing for the burial place of the New Jersey Soldiers who died in Andersonville prison pen was before the House. Mr. Hopkins spoke as follows. He was there himself, but he survives to tell the story. The bill provides for the expenditure of $1,800 by a commision of two to be named by the Governor. They are to be men of sufficient patriotism to do the work for the love of the cause:

Mr. Speaker: It is my pleasure to speak for this bill, and for the time being I would that I were a Griggs or a Scovel that I might do it justice in eloquence.
This is a righteous bill. Carried out it will reflect credit upon our state. We ask not for the living to-day. Our thoughts turn back a third of a century to scenes of conflict, glorious victories, disheartening defeat, and the horrors that sickened the heart of the stoutest, who faced death in scores of battles without a tremor. We speak for those comrades whose sufferings and death were such as make Dante's Inferno seem a paradise. The acts of Caligula, Nero, or the Inquisition were not worse. The horrors of the Jersey Prison Hulks, or that of infamous Spain's famous Moro Castle and Fort Cabanas with their subterranean hells beneath the ocean, did not eclipse them. And this is in the 19th century.
By the personal appointment of Jefferson Davis, was General John H. Winder, chosen as a man of "Christian-like qualities." of whom the people of Richmond-though not differing in sentiment as to the war, yet when he was ordered to Andersonville said, "thank God he has left Richmond, but God help those to whom he has been sent." They knew the man, the most cruel of tormentors, the most arrant of cowards, the most heartless of mankind. His father gave Washington to rack and ruin by the British in 1814, by his cowardice at Bladensburg. Tis true in this case "Like begets like." Winder was the arbiter of the fate of 15,000 (in Andersonville alone) of the youth, vigor, aye! the heartsblood of this nation.

They were the product of that sturdy northern blood that conquered in every field since the fall of the Roman Empire. They learned their lesson of honor, patriotism and fidelity to their principles, in our common schools and churches. And well did they bear them out. They boasted not of honor, they knew not of chivalry, but did their duty in defiance of death and torture indescribable, with a calmness not excelled, if not equaled in all the six thousand or more years of grim war. Constantly facing death in prison, daily reading their own fate in that of the thousands of dying comrades lying about them rotting by inches of horrible and loathsome disease. Helpless, hopeless, mocked and sneered at, in their terrible sufferings by their tormentors, taunted with the assertion that our Government had abandoned them to their fate; proffered employment in the Confederate service as non-combatants, to fill places for the Confederates who might be sent to the front to fight their comrades. The conditions were that oath must be taken to make no attempt to escape, nor aid or abet the United States in any way against the Confederacy. To accept meant life itself to many thousands; to all, comfort, temporary liberty, fresh air, and freedom from contact with loathsome diseases. Was this temptation, think you? Aye! but not for any Jerseyman of whom we knew and have yet to know, and have no desire to know.

Those faithful, honest, devoted boys rose superior to every blandishment. They prefered death before dishonor. (With) no question as to their rights, no complaint against government; accepting calmly, unflinchingly, fate as dread fortune might decree.

We long since have expressed our belief, and still believe, and love to believe, that when those sorrowful, saddened faces appealed to the righteous but knightly St. Peter for admission within the Pearly Gates, no matter what creed, denomination or belief, his reply has been: Enter, my heros; the gates are left ajar for you; you have suffered your full measure.

When fifteen years will have passed away, so will the souls of nearly all we call comrades to-day. Those who are here now would fain have our state pay some tribute in a plain, unostentatious way, to the memory of those noble dead, who died not on the front line in a halo of glory. Commence now, that the living may see the fruition of their hopes.

Upon the granite for which this bill provides, we would have graven: "Go, strangers, to New Jersey; tell her that we lie here in fulfillment of her mandate and our pledge,-to maintain the proud name of our state unsullied, and place it high on the scroll of honor among the states of this great nation." And they did. on the reverse side we would inscribe, "Death preferred before dishonor." They did. God bless them.

When Charles Hopkins returned home from almost ten months of imprisonment, his struggle for survival was not yet over. He took nearly a year to recover. Doctors were most anxious to amputate his badly swollen feet, fearing death would soon occur if they did not. Hopkins professed that if he had to die, he would prefer to die intact. After all he had been through, the fear of death was hardly worth a passing thought.

After recovering somewhat, Hopkins began a small harnessmaking business in Boonton, N.J. and in 1867, married Miss Hettie Anne Van Duyne. The couple were married over sixty years and had seven children. In post-war years, Hopkins became more involved in local issues and politics. In 1880 Hopkins was elected Mayor of Boonton, New Jersey. Other offices and honors were bestowed upon him, such as New Jersey State Assemblyman, Morris County Freeholder, Assistant Sergeant of Arms of the State Senate. He also served as Postmaster of Boonton for nearly 20 years. And of course he was involved with the many Civil War Veteran organizations that flourished after the war, especially the Grand Army of the Republic.

In the book, *Biographical and Genealogical History of Morris County, N.J.*, published by the Lewis Publishing Company of New York in 1899, there is a fine description of Charles F. Hopkins, the man:

"Mr. Hopkins is an active man in all affairs that pertain to the welfare of his town and never shirks a duty that devolves upon a good citizen. He has been a Grand Army man since the formation of the order and is active in its support. He has many times served as post commander, and is now occupying that position in John Hill Post, No. 86, G. A. R. He has also been a department officer, is a member of the New Jersey ex-Prisoners of War, and is always found in attendance at the re-unions of the veterans of the Civil war held in New Jersey. He is a man of genial manner, kindly disposition and courteous deportment, holds friendship inviolable, is generous and benevolent and quick to forgive. Whether on the field of battle, in public office or in the walks of private life he is the same loyal citizen, having the best interests of his country and of humanity at heart."

Throughout his long life, Charles Hopkins never lost his sense of duty to his community, to his commander or his beloved country. He was a model American, for all Americans to be proud of. God bless him.

In the late 1920's, Hopkins, who was approaching ninety years of age, was visiting the battlefield at Gettysburg, Pennsylvania. After a day of touring the field on foot and in an automobile with his son Emmett and his grandson Thomas, Charles Hopkins spotted a nearby airfield with an aeroplane belonging to a local barnstormer. The elderly Hopkins cunningly asked Emmett to drive him and young Thomas toward the airfield; supposing there was still some part of the battlefield they had not yet toured. Charles Hopkins approached the barnstorming pilot and asked, "How much to take the three of us up for a ride?" Despite the loud and unheard protests of his son Emmett, the three were soon piloted high above the battlefield. While the screams of joy came from young Thomas Hopkins, they were mixed with cries of terror from his father, Emmett, as the biplane swooped down and around such sites as Little Round Top, Culp's Hill and Cemetery Ridge. For Charles Hopkins, the soldier who marched off to war to fight at Gaines's Mill and at the Wilderness, and to survive the hells of prison life at Andersonville, the flight was perhaps the most exciting moment of his long life. With a gleam in his eye as he was helped from the cockpit, Charles Hopkins only comment was, "That was good!"

In February 1934, Corporal Charles F. Hopkins passed away. New Jersey's last Civil War Medal of Honor recipient. A bronze Medal of Honor with the word "Valor" is on his tombstone.

This book pays tribute to his memory.

As did Charles Hopkins, I have the utmost admiration for Major General Philip Kearny. As a Civil War historian and having lived in the town of Kearny, New Jersey all of my life, I naturally studied the general's career for many years. During the research for my first book, *Letters from the Peninsula: The Civil War Letters of General Philip Kearny*, I frequently came across the name of Charles Hopkins. The more I found out about this soldier and his loyalty to his old commander, the more intrigued I became in him. In 1987 I discovered that Charles Hopkins hailed from Boonton, N.J. I explored the possibility that some of his descendants might be still in the area. It was my good fortune to meet and interview several of Charles Hopkins' grandchildren. Their assistance and contributions to my book on General Kearny will always be very much appreciated. The more I learned about their grandfather's career, the more fascinated I became with Charles Hopkins.

The Civil War memoirs of Corporal Charles Hopkins of the First New Jersey Infantry are being published here for the first time. The memoirs were written in the 1890's by Hopkins, using the diary that he had kept while a prisoner at Andersonville. In 1983 Gerald Hopkins sent the memoirs of Charles Hopkins to *American Heritage Magazine*. Due to limited space, American Heritage only printed a small portion of the memoirs. Also, small excerpts from the memoir appeared in the book, *Boonton Was An Iron Town*, by Peter Wendt, Compton Press, 1976.

Upon reading the memoirs I felt that the fascinating story would make an interesting book. It was the wishes of Thomas Hopkins to publish the complete work for all Americans to enjoy. I began my task to edit the memoirs into a form which the reader could easily comprehend. I decided where chapters would begin and end. I also divided Hopkins' page-long paragraphs into reasonable lengths. Charles Hopkins wrote his memoirs for himself and his family and so wrote in his plain language prose. I chose to leave ungrammatical sentences unedited except where needed for clarity. It was my decision to insert pertinent excerpts from Hopkins' diary between sections of the memoirs. The diary excerpts appear in italics and serve the purpose of bringing the reader back in time to the misery of prison life during the Civil War. One should not forget the circumstances that the writer of this diary was under: poor shelter, inclement weather, inadequate food and medical care and all under the wary eye of a hated enemy.

My comments, when needed, appear in heavy italics. I also chose to illustrate the memoirs with actual photographs of Andersonville taken in 1864. These photographs are the proof of the indefensible horrors of Andersonville. Along with post-war drawings and illustrations, there are several additional photographs taken by Charles Hopkins when he returned to Andersonville.

While I was working on the manuscript, a sense of duty overcame me. I felt that I owed it to Charles Hopkins, General Kearny, and the rest of the soldiers of the American Civil War to show future Americans what those men had to go through to keep this country free and under the American flag. I am very proud of Charles Hopkins and Philip Kearny. I hope that readers will feel the same way as I do when they are finished with this book.

PREFACE

By Charles F. Hopkins

This story is not intended to embrace the whole area of the Civil War, nor yet, a small part of the movements, by quoting from the work of others. The story of the personal experiences of the individual will give more real history of the War, the hardships, suffering and mental anguish than any attempt to cover the movements of the Division, Corps, Regiment or Company.

The personal reminiscences will be read with much more interest by the general reader. The man in the ranks naturally, from his narrow scope of action, knows little, if any, of what is taking place beyond the limit or bounds of his own Company, or Regiment at best.

The interest of the writer is only to tell in an unvarnished, plain and commonplace manner, as sitting among his comrades at a campfire, or elsewhere and in his own language, of his personal observations and knowledge, without exaggeration and overdrawn statements.

To be plain, it is scarcely possible to overdraw on imagination, the borders of the Confederate prisons, such as the writer has participated in, and been a part of.

Language to the writer is difficult and perplexing in his conversation, but were he fluent and prolific in that line, exaggeration could find no lodgement in this story.

If the perusal can convey to the reader even a crude idea of what it means to be a prisoner of war in the hands of an implacable enemy, the object of the writer is satisfactorily accomplished. While it is not good manners to make oneself the hero of his story, my apology is, who can it be? Each reader will pass verdict according to his own view.

The writer was born in the quaint old Moravian village of Hope, Warren County, New Jersey, on May 16th, 1842, and the inspiration of hope that remained within him through the details in the following story, was, the one sentiment that kept him alive, when the thousands miserably perished, a prey to mental depression that lack of hope produced. The towns and cities throughout the South, had for years, been maintaining military organizations, and were given the best military training and instruction possible as the majority of trained military men of the country came from the South, and for the reason that, the whole Administrations of Government had been dominated by the Members of both Houses of Congress, from the Southern States, consequently the Army and Navy schools were in turn predominately filled with Southern born young men. Every planter, or business man of the South deemed it a duty to have his son educated in the United States Military or Naval Academies, as their wealth would permit, and the young men were not supposed, nor inclined, in those days, to do anything in the line of menial labor for their maintenance.

A view of Boonton, N.J. taken in 1854.

Slaves earned their living for them, hence, they could be military or naval gentlemen, or aspire to be rulers in Congress of the United States. Anything but menial labor. With this hard-earned money, slaves were made as miserable as possible, leaving their owners to spend lavishly in idleness and otherwise, not commendable. Not so with the young men of Northern birth; they were to make their way, first, to earn and learn some self-supporting trade or business that contributed brains and bond labor, and when they had made a competency, they could, for past-time and recreation, branch out into politics, or travel, as their desires dictated.

In the North, it was thought there was method in the Southern idea of maintaining the military organizations, for several years prior to the Civil War. It may have been so. However, the young men of the North took up the Southern idea a few years before the great struggle, as a pleasing pastime and beneficial exercise to train and develop the muscular system. Every village that could boast of enough young men of this trend, had their company of Militia, either mainly supported by the purses of the members and their enthusiastic friends, or partly from the State. In the latter case, such companies were a part of the regular organized Militia and under the control and regulations of the State Authorities, subject to specified inspections, drills, etc., and ready on call for duty when the State gave notice. Boonton, New Jersey, a beautiful hillside manufacturing village, boasted of one of the best Companies of the National Guard of the State of New Jersey, so proven by competitive drills and inspections, maneuvers and other tests, against the Crack Companies of the State. The writer became a very enthusiastic member of Company G New Jersey State National Guard. This Company had for its Captain, Edwin Bishop, First Lieutenant, James Plant, both of whom had served seven or more years in the world famous Seventh New York Militia, and were very competent men in that line. They, and their men, were enthusiastic, and were brought to such a stage of perfection, military bearing, appearance and performance, that in competition with the widely known Tucker Guards of the City of Newark, known as a crack military body of men, and the State celebrated Morris Greys, of Morristown, New Jersey, who were commanded by the late Major General Revere; Company G, of Boonton, carried off the honors on both occasions, and defeat was heartily admitted by both of the competitors. The plain, but neat uniform, consisted of Seventh, New York grey suit, black sleeve cuffs, collar and pantaloon stripes, white body and cross belts, high regulation hat and pompom. When they appeared upon the streets, they were the cynosure of all eyes. Muskets polished like glass, belts of the whitest, brasses like polished gold, shoes with the highest possible polish, suit without a wrinkle or spot to mar. Every man prided himself upon his neatness, manly and soldierly bearing, as well as faultless marching. Indeed, Boonton was proud of her soldiers, and never stinted their praise. The Company had existed about three years, when the sullen mutterings of discontent, both North and South because of the agitation of the Slavery question, were heard. The South contending that slavery of Negroes was a lawful and Christian institution, and should be permitted to extend to all the States and Territories, south of the Mason and Dixon Line, from the Atlantic to the Pacific Oceans, and into some of the Louisiana Purchase, north of said line. The North insisted and maintained the argument that the institution of slavery was inhuman and debasing, intolerable in a land of freedom that we prided ourselves upon, among the Nations of the World; that Slavery should not be extended beyond the States then occupied by Slavery. Kansas was a battle ground occupied by those who emigrated from the Northern and Eastern States, who declared that Kansas must be a free state. Compromises were attempted in several ways, but all were violated by the dominant power, whose head was at that time, James Buchanan, a man of the Northern birth, and came from the great liberty-loving state of Pennsylvania; and who was, by his election as President of the United States, committed to Slavery as it then existed, and was too meek to stand the pressure of his party, and make for himself a name in history - a man of stamina that knew the right, and obeyed the instinct. He submitted himself to the Slave Oligarchy and fell to dishonor and obscurity. There let him remain forever. Throughout the North, the many branches of the Underground Railroad to freedom were doing a lively business, in helping runaway slaves to escape to Canada and freedom. Boonton was a principal station on the line, and many slaves, on their way to a land of liberty, had good cause to bless the names of such men as Dr. John Grimes, John Hill, William G. Lathrop, Charles B. Norris, Thomas C. Willis, Philip Wootton and Nathan Hopkins, the father of the writer, and a number of others, whose names have escaped by memory, yet, they were as loyal as any in the cause of freedom and humanity. Very few people of Boonton and vicinity knew of this work, but were most loyal.

The writer has been the medium that passed many a slave to the next station, though but a boy, by instructions from his father; had driven many a stormy, dark, lonesome night, either by way of Pompton Plains to Canisteer, or by the way of Splitrock and Charlottesburg, or to Rockaway, Berkshire Valley to Milton, thence to Canisteer, the regular station; often not exchanging a word on the route, peering through the darkness to discover a pursuer, who might be anxious to capture the hunted slave, for the reward which ranged from a hundred dollars to fifteen hundred dollars. Many slaves passed over the line, being considered safe though near New York. Many tricks were resorted to that would lead the reward-hungry officers on a false scent. Yet twice, the call was a close one, but a speedy mare and a frightened boy accomplished the end. The boy was not frightened at the pursuit of the officers, nor the legal result if arrested, but more of what the result would be on his return home to acknowledge failure, which, while not meaning punishment of any kind, would mean something worse - disgrace of failure.

It was natural that our mind was alert on the question of the abolition of Slavery, as we had with great avidity, read the "Book of Slavery" by Wilberforce, "Uncle Tom's Cabin", by Harriet Beecher Stowe, "The Impending Crisis" by Hinton Rowan Helper, as well as being raised on the "New York Tribune" by Horace Greely, which was the "all in all" in the household and ranked next to the family Bible. Born and raised in a Whig atmosphere, schooling in abolition of Slavery - hearing it and reading it almost hourly, everything that treated of the subject favorably, the transition was easy to become a fighting champion for the annulment of, or the stopping of, farther extension of the vile and wicked practice of enslaving human beings and treating them as cattle or worse. In the heat of debate in both Houses of Congress, there soon followed the brutal attack upon Sumner by Brooks, the justifiable knock-down of Kieth Crow, and the other detestable bullying practices of some of the Southern members, who long in control, became insolent, abusive, defiant and aggressive, knowing that they held the reins of the Government. Then the Massacre of the Unionists at Leavenworth, Kansas - men who emigrated from Northern and Eastern States to make homes, and they insisted that it should be a free State. Quantrell and his gang of murderers, instigated and financed by the slave owners, swept from life unto death, without trial or hearing, every Unionist in Leavenworth they could lay hands on - women and children not spared! The Sioux and Apache, whose Indian traits were of the most brutal and fiendish, could not have done worse than did Quantrell, who, in the Civil War made himself famous as a brute of the most cowardly instincts - killing the wounded and helpless, and taking no prisoners. Events, now, were moving swiftly; and the excitement in the South gave vent by the more frequent drilling of the Militia, with threats of dire destruction to the ''Mudsills'' of the North - should war come. The exciting and warming up of the blood by Lincoln and Douglas on the stump which ended in the defeat of Lincoln as Senator, and later defeated Douglas for the Presidency, thus placing the uncouth and ungainly rail-splitter, but thank the result as ''God's Choice,'' - into the chair of the Chief Magistrate of the Nation.

Private Charles Hopkins of the 1st New Jersey Volunteer Infantry. This photograph, taken in 1861, shows the young, healthy man, full of patriotic confidence, that was common early in the war.

CHAPTER ONE
TO WAR!

Turbulence reigned supreme from now on, and no one could predict for a month, aye, scarcely a day as to what would happen. The Militia of the North took on new life, a more frequent drilling, perfecting organizations in every possible way, new companies formed, but not equipped, etc. The North was being aroused to action. The South threatened and fumed. The Saxon blood of the North had not yet become overheated; while the hot blood of the Chevaliers was at the point of combustion. In Congress, matters looked serious, yet the man at the wheel of the Ship of State, was cool, vigilant, hoping to satisfy the discontented of both sides of the controversy in an honorable way, and save the fratricidal and dangerous arbiter - War. The waiting and waiting, with bated breath, that every loyal heart in the North could be heard of its own beating; waiting with anguish, - patriotism in every thought; hoping against hope that the worst might not come; that a war of families of the same blood, that father and son, brother and brother, should not be found as the murderer of each other. The strong bond of Union made by our wise ancestors, was being strained to its very limit. Oh, God, will it break - and send us into a struggle that will cause such a holocaust of lives so precious, and suffering of those who are left to mourn - the widow, orphan, and the darkened life of the loved one? Heaven forbid! The silence of death is about us - then the fatal boom, Sumpter's gun was fired upon the Flag, April 9th, 1861! That boom was heard on the quiet hillsides and valleys of the North. Boonton was thoroughly aroused, and the spirit of war was intense. Company "G" was ordered out for drill and a full inspection. Fifty-eight members reported "present" in response to the request of the Captain! "All who are willing to go to the front at a moments notice, please step three paces forward!" All but two promptly responded - those had good reason for remaining, though tears ran down their cheeks to think that they could not answer the call - but they were cheered by their comrades, that they should feel no shame for their manly action. The Company, when actually called in the latter part of May, took with it, almost the entire number. Among those who had more war spirit than discretion, was a youth of very boyish appearance, yet, so full of fight (naturally distance enchanted the view) that he could scarcely take time to eat or sleep - but was more than willing to do both later on, when the actual fighting was not as rosily-hued as the dreamed-of-glory to be attained on the battlefield. Quite unwilling to await the seemingly slow process I though found sufficiently swift a few months later, I offered my services and being accepted in the Company; with more patriotic ardor than good sense, on the 3rd of May, 1861, without due parental notice and sanction, I startled the family at the breakfast table (minus the head of the family who had left early to be absent the whole day), with, "Ellen, I want a clean shirt, I am going away!" Ellen, who was my stepmother, and a good one, and her two daughters, who to me were as my sisters, were the only persons present - the one whom I did not wish to consult on the question, my father, was absent, as before stated; I had chosen this auspicious time, in order to avoid a collision that might prove all my nicely-laid plans abortive. In reply to my good stepmother's question, "Charlie, where are you going?" "To war!" came the prompt reply; and I imagine there may have been some bombast in the tone, for I was chuck full of enthusiasm to go to war - not the quality of "enthusiasm" that filled the Irishman when he met a half-starved Scotchman and received a damaged countenance - for I did not indulge at that time. (To remove the suspicion that the last statement may give rise to, I may be permitted to state that I hardly ever now, have recourse to stimulants of that nature. With the tears and pleading of Mother and her daughters, I had to brace up pretty firmly - and won! The bundle was neatly wrapped, and many other things were urged upon me, but I was no pack horse then, no matter how much of a pack mule I was later on. I pleaded stage time which was close at hand as I could hear the rumpling of Jake Meslar's thorough-brace, old, rocking stage. Hastily embracing and kissing them all good-bye, not forgetting to leave a good-bye to the absent father, the stage passed the door - and I became an unexpected passenger.

I sprang on the boot at the rear of the old Ark, crawled to the roof and surprised Old Jake, who gave me a dark scowl as I paid him the usual thirty cents for an uncomfortable ride to Denville. To all his inquiries, as to where I was going - believing it none of his business, I was both deaf and dumb. This was strategy I was practicing, for he may have flanked my position and surrounded me, as he knew I was under age, and had not the consent of my father. These two were great friends, though they differed to the very extreme in politics; but 'tis said that politics sometimes make strange bedfellows, which was indeed true in this case. We reached our goal, New York City, and visited the Battery, intending to enlist in the Second Militia Regiment of New York, from which some eight hundred had already gone forward to Washington, the front. When about to enlist, we learned from the newspaper, that there had been a mutiny among them at Washington; and thereupon, we stoutly refused to become that kind of a patriot. We searched from one headquarters to another, until finally, in much disgust, we crossed the Hudson to my native state. At Hoboken, I was "taken in" in right smart order, along with a Yankee, whose acquaintance I had made at the Battery, by his proffer for me to share his "bombashoot," properly, an umbrella. He hailed from the land of Wooden Nutmegs, and this friendship was to ripen into a long life comradeship, both in the service and to this hour - with seventy eight years to my credit and eighty five to his. We were sent to Trenton, New Jersey, on the day following our visit to Hoboken, and became members of Company "I" 1st, New Jersey Volunteers.

Quite contrary to our hopes and expectations that we should speedily go to the seat of war, and become busy at the vocation of quieting rebels, we remained at Trenton, drilling and doing monotonous camp and police duties, waiting impatiently for uniforms, arms and other requirements. To tell the truth our ardor for military duties and rebel-quelling spirit was fast being cooled by the delay, and consequent constrained conditions of camp life. The arms we were using to practice with, were old flintlocks of the Colonial age - some flintless, some lockless and some with the bayonets missing, mostly so - the odds the difference when ordered to stack arms, we just jammed the old flinters into the ground, muzzle first, thus loading them each time with a fresh charge of Mother Earth, until the barrel was full to the muzzle. No thought was given to its historic memories of the past - they may have slaughtered the Red Coats at Princeton, Trenton or Monmouth, in the first great struggle in the name and cause of liberty and freedom. The flinters, only weighed thirteen pounds when clean - we never cleaned them, and everything was in keeping. To match the useless arms our very much abbreviated clothing suited well. We had not been careful with the clothing brought with us, for we had daily expected better - at least that was the daily rumor and report of our officers, and of course they knew (but little more than we did) - hence, many were shirtless, except the nether shirt, shoeless, hatless, and pantless - in fact, were quite "less" in every way, even getting "less" on patriotism, and chafing under the long delay. The uniforms on drill were fantastic - some self-made paper hats, tri cockade, square and round, as fancy designed; others, for pantaloons, had their blankets folded over a string much like the Kilt of the Scot, bound to the waist by a knotted cord, or a wooden skewer for a pin. Truly, we may have been taken for some of our forbears, who had risen from their tombs and wandered over from Valley Forge to give us inspiration for the awful struggle yet to come, which no one of us, looked upon in a serious light, all nearly with the view that it was to be a holiday only.

Finally, we were ordered to appear at the unpretentious, quaint little octagon shaped, or six sided building, and our memory to verify which. This was located on the Delaware River and known as the State House. Here we were to be sworn into the service - the uniforms and arms to follow, of course. It was well that the swearing in process was done for we felt awfully prompted to swear very hard and loud a short time after when we passed the Camp of the Second New Jersey Volunteers, and to our astonishments, we saw our old Company "G" from Boonton; and back rushed the thought of the haste we were in to get away to the front - not to wait for the acceptance of the Company. Tears would avail nothing, even if in that mood our temper was up in the clouds and time would only bring it back to earth and moist atmosphere. Protests and pleading with the Captain were futile. My ardor for war, was sufficient to hurry me from home, yet I had gained no time over the Company so all we could do was to think very, very hard and it was well it was not loud - it may have been mistaken from the "swearing in" with some variations.

At last arms and clothing had arrived - the latter sadly needed - and the variety of fits and misfits was laughable to any one except those most concerned. Had the suits been fitted by a Broadway "Nicoll" there would not have been so promiscuous a fit. Some did truly fit but very many did not by a long shot. Imagine a four foot five banty, with six foot four pants, coat, hat and all, to keep company.

Then another picture - a stalwart six footer, with pants that gaped at the pockets and elsewhere, that caused a shrinkage of the legs, halfway to the knees; a coat or blouse that fitted like a straight jacket and left the forearm bare to the elbows, ready to sever relations with the buttons in front, seeming like an over-filled balloon; next a fatigue cap to crown the whole, which resembled a four quart measure on a hogshead top. However, matters evened up later on and fits became in normal shape. We were now the belongings of Uncle Sam, to be whipped into shape of real soldiers. Our arms were of good make for those times, being the smoothbore, calibre fifty-eight, Springfield pattern, and four pounds lighter than old 1776, formerly used. We enjoyed all the advantages that go to make up the life of a soldier - hardtack, salt horse and sow belly. (I should have said "stomach," but used the familiar term of expression, for, disgust was stamped on every countenance when the "mess" came into view on pork day.") Included was that wonderful and world-renowned legume "the bean." Misfit garments and contents, as they were now on the market and no partiality was shown - for everybody that claimed to be regular, was obliged to accept the contents, it being an "indispensable," though very troublesome at times, I may say at all times - still, they were a source of employment of course, and kept one's mind off the more serious matters. In a word, I may say, that they were hunted at all times by men, and were invariably found in abundance, but we had licensed to hunt them.

We were ordered to the seat of war and left Trenton for Washington, arriving the next morning in a downpour of rain - only such as the South can produce and enjoyed a stretch on a "soft and downy" bed, down on the steps and sidewalk in front of the Treasury Building. This spot was chosen, no doubt, in order to stimulate dreams of the enormous sums we should draw from there, each month for our services. ($11.00 per month at that time). Well, we followed the sun; but after it was high in the heavens and had kindly dried us out and made the sidewalk so hot, sleep became too much of an exertion. Our officers put us in motion; we were seesawed and repeated again and again, marched and countermarched, (all this time in the sun, at from 95 to 100 degrees), with woolen suits from hide to daylight - we thought the heat must have been about 500 degrees. If this exercise was meant to get our blood up, it was a complete success - from the tone of voice and language used. Finally, we marched through the "Soldiers" Retreat, near the great Pennsylvania Avenue, which when not in use as a highway by the incoming and outgoing troops, was a wallowing place for swine - all of which made it a bed of liquid mud of real color and clinging quality - greatly enjoyed, of course, by "un Mudsills." We passed through the "Retreat" without a halt along tables, laden with tin plates, cups, cold and drowned coffee, salt pork - a slice as big as a foot, "Trilby's" - and slices of bread of ample size. You snatched two pieces of bread and pork ditto, slapped the "ditto" between the slices, grabbed a cup of coffee and continued the march, eating on the move, this was probably done to avoid an attack of indigestion. The cup must be left in the building where you made your exit; hence, you must be able to gulp it before reaching the point of departure. I did not think that a hard stunt by any means, for although it was cold, there was no ice to break and could have drunk twice the quantity had it been hot, and felt more grateful than I did. From the sulphurous language we heard, we concluded we were not alone in the light of the past. We now feel that we were quite ungrateful for so many times since then - oh, how wistfully we thought of, and wished that we could have had, even that cup of cold coffee and the much despised pork!

Our march continued until at last, in late afternoon, we were located on Meridian Hill and camp, moved and camped once more and then moved to Roach's Mills, a short distance from the Lee Mansion, on Arlington Heights. This was named Camp Trenton. Here we were being molded into soldiers, from day to day under the eye of that Mexican War Veteran, Colonel William R. Montgomery. We wore the Regulation hat - black, stiff-rimmed, disagreeable to wear at any time, much less in the hot sun at 90 degrees in the shadiest place one could find; and ornamented with a brass excutcheon of the United States, covering nearly one side of crown: and finished in its elegance with a long, black feather, not related to the Eagle family. Really, we looked very fierce and warrior-like! The boys rebelled at wearing the hat in that climate and found ways of disposing of them; though at their own expense, as they were charged with each article of wear, and must account or pay for them. "The damn stove-pipes!" I never knew why that term was used in that connection. My hat did not fit my head, nor suit my taste, and in a frame of mind not soothing, my hat was made open at the crown by the use of my foot, so although useless as headgear the top acted as a sort of a valve.

A Union soldier with his dreaded "stove pipe" hat resting on a pedestal. The regulation Hardee Hat was often lost at the first opportunity by the soldier.

Camp Trenton was demoralizing in some ways; but doubtless the steady drilling was to benefit us in the near future - for on July 16th orders came for us to go to Vienna, a straggling village of 150 to 200 well scattered inhabitants; hold the Rebel Army in check and save Washington. (We thought of course that we did it). After a hurried march to the position it was discovered that our "tack" and other provisions had taken a wrong tack and had not followed us; so could not find us nor we them. Here was a serious dilemma - three days rations lost, and the same term of possible hunger, 'unless' the strict order from Headquarters against foraging was violated. Nevertheless, the hunt for grub began - though forbidden fruit - on that sacred soil. Orders were made as the laws, and laws were broken by men - for these men were only human! Well, there was nothing in that town or near vicinity that could be defined as "forage" except short, sunburnt grass and pine scrubs, but they were dry eating at best. Blackberries and dew berries were plenty but close to the rebel lines and under fire; at all events, they were outside of our established lines. Now what was to be done while waiting for that everlastingly slow "grub" to reach us? It was to come by an Army railroad, which at that time was under repair, as the rebels had been so discourteous as to tear it up in our rear. The Camp seemed about as disconsolate a crowd of hungry men as could be. One day, as the Captain was gloomily staring into a fire, being uselessly burned as we had nothing to cook, I asked him if he was not hungry. His surprise may be imagined at such a question at such a time. I assured him that I was not crazy or drunk, (as drink was harder to get than grub, aside from poor water) and he replied, "yes, I am hungry! Why do you ask?" I asked him if he would account for me at roll call (there being four a day, of which I had already answered two) and he said he would. I knew that I was safe on that score, provided I reached Camp again. I sauntered out to a sentinel post of the outside guard, who knew me, and under promise of something to eat if I made a successful trip, he did not see me pass over the line. I had made a chum of another Company and he had done the same with a mate of his. We met outside of the lines and were carefully picking our way, when we met four others of our Regiment on the same errand. Moving as cautiously as possible in the brush for about a mile, knowing all the time that we were treading dangerous ground, we separated a little - my companion and I together, when we heard a rooster crow. Well, we could not resist that music even if beset with danger. We found him perched on a post, that had forgotten the gate of former days, in front of a little log hut, which, by its dilapidated look we took to be uninhabited. We gave that rooster the contents of our "58", the bullet passing into the hut just above the door. While picking up the fowl, after a keen searching look all about us to note if our shot had startled anyone in Rebellion, to our utter surprise the cabin door opened and two black, snowy white-headed, apparitions appearing in the opening. They were alive and very respectful, and bowed meekly, and we felt ditto. We caught our breath and said "Uncle, is that your rooster?" At his "Yes suh, Massa," recollections of past years came back to me and after a moment's deliberation, I said to myself, "Charlie, your father always stood up for the slave, and you were a young conductor on the Underground road to freedom for them, under his instruction; it won't do to injure the slave now." A few days before leaving Camp Trenton, I had received one months pay - eleven dollars in gold - and had nine left; and although I felt very much like keeping them my conscience was alive and busy (much more so than the years to follow) and finally, I produced one of the "shiners" and asked, "Uncle, will this be enough for the rooster?" How those two pairs of eyes sparkled and how their dark faces became wreathed in smiles! "Massa, dats too much for de chick" (chick, indeed, he was old enough to vote) "yo take him, we got mo." "Yes, but Uncle, you must take it. I can't take it from you without paying." "But Massa, yo is Massa Linkum's men, we know it, and yo may take de chick." "No, Uncle we can't do it. Here Auntie, you take the money." "Yes Massa, but yo must have mo chick." And away she went into the cabin to return a little while later with two fine, fat hens. "There, Massa, you take de chicks, we git mo chicks but we done got no mo dollahs like dis here one!"

At a little distance we saw a respectable looking house and asked if any Rebs had been about. "There was," said the darky, "in de mawnin, but not jes now, but yo must keep a right smart lookout as de Rebels been all about heah." We went to the house and found our other friends there. We got some buttermilk and offered pay though none was taken. After helping ourselves to some cherries we were invited to stay and they would prepare a meal for us before returning to Camp. I noticed that someone was missing from the house, took the hint and quietly spoke to the others about it. Although the lady of the house was awfully pleasant and entertaining and pressed us to stay for the lunch she was preparing, we thanked her for what she had kindly done for us (and in fact we were not hungry then; and truly none of us were in a waiting mood,) when noticing a colored girl making motions from the rear of the house for us to go away, we hastily left the house, for fear that a short stay then might be prolonged by a visit to Richmond.

In passing a small piece of woods my comrade and I heard a noise that sounded ominous and made ready to enter into a business contract with the Rebels. We wished the other party was with us but they had gone in another direction after leaving the house. After some listening we found that the noise came from a razorback a genus homo of southern breed, that has no home nor owner till killing time, he roams the woods, lives on acorns and grubs, and when found is owned; in appearance it resembles a hyena, long legs in rear, long sharpsnout, high thin backs. We interviewed him over first sight of our "Springfield," and he lay down. Intent upon dressing him out we were startled by a distant shot which did much to hurry us. Without skinning we cut him in four parts in order to carry him better. The shot had drawn two of the other party toward us and the load was generously shared; for although we could have used the razorback for ourselves and

Union soldiers occupy Southern fortifications in Northern Virginia.

it was not heavy, we wanted company - something told me there was trouble in the air.

One half and the head went to our friends, the balance of the ham went to my comrade - this with the chickens, was the load we had to lug back to Camp. We sneaked away for Camp and on the way, about a half mile from safety, stopped to pick some blackberries of the low bush variety ("dew berry" the southern named them). All this time our meat was being flyblown in our haversacks and the grease working its pleasure on our clothing, contented and happy, without fear of trouble, almost in sight of camp, - when we were fired upon from the rear of a barn, which, in our greed for berries, had escaped our notice. A stone wall a few rods away seemed a good place to take shelter. We were four to the unknown and made double quick time to place the wall between us and the enemy, whose shots were falling too close for comfort and peace of mind. Loaded as we were, and the low tangle of briars and vines tripping us several times, giving us the appearance of having had a lively and bloody scrimmage - hands and faces cut and bleeding seeming to come from every pore; clothing looking as though we had waded in blood of a dozen colors - our light blue pants particularly showed the effects of our fall, crushing the ripe berries and wanting the luscious juice on our arms, elbows and knees, - we finally managed to get the stone fence between us and the manhunters. We halted to recover our breath and equanimity, laughed at each other and our forlorn appearance, held a council of war and concluded to fight for a change when we could discover our tormentors. They were found in the barn - we placed our caps on a stick and made ready to fire through a crevice in a stone wall, when we saw the smoke that would tell us just where to fire.

During this interval we were joined by two others of our party on the run to cover. Up went our caps, bang! went four rifles from the barn, and three of our rifles replied. Our caps came down and quickly up again as we loaded again; three shots from the enemy, followed quickly by ours; caps up again, but no response came from the barn. We crawled along the wall to a point where a better view could be had of the rear of the barn. Oho! we had checked them, as two men were helping one in distress, while another of their comrades was carrying rifles. We quietly rejoiced in our victory, not giving heed to the fact that we were outside the lines, and in danger of capture; nor at the fair chances of being caught in disobedience of strict orders which would mean court martial with such punishment as made by the court. Both dilemmas were unpleasant, but, of course, we chose the latter as our preference, provided the Rebs failed to make us accept their choice. Suddenly, we heard a clear ringing bugle note and we knew that it was either Rebels or our troops, attracted by the firing. We crept, walked and ran in a stooped position until we found ourselves in friendly woods. After resting we took a circuitous route homeward and reached Camp about six o'clock in a dilapidated condition as to appearance, and physically done up; our meat most beautifully fly blown and ill of smell. We paid the guard on duty, the "open sesame" promised to the fellow who had let us out. We just lived that night, you can bet, although it took from about seven p.m. to two a.m. before we had the "gorge." The cooking was primitive but complete. My individual share of the day's "hunt," was the rooster, a hen and part of a ham. We dug a hole; filled it with stones; piled wood and brush into it, made a big fire; let it burn down, thus heating the stones; meanwhile made a great mud pie of clay; rolled the chickens, feathers and all, not dressing them in any way - ham, bristles on, fly blows and all, into the pie clay crust, each by itself (crust being about one and one half inches thick) put them in the coals on the stones; raked the coals over them thickly; and then just waited for results, anticipating a square meal, minus square tack, salt or seasoning of any kind. When the "savory" dish was done, we were notified of the fact by a thread of steam making its way through the broken crust. The meal was served in a primitive a way as the cooking. The officers, contrary to the order on "foraging," actually partook of that meal and agreed that it was good. Though it had cost considerable anxiety, and some danger, not forgetting my gold dollar - one eleventh of a month's pay - it was worth it considering that we came through safely, free from death, wound, capture or court martial.

On Sunday, July 21st, we could plainly hear the boom of cannon, and were ordered to march for Bull Run via Germantown, Fairfax Station and Centreville. During the march the firing became plainer as we drew near the battlefield. Thousands of our soldiers were met on the way, Confederates as well, in small numbers, citizens, slaves, Congressmen and other National officials, as though there was a gala day, but they all seemed to be in a great hurry to get home, or somewhere nearer Washington. I noted a lady, sitting in a buggy alongside of the road, as cool and calm as could be. She proved to be the wife of a physician who was giving aid to the wounded, sitting or lying about on the roadside. Near Centreville Heights we met the panic stricken hordes leaving the field of carnage in a rout, without cause or reason simply wild with terror at a senseless rumor. By order of Colonel McAllister we formed a line across the road deploying into the field on either side and woods adjoining, and with fixed bayonets called a halt. The oncoming crowds surged upon those in front, broke right and left like a flood, to be in turn surged upon. Among this panic stricken, fleeing mob was his Lordship Earl Russell, Minister, Plenpotentiary, etc. from England. He demanded that he and his suite, etc. should be allowed to pass, but the sturdy, cool headed McAllister said very emphatically "no, not until this rout and disorder is checked and men no longer demean themselves as craven and cowardly!" His Lordship informed the doughty Colonel that "He" was Lord Russell and "he" insisted that "he" be allowed to pass. The Colonel replied that he did not care who he was, he must halt his equippage, and he did, with mental reservations and other mental "prefixes," no doubt.

Lt. Colonel Robert McAllister of the First New Jersey Infantry.

After bringing fairly good order out of the chaos we moved on to Centreville and lay on the field until almost daylight, then ordered to fall back to Washington - and it seemed quite proper to say "fall back" for we were so worn by the forced march of 27½ miles under a sun heat of 90 degrees or over, that we could "fall" almost anywhere and forget it. The march to Washington of 29½ "Virginia" miles was begun in a muggy, warm and sticky rain. Wet to the skin, with very short halts and very few of them, foot-sore and disheartened, the day seemed long to all. Though this was the condition of our men, they were enraged at the tauntings and flings of the women of the villages they passed through - derided, insulted, and villified in every way possible - yet none could find it in his heart to do injury or insult, by word or deed, to women who would so unsex themselves by doing these things. During that day my mind constantly reverted to the time when I was in such a hurry "to get away to the front." Pride and "my Uncle Sam" barred my way as I sometimes thought that any place was better than in an Army, in this condition. We reached Arlington Heights and that night at about eight o'clock, reckless and careless as to where to lie down, and simply fell down in rank in a growth of clover, dead to the world. The hot sun awoke us in the mornings as "bugles" were as done up as anyone. Here we camped a few days to rest up after that weary and dispiriting forced march of fifty-seven miles. The rest made things look better and the experience was a thing that had done us no harm as was to be proven by the future. From there we went to Alexandria and camped on St. John's Seminary grounds, and did little but make prepara-

The Camp of the First New Jersey Brigade at St. John's Seminary.

tion for what was to come, and what was to come was a revelation to the armed mob that came from Bull Run, from that disastrous Sabbath Day struggle with blistered feet, sore at heart and some misgivings as to the final result. But now we were about to get some knowledge of a character that made name of the First New Jersey Brigade world wide known. In August we were placed in company of a man celebrated for his soldierly qualities and strategic fighting ability, with actual experience in the art of war, the matchless Fighting Phil Kearny was appointed to command the Brigade of Jersey Blues, the First, Second, Third and Fourth New Jersey Regiments.

Brigadier General Philip Kearny in civilian dress.
Kearny looks much like he did when he first encountered his Jersey Brigade.

Our first introduction to this "Bravest of the Brave" as General Winfield Scott called him (under whom he fought in Mexico) was, as we straggled into our temporary camp at Edge Hill one afternoon in August 1861, and we were not all well trained by any means, but, our company Captain, John DePuyster Mount, a small man in stature, but a perfect military man, a martinet on duty, but gentle and pleasant personage who mingled with his men, knew their wants and made sure that they had them supplied, he was the big, little man that every one of his men liked and obeyed. Those who failed to obey or attempted to shirk duty had some thinking to do and ample time to do it. Mount knew Kearny at sight and when we were marching through the lawn in front of Headquarters, which was adjoining a peach grove, our orders were to keep in order to pass in review as it were, in soldierly manner, we did it in fine style, so well, that the Captain was recalled after passing and Kearny paid him a high compliment for the manner in which his Company indicated fine discipline. Not so with other companies who lacking discipline, broke ranks and scurried for the peaches, though they were not near ripe, pulled down branches, broke them, in fact became an unruly mob which their officers could not control. Kearny saw this lack of discipline and reckless destruction of the fruit trees and green, unripe fruit, and while I had heard of Kearny I was so convinced that he was the real Phil when I heard some of his expletives; so rich in color, if red and blue, with a sulphury smell, were a good combination. Kearny was not in uniform, but wore a seersucker coat, bareheaded, only his pants were of his uniform, hence, to the uninitiated, looked the civilian more than an officer of rank. This non military look deceived a Sergeant of Company D, a big burly, loud voiced fellow, who paid no attention to the demands of Kearny to stop the destruction of the trees and fruit, but in derision yelled at Phil wanting to know "who the hell he was" and denounced as an old Secesh (meaning Secessionist) and used some lurid terms not in a very accomplished vocabulary, not nearly so accomplished as that of Kearny's to follow, after the General had an opportunity to make known who he was; but Phil did it in fine fashion. "I am General Phil Kearny, you damn thieving Jersey scoundrel, you (this was not the terms the General did use) get in the ranks or I will have you shot." That big noisy braggadocia was as stiff as a ramrod for a moment then wilted to dimensions to fit a pinhole, so cringing and beaten. From a dirty unshaven, long-haired, misfit clothed mob we were now to have someone to make us over into disciplined, well trained, well fed, well dressed soldiers. This job, to anyone but Kearny, would have seemed one long drawn out performance, but, he was not to be tampered with, nor hindered, nor was any officer of his command any better to him than the private; all must do their duty or get off the job for a better man. His commands were religiously attended to as to food, clothing, proper medical aid and best of equipment possible.

We moved to the St. John's Seminary grounds where everything for comfort of the sick or wounded, the religious attendance, health of camp and drill grounds were of the best, then the rejuvenation began, as Kearny could not wait the slow process of getting government equipment, and from his own purse he clothed the Brigade from head to foot. Rifles of the best then available (Springfield rifles) and every detail that man needed was looked after as we were to enter a strenuous period of drilling. Drill and manuevres were the order of the day, fatigue duty, camp duty, and reconnaissance, and other duties that seemed they would last forever. Some swore, some prayed - not very reverently - to be delivered from the thralldom of Phil Kearny, all to no purpose as Phil had it in his mind to make soldiers of us worthy of the name. The privates were not alone in their harsh feelings of resentment of such laborious duties as building Fort Worth, roads, and etc.

Some officers kicked and were asked to resign or be dismissed and Kearny made it very plain that he was in command, and would have discipline or heads. He secured a discipline that was the marvel of the times and made a body of men he was proud of and they proud of him; notwithstanding their prior feelings they saw the light. Kearny did not spare himself nor his Staff, demanding the same of every officer of the Brigade. Kearny praised his men and prized them highly, he asked nothing for himself or his officers that was too good for the private. He was training us to meet what he saw to be inevitable as he knew the Southern officers to a man, their intent and preparation for war, not a ten day picnic, and he knew the temper of the South.

After wintering at the Seminary Camp, spring came. We were what might be called thoroughbreds in training, ready for the fray. With March came the order from Headquarters (urged by the cry from the North "why doesn't the Army move?") to move upon Centreville where the enemy was supposed to be in force and of great strength. Some part of the Brigade moved up to Fairfax, had a little skirmish at Sangster Station, on to Centreville and its wooden guns. Kearny swept on to Mannassas, following the retreating rearguard of the confederates when stopped by orders from Headquarters (the mistake criticized by Kearny) and returned to Fairfax. Here came orders for Kearny to take command of Sumner's Division and he asked to take his Brigade with him, which was refused by Franklin, and McClellan, being a friend of Franklin, refused the request of Kearny whereas Kearny refused the promotion of Major General, saying he would rather command the First New Jersey Brigade than that of any Division in the Army. He came to his disheartened men who, when the orders came for him to leave us were so stricken that strong men cried and damned their Government from Dan to Bersheba and talked mutiny, but they knew Kearny would turn on them his ready and fluent vocabulary of wrath, and choked with bitter feelings they hushed and waited with bated feelings and hoped for relief; downcast and gloomy and mad. But, about four o'clock p.m. who should come riding in camp but the one man that the Brigade would follow, Kearny, no matter where he led as long as he was with them. The ovation he received! The men shouted, cried, wasted their head gear with abandon, a Brigade of lunatics for the time being.

One-armed General Philip Kearny. Kearny lost his left arm in the Mexican War and, in subsequent battles, rode into action with his horse's reins in his teeth.

A happy lot they were to think he preferred being a Brigadier with them, rather than a Major General with any command. This condition remained until after the fiasco of moving on to Centreville. (This was the route that Kearny believed should have been followed, from Manassas to Richmond, thus, keeping the Army between the Capital of the Nation and the enemy, and he predicted failure of the route via the Peninsula, and the return of the Army would be by land and back to Manassas and Bull Run, and he was correct). Kearny was the most experienced, the best strategist in the Army while in it, having the instinct to fight and not to dig, and the knowledge of War in the latest lines. He had fought Indians under his Uncle Stephen Watts Kearny; had fought in two wars in Europe, the French-Algerian; had been twice decorated by the French King; and was the hero of Magenta and Solferino, decorated by the Italian Government, in both instances fighting the followers of Islam; was the most reckless and desperate of fighters, barbarous, fanatical, to whom to die in battle was glory. His African-French campaign was one of daring and success. The French followed him as they would a Murat or Ney, yes, even the Little Corporal himself. His delight was in the battle front; his troops never gave up a foot once obtained. Kearny was the Ideal Soldier of President Lincoln, and the whole Army loved him as he was a fighter. In the brief thirteen months, he became a Nation wide favorite, the real hero of Williamsburg, where he saved Fighting Joe Hooker from defeat and consequently McClellan's army form a possible surrender. Again, at Fair-Oaks-Seven Pines, he came on the field just in time to save the Divisions of Couch and Casey, fought out and cornered between a victorious enemy and the Chickahominy River either to surrender or be destroyed. Again, at Charles City Cross Roads, he arrived on the spot in time to prevent the severing of the Right Wing of the Army. One more, and the last, a most costly blow to General Pope and the Nation also, at the second Bull Run-Mannassas, where the fighting was most desperate on both sides; one, the elated enemy fighting to break the lines of communication and destroy Pope's Army; the other, the disheartened but sullen and undefeated, defiant Army holding their lines intact until the hard pressed Army of Pope could reform and get to the cover of the works near Washington. The crux of the situation was the use of the Little River Turnpike to Pope's Army, the only possible road to move his Army in retreat, and the Ox Hill road--a road of no very great width, but was a cross cut to the Turnpike. Here at Chantilly, though Chantilly was a few miles away - known by the confederates as Ox Hill and three miles south of Fairfax, Kearny and Stevens fought Lee's victorious troops to a stand still in one of the worst storms of rain and flood, the thunder and lightening never ceasing during that desperate human struggle, which only nightfall brought to a close. The play of lightening dimmed the blast of cannon and rifles, and the crash of the thunders drowned the roar of the cannon and the steady drone of rifle volleys. It was in this terrible din and flash that the souls of Kearny and Stevens passed to their Maker; Kearny being the last to fall in the shades of that awful first day of September evening. The army and the Nation mourned the death of Kearny and his adopted State was stricken sadly. He was buried from his beautiful home at Belgrove on the Passaic, East Newark, N.J., on September 5th, 1862. The route of the cortege was one mass of mourners to Old Trinity, Broadway, New York City where he was accorded a beautiful service and interment in the John Watt's vault - then his own - as his grandfather had devised in his will.

Having deviated from the campaign I will now return to Camp Seminary after the Centreville move. The return to camp brings to the first Regiment a new Colonel - Col. Montgomery being made Governor General over Alexandria. The Lieut. who mustered me in at Trenton - Alfred T.A. Torbert - was made Colonel of the First. He was a West Pointer; a handsome man in feature and figure, afoot or horseback; he knew his business, was a strict disciplinarian, a martinet on duty, but a very gentlemanly person and democratic socially. He, like Kearny, was a master of his calling and saw to the wants of his men and demanded service of them in the making of a good soldier. His eagle eye detected the fault in a man at a glance. If an officer, he weeded them out as they were better at trades than the command of men. Torbert was a commanding figure in any assemblage; his knowledge of the art of war being well based, he knew every branch. Infantry, Artillery and Cavalry, and was a fine figure as a Cavalry Commander, which he did later get as Division Commander in Cavalry. He was drowned off the Keys of Florida on Sept. 27th, 1880, when the steamer Central America was foundered in a hurricane as he was on his return from Bermuda as a Minister of the U.S.

Colonel Alfred T.A. Torbert

John Kuhl

Kearny again put us in shape for the Peninsula campaign. Via the transports, on the order to take boats at Alexandria, we proceeded down the Potomac, up the York River to Ship Point, disembarked for a few days for rest, drilled, and a free lunch on crabs, oysters and fish which were plenty and easy to take when the tide went out. We lived high for two weeks; then came a calamity : - Kearny was ordered to take command of Heintzelman's Division on the front line and under fire. On dress parade, orders were read wherein he stated he still would prefer the command of his Brigade than any Division, but he could not refuse command of troops under fire and must obey the order. He was leaving us with regret but was sure we would accept his leaving like the true soldiers he had hoped to make us. Very sorrowfully we accepted the edict, cheering him loyally while our hearts were sore. Col. George W. Taylor took command ordered us to reembark for West Point at the junction of the York, Pamunkey and Mattapony rivers. After some considerable delay on the boats, we arrived at the point of debarkation, West Point, Va., the junction of the above three Rivers, the enemy only two miles away in large numbers

Col. George W. Taylor (left) and Gen. Philip Kearny (right). Both men would die on September 1, 1862.

and in a strong position, but were surprised and prevented from attacking by the presence of gunboats, which shelled them while we landed.

Our forces consisted of but Newton's Division at time of arrival, while the enemy was eighty thousand strong within six miles, with over two hundred guns, yet the fear of the gunboats kept them at a distance until too late to stop our landing. We disembarked from the transports; ie, rowed in a yawl to within fifty or more yards from shore, then made to wade through the slime and water, loaded like pack mules - which was not easy, proving disasterous to many, but a soaking was only an incident, for after getting on terra-firma, which proved to be an old corn or tobacco field, and lying down to rest, night come on - and so did a Virginia rain storm, which most cordially filled our pores and everything else that was porous. The ground having been ploughed, we spread ourselves across the furrows making the most comfortable fit we could; but somehow the furrows did not exactly conform to the contour of our bodies, consequently we were extremely uncomfortable. Besides all this, the Johnnies were keeping bad hours and found some enjoyment in throwing the shell in our direction, which reminded our officers that we would present - less "objective" to both shell and rain, if standing up and sleep, which we did, to the best of our ability, in that new line until daylight, and was it a long night? It seemed like a month!! The sun beamed upon us - he could have spared many of his lavish rays, and made us happy. We had hardly swallowed a hasty breakfast before orders came to support the 2nd U.S. Artillery.

It was a short, sharp fight that had ended at nightfall. The first real fight on the Peninsula, and had the Confederate General in Command, at that time and place, known that he, with nearly 80,000 men and several Batteries nearby, had only from 10 to 12 thousand to contend with, he would have driven us into the river or captured what was left after the fight.

Gen. George B. McClellan, Commander of the Army of the Potomac. On the Peninsula Phil Kearny called McClellan a "coward or traitor" for refusing to engage the enemy.

Our regiment reached the Village of Mechanicsville, from where the church steeples of the much coveted city of Richmond could be seen, "The bonny bunch of Roses" that McClellan would have liked to obtain, but like his predecessor. "Napoleon lost, never for him to recover the prestige once his," and, as in both, "Napoleon" and the "Little Napoleon," of the Potomac Army, missed the fame they so much desired. Had "Little Mac" been more aggressive, and active, Richmond could have been his, and his fame would have been world-wide. But alas! that seven miles stood between. A change came suddenly, out of the northwest - the flying columns of Stonewall Jackson, whose unique name was attached at first Bull Run, and now was again to add laurels to his fame by an attempt to flank our right wing, compelling us to fall back to Gaines Mills and later to Gaines Hills, near the house of Dr. William Gaines, where on June 27th, 1862, the

The house of Dr. William Gaines.

unlucky Friday, so called, we engaged the enemy in a hotly contested fight, in which the writer was twice flesh wounded, and while falling back found Sergeant Richard A. Donnelly of my company, and my close friend, badly wounded with a shattered leg. He wanted to be taken from the field of carnage, then raging like a holocaust of Hell, and the chances were as one in a thousand that both of us would fail to reach cover. I would not refuse my friend, Dick in such a case, and under a terrific, galling cross fire carried him to a supposed place of safety into the hands of comrades of our Company - though he was made prisoner later on - and after recovering from the temporary blindness and exhaustion due to a 1200 yard dash with load of no mean proportions, as my comrade was over six feet and I was only five foot nine, I again took to fighting and after about twenty minutes was shot in the left side of the head. To all appearances, my comrades said, I must be dead, and they passed on in that belief, and reported me "dead upon the field of battle." I slowly came back to the world as, during the shock, I had passed into strange places as well as having a vivid panorama of my whole past life in that short time of, not over ten minutes, while it was not all virtue I had not much to deeply blush for, perhaps because I had not lived very long and was country bred. I managed to struggle to my feet and attempted to make my way to where our men had formed a line to stay the onrush of the elated enemy, and was almost run down by the charge of Rush's Lancers who swiftly came on to meet the advancing enemy and but for the quick thought of the left guide of the Squadron I would have been trampled to death beneath the feet of the close column of horses. Reaching the line of battle, with the aid of a strange comrade, I was passed through to the rear; taken to the field hospital, which was near the Woodbury or Engineers' Bridge; and placed under the low hanging branches of an apple tree to wait my turn for surgical treatment, which came about two o'clock in the morning. A ball and two buckshot were removed from the wounded head and neck. They placed the "Ball and Buck" in my pockets and then returned me to the shelter of the tree to die from bleeding or saved by Nature's choice.

The Engineer's bridge through the Chickahominy Swamp.

We were to be taken over the Chickahominy in the late morning and about six or seven a.m. were roused from our stupor by quick and heavy firing on the road to the west of us. Among others we found our way to the causeway leading to the Bridge and the only crossing near, when to our surprise an attack was made upon us from a supposed friendly quarter, and by men in our uniform of the Cavalry service. A number were killed in our wounded line, others again wounded - as this whole body of men were wounded, and none armed whatever. Finding the enemy was upon us we made every effort to reach the bridge and when it was discovered that the enemy was charging, the bridge was blown to atoms by those in charge of it, and our escape was cut off. Many of the men jumped into the slough of mud from the causeway and disappeared forever - others simply stood or fell to the ground awaiting that which might happen next, helpless as they were, death or imprisonment. Among those who decided, and take consequences, was the writer, and was made a prisoner of war. We - I mean those who were prisoners, - and they were in the hundreds - were marched up the River to near our old camp at Mechanicsville, crossed the river, and marched to the "Rocketts," just below Richmond and near the James River, where thousands of "unfortunates," like ourselves were collected, awaiting disposition. Very many of those were badly wounded and during Sunday orders came that: all Yankees that could walk would be sent through the lines to join their own army. After a careful inspection to make sure no unwounded "Yanks" were released, the line of pitiful men was started for the Williamsburg Pike which would bring us near Savage Station, which was still in our possession and was a great Hospital filled to overflowing with wounded and hundreds lying on the ground under improvised shelter. We were barely made comfortable when orders came to have all the wounded that could walk make their way toward White Oak Swamp Road to Charles City Cross Roads, and those who could be moved were placed in Ambulances as rapidly as possible and all stores of food, fodder, ammunition and clothing were collected and burned - rifles by the thousands, as all this stuff could not be removed in so short a time. General J.B. Magruder, of considerable fame at that time made three desperate attempts to break and destroy the rear guard who were protecting the safe retreat of the Potomac Army across the Peninsula, and as many

Federal wounded after Gaines's Mill. There may be a possibility that Charles Hopkins is among the wounded in this photograph.

times failed after most stubborn and costly fighting. We followed General Newton to Malvern Hill, near the James River, and after a most terrific fight by rifle and cannon from both sides, that lasted what seemed forever, the wounded men were shipped by boat to the Hospital in all parts of the North. The steamer John A. Warner was our refuge.

Our wounds were dressed for the first time in five days. The Doctors shook their heads but spoke as cheerfully as though it was a comfort, and it was, yet we knew that there was danger from the first as the surgeon who had performed the operation intimated to his assistants that the changes were not very hopeful - not knowing that I was conscious enough to comprehend his remark. We reached Baltimore on the "Natal Day" and there was but little evidence of jubilation, and no wonder, as the whole work of a year, costing millions of dollars, thousands of lives and thousands maimed and disabled - was all gone!!! And conditions were not better, really worse, than on the fatal 21st of July, 1861 at Bull Run. Gloom and discontent in the North, Copperhead sentiment openly avowed, plots and counter plots to undermine the loyal sentiment at the North.

While this was going on our stay was made at Camden Street Hospital, Baltimore. I had hoped to go home but the surgeon refused to allow it - as I learned later - because I was a subject of treatment at such a place, in order to have a chance to recover, provided I could. While here, memory became deficient, could give no coherent statement, forgot who I was and where my home was, no facts about my people. After an operation by Chief Surgeon, and some coaching I was able to recall to my mind some things the most recent before my arrival at the Hospital, and finally, piece by piece my memory returned. After some time I demanded my return to my company. This was finally made possible despite the strong opposition of the Surgeon, by my personal letters to Secretary of War, Stanton.

I was returned to my Regiment, and passed the winter at Camp Hazel Run, Virginia, surprising many of the company by my return as I had been reported dead June 27, 1862. Among those who were greeting me was my old friend and mate, Alfred L. Lincoln, who had been wounded at Salem Church, and who had become quite a "melancholia" for several reasons - he was disgusted at and disheartened by ill treatment and his untreated wound. I think my return did much good, as he had no one to whom he could freely talk his innermost thought to - yet he would to me - and he had my sympathy. At all events he became cheerful and responded more readily to the inevitable. After almost dying with appendicitis, as now known, he recovered partially and in March we had orders to support General Jud Kilpatrick in a raid upon Richmond to aid in the release of the Libby, and Belle Isle prisoners, which raid resulted disastrously - costing the life of the gallant Dahghren - and the result of the above raid also caused relapse to the writer who had to go under treatment again. After a long and tedious march - mud galore, and sticky, cold raw weather, and no "game" returned to camp, and as I had left camp despite the doctor's orders, having been very ill, that Dr. Miller said that my death was near at one time, of peritonitis, and that I did not die was a surprise to him. when he said to me, "you must die, I cannot do more to help you," I differed with him and said "I will not die." I was spared for other trials.

CHAPTER TWO
INTO THE WILDERNESS AND CAPTURE

In May, 1864, as the Union Army of the Potomac prepared to begin its spring campaign against Confederate General Robert E. Lee's Army of Northern Virginia, all the soldiers on both sides knew that this would be the bloodiest struggle of the war.

After three long years, Corporal Charles Hopkins had seen more than his share of death. He began to record his experiences in a small pocket diary. The first entry in the diary is May 5, 1864. The day his regiment, the First New Jersey Infantry, moved into the wilderness of Virginia.

Thursday, May 5, 1864

Broke camp at "6" O'Clock AM. Marched to the place of organization of line of Battle which was in the most impenitrable thicket I have seen for some time, our troops drove the Confederates for some 4½ miles before we were engaged which was about 1 O'Clock PM. and at that time they were falling back to their breastwork in a swamp. We fought hard until night. Nearly 6 hours fighting.

The campaign opened with Lee. We met him at the Wilderness, May 5th and 6th, 1864. On the march from our winter quarters at Hazel Run to the Wilderness there were some raw troops that had been doing duty about the mines of Pennsylvania. In the strike region, they were supplied with all kinds of wearing gear and everything that a soldier in a permanent camp could wish for - from cap to shoe - and much more "tailored" than the men in front had, or could use. This march tried them as never before - loaded like "jackmules" - and being placed in line between Regiments of hardened veterans they soon displayed their weakness in hard gruelling and marching. To make matters more unpleasant the old Vets would laugh and jeer at them for carrying so much while the knapsack

The soldiers of the Federal Sixth Army Corps cross a pontoon bridge. This was the opening of the 1864 Spring Campaign, which soon resulted in the Battle of the Wilderness.

and blanket roll for the Vet was like a wallet, the day after the circus was in town. Comparison became odius. They were given voluntary advice by the Vets to unload their surplus and only keep a single change of undergarments. The sly old Vets! Away went the fine shirts, collars, shoes, blacking and brushes, boots, overcoats and all that the warm season would not require. It was like pulling teeth to part with some things. Most of the clothing had been made over by the "handy man" of the Regiment or Company, or the Village tailor, where they had been stationed, and fitted them decently, while the "old Vet" had the Regular Army "fit" (i.e. no fit or too much fit) but they were useful and the shoes were truly comfortable. The longer the march the greater the unload by the "recruits."

The road, for miles, was strewed, not alone with the shuffling "off" of the new levies, but those of the crafty Vets in exchange for articles better than their own. What was left on that line of march would have supplied a small army completely with clothing.

Thursday, May 5th, we crossed the Rhappahannock at Germania Ford and by afternoon were in line of battle and under fire in the Wilderness. It was a spot on the face of Nature well named "The Wilderness," but if anyone was lost they were soon found by the "Confeds" of Gordon or Early. Such a battle as waged there for two days, of the three, seemed like Hades broken loose. Six thousand men, lost to Grant, were killed, wounded and missing - no one will ever know exactly, as many of the badly wounded met a terrible death - in their helpless condition; they were burned to unrecognizable crisp; some in their last struggle to get away from the fire had partly pulled themselves to their knees clinging to the trees and were tortured by burning in that position. Numbers were literally a mass of crisp, like burned leather - the woods and underbrush had taken fire, and the pine trees of all heights flamed like giant torches, shooting to the skies. Horrible sights in the shadows of the "Wilderness" for three days and nights - scenes that harrowed the soul and gave rise to gloomy thoughts, and sleep unknown, only to those who could stand no longer vigil.

Friday, May 6th still found us in the "Wilderness" hoping for a Moses to lead us out. Grant was the man but he was not my "Moses," for about 5 p.m. our right wing under General Seymour of Olustee fame, with his "Black Brigade" of negroes who had proven themselves fighters at Olustee, was turned by General J.B. Gordon with his "all Georgia" Brigade. That was the beginning of the end of that terrific struggle to shake off Grant's clinging hold in the Wilderness, and many would have been glad to have walked out with some Moses before the fight; but Grant led though it cost blood in plenty, and precious lives. Those who followed where Grant led came out of the Wilderness; i.e., the unharmed and not seriously wounded. Some of us, however, followed Lee that night, not because we loved him, or feared him, but because of his affection for us - as we were wanderers in the Wilderness, wounded and sorely pressed, strangers within his gates - and he took us in.

Friday, May 6, 1864

We lay on the front line of Battle all night and until 1 O'Clock PM. and then we were relieved by the 7th Maine and we fell back 50 yards and threw up a wide breastwork and held it until we were thrown back, for to give the 77th N.Y. a chance to try their powder & ball. At 4 O'Clock the Rebs made a flank movement on our right. And the first line of Barrier gave way.

6 O'Clock finds me a prisoner.

The end of that day that gave us to the enemy as prisoners of war, was a day of individual fighting, as the force that met the final charge of Gordon's Flower of Georgia, and repulsed him twice, was made up of all kinds of Regiments, in knots of ten, to fifty, more than a dozen different Regimental colors were massed in small space, surrounded by the homogenous mass of loyal men, all of one thought - check the enemy - and save our right wing, or all is lost in vain, after three days of most desperate and costly fighting. We checked him at awful cost to Gordon as well as to Grant. I distinctly remember seeing the colors of the 1st, 2nd, 3rd and 4th New Jersey, and the 1st Long Island, 42nd and 63rd Pennsylvania, and 45th New York. Colonels, Captains and all ranks of officers were making effort to get their own organization together and all efforts were in vain, however, the men seemed willing to fight with any organization, or none, under anybody who could command them; they seemed engrossed with the idea of Phil Kearny, "there was damn good fighting" at any point in the line - and indeed, there was enough to go around and satisfy the most plucky. From 1500 to 2000 men so successfully checked the terrible onslaught of Gordon as to permit the gallant Shaler to so reform his lines as to repel the bitter assault of the Division of Jubal Early, who confidently expected to crush our right wing and close in on our rear. He counted upon an easy flank movement, but that brilliant ideal soldier, "Shaler" was to be reckoned with, and Early failed. So ended the Wilderness struggle so far as your humble servant was concerned, for he was wounded and a prisoner.

Now, came the real troubles of the poor devils, so unfortunate as to be made captive, as very, very many were badly wounded, very few among them not having a wound of some kind, beside a grievous and wounded spirit. The writer, having been twice wounded that day, and ordered from the line by his Captain with orders to go to the field hospital, and to Acquia Creek, and, as my time was out in three days, he said that I should go on to Washington for discharge. I contended, that to go to the rear was as dangerous as to remain with the Company, and remain I did though three days more would have let me out of service. I remained longer than intended and the future came very near leaving my remains only - and not much remainder either.

Now comes the beginning of a life that seemed the realization of that place, which, as a child we imagined the abode of the wicked. No doubt some of us were yet each supposed of course that it was the other fellow - though I never posed as an angel. Later on we came to think at least, those of our comrades who so awfully suffered in those "Hells" on earth should be allowed to pass the "Gates ajar," unquestioned by the good Saint Peter. Perhaps this view was colored by the fact that we expected to end our days in those places - but who could blame us? Our comrades died the most horrible deaths, all for their country and its honor, and to maintain the only flag which spoke in plain terms, "Liberty and Freedom." Many of those who still survive may feel that they also be shriven - no doubt, would have been long ago had they been willing to do less, than to suffer as then, with no chance to lose life and all its pleasures, but would win all. But you know how it is yourself. I find that my ideas have "changed base," so will return to the subject.

Saturday, May 7, 1864

Seps Robertsons Tavern at 6 AM. marched to Orange Court House 19 miles, "Virginia miles". I never was a more debassed man for a companion. A Capt. of C.S. had charge of us to the above place.

Monday, May 9, 1864

10 O'Clock the train came for us and we started for Lynchburg where we arrived at 4 O'Clock PM. March about 2 miles to camp.

    The night of disconsolation passed at Robertson's Tavern but we did not find quarters there. The tribe of the Lost Children in the Wilderness was located about the Tavern - by the way, the host was not there to greet us - in the open lots, the "Big Fish," as Generals, Field, Staff and Line officers were not much better off than the "high" privates except they were enclosed in a circular worm fence that had at some former date encircled a hay stack. Among the officers we recognized General Alex Shaler, the redoubtable fighter and tactician; General Seymour, of the Dusky Brigade of Olustee fame, with some seventy odd officers of all grades, and being in such good company none of them seemed happy; and, in fact, there was nothing to feel very happy about - unless we could find comfort in making our captors jubilant because of our presence. Among them, as from their performances and language, you would think they had captured about all of Grant's highest rank. An incident of that night's bivouac will give an idea of the real chivalry extended to the unfortunates. I made acquaintance with one Corporal Millam of the 14th Alabama of Gordon's Division, and he wanted my rubber blanket and I suggested he may as well have it as to have it "confiscated" by some other Confed. Indeed, that was polite and to the point and of course he did not want to take it without some compensation so offered me some Confed. money - five dollars of which was equal to nothing in greenbacks; and as my greenbacks had been sent to the rear by my tent mate on Friday, just before our capture, along with some letters, pictures, and other trinkets I wished to be safe in case something happened - and it did happen. After thinking over the deal I was getting, and of the fellow's honest intent, I concluded that I would be $5.00 Confed. in pocket, I closed with him and also "swapped" him a "portmonie" - a pocket book - that cost me $3.50, for his patched, empty, rusty, little, clasp purse, and a "blockade," black lead pencil; and to my chagrin, when too late, the day following, I discovered that I had left a gold "Kearny" Maltese cross, with my full name, Company, Regiment, and my address inscribed thereon, in the pocketbook, and a note for $90.00 against a man of whom I could have collected. Alas, too late! Yet I did not then, nor do not now, make much ado over it - he was a decent fellow, and truthful, as I found later; also, he broke bread with me that gloomy night, his own corn pone. May 7th - oh, what a day! A march over the hot dusty roads of "Ole Virginny" with a mixed column a mile long composed of all ranks in officialdom, and last of all, the rank and file, the bone and sinew of any army, many of whom had been through that three days storm of whistling bullets, and the hurtling shot and shrieking shell - reaping by the thousands the best blood of the loyal North and misled South. In that long line were loyal bodies with probably an arm or leg missing,

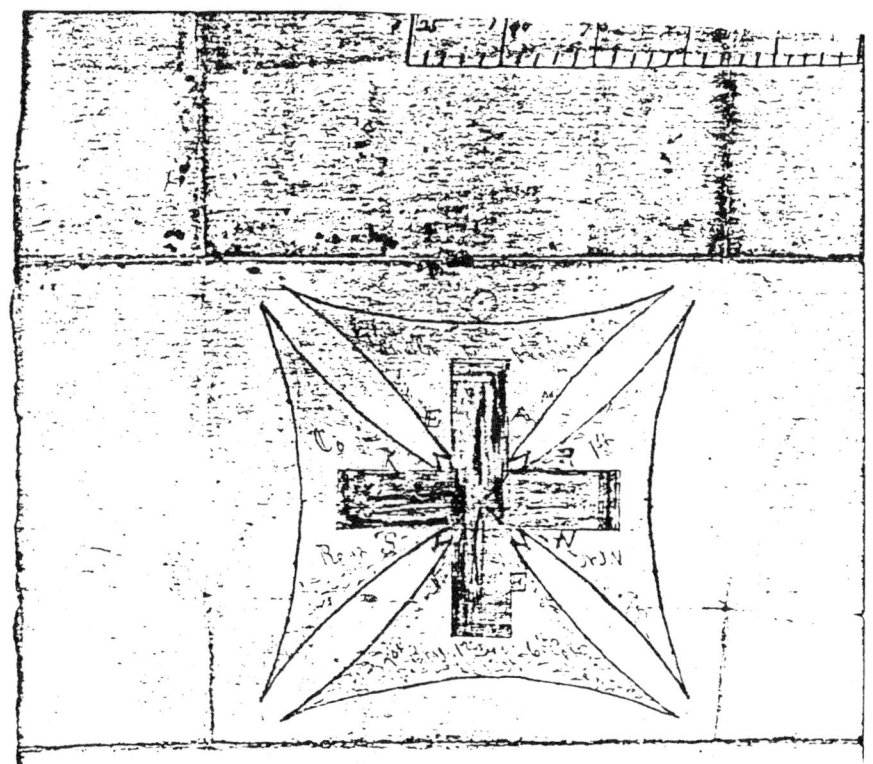

A sketch made by Charles Hopkins of his Kearny Cross identification medal, which he lost in a trade with a Rebel.

or one of each; perhaps, both eyes gone; wounded men of all descriptions representing a hundred or more separate and distinct commands, smoke-begrimed, bloody and exhausted almost to breaking by the tireless struggle, with its sleepless nights and gloomy thoughts, - yet, defiant, loyal as ever, and proud of their Flag and Country.

The Confederate officer, a Captain, in charge of the troops serving as guard to this lot of unfortunate captives, was a Georgian, by name of Fletcher and he was unfit for officer of any rank - neither a gentleman, scholar nor soldier, as proven by his language and bearing, but was the personification of a brute, idiot and coward - he made our dusty, sultry march of twenty-eight miles to Orange Court House a march of indignation, misery and death. Men who were wounded and unable to march further were speedily furnished with a quick remedy for all the ills of life, brutally murdered and left by the roadside to become the prey of the razorback hogs, and dogs, if any there be - or rot away in some unknown locality - their bones left to bleach in the enemy's lines, never to be identified or what had been their fate - while loving ones at home waited for some tidings of them. It is a fact that hundreds, aye, thousands of such cases were reported as "missing in action" or were reported as deserters - their fond parents, widows and orphans were compelled to mourn in silence and shame for such a record, for while in their hearts they could not believe it to be true they had no proof to the contrary. The writer knew of two such cases personally, marked as deserters, while their loyal hearts had been broken and their bones lay mouldering in the Hell at Andersonville. These two cases were corrected - but one of them not in time to save a poor, fond mother, who never would be convinced that her William had been a deserter, from being sent to her grave. The action of this brute of a Captain in disposing of the helpless, maimed and overdone victim, was of course an incentive, and a strong one, to those who were ready to drop from exhaustion, forcing themselves to struggle on and on, until Nature had been urged to the limit and could no longer stand the strain, and knowing their fate from what they had seen they would hopelessly sink to the earth, and without a tremor await the executioner, who came soon, though in most cases there was but little life to take. To our personal knowledge, being near the rear of the line, we saw several of those loyal patriots murdered in cold blood and we forged ahead in the line in order that we might not be so close to the rear-guard. Any pretext was good enough to shoot a Yankee. The feeling and desire to murder, which rankled in our hearts that long and trying day, toward that brute, Fletcher - an Apache Indian, in a Confederate uniform, would have found vent, but for the wholesale slaughter, that would have followed to the wounded that still struggled with the hope that they would yet get home to their mourning people by the process of parole and exchange. (The vent, above mentioned was the quiet passing of the word along the line that a break might be made to escape - but this was abandoned at suggestion of General Shaler and General Seymour, who were ranking men, and gave as reason the above possible and most likely procedure of Fletcher).

But alas, it was never to be to very many of that long line of valiant men. We, I mean all the line, were systematically robbed at each halt by this animal, Fletcher; and even his men were ashamed of his greed and brutality, for some of his men had seen service at the front, but not all of them - there was a marked difference between the two. From a Union soldier with a fairly good hat, he would take it or else demand it at the muzzle of a revolver - giving in return, his own, or that of one of his men's filthy head coverings and found pleasure in continuously making "swaps." He would say, with a sneering grin on his countenance, "Fair exchange was no robbery." His collections were made up of watches, jewelry, knives, money, both wool and rubber blankets, postage stamps, shoes, boots, in fact anything and everything of any value or comfort to those poor men. Perhaps, a photo of a wife, child, parent, sweetheart, sister or brother, or someone near to them; letters were taken and read to those about and jeered at; some destroyed in the presence of the owner; yet all these were so precious to the owners, and would be so much more precious to him now that he was fastmoving toward a place of misery and suffering unknown. Those letters - Ah! what a comfort they were to those who were able to secrete them from the prying eyes of that thief, murderer and outcast of Hell - to read and re-read so many times over in the long weary days and months of mental and physical suffering; and to those who died with them pressed closely to their speechless lips, they were indeed a comfort, though of a poignant degree, yet, they were almost envied by those who had no such consolation in kind. The writer had saved some papers and a few trinkets, retained at time of sending his money and some pictures to the rear on the day of capture, which he managed to secrete in the double seat and legs of his pants; thus was saved my little "housewife," including the contents, which consisted of needles, small scissors and some thread, also saved two pictures of friends, and a New Testament given to me by my sister Rebecca. (All of which are still in the family).

This awful march ended at the close of the day and we were free from the contact of that demoniacal coward. We were now at Orange Court House, in the grounds that were known as the Court Yard, and placed under guard of men, all of whom had seen field service and had hearts of men; yet, they loved us not as we had held them at bay, and badly wounded their favorite Division Commander Longstreet, I learned right here - that information given me by Corporal Millam, with whom I had swapped purses with, was literally true, as everything of value or benefit to men in the field was asked for and if not handed over at once, you were "relieved" of it by persuasion and coaxing that was simply "irresistible."

We lay all night in the Court Yard and we really slept. Our first salutation in the morning was "Hey thar you-uns, if yo want to see a nigger hang look 'round right smart." We were just opposite the opening of the basement and sure enough they were just pulling up one of Burnside's black heroes in full uniform! We were born Abolitionists, if you like, or rather utterly opposed to Slavery; and knowing we had good reason to believe that our remarks would not meet with favor, we, nevertheless, could not contain our wrath and remarked to the sentry nearest us "that the soul of that colored patriot had gone to meet the soul of John Brown, in Heaven - John Brown, who had been murdered in the same way by the same people of Virginia; and that no Rebel soul, engaged in that kind of work, or the unholy war, would ever room in Heaven or meet that of the martyr they were hanging! God bless that colored Veteran!!! That was a long speech under the circumstances and the immediate surroundings did not impress me as I only saw the swinging form of that sable hero.

I was suddenly brought back to earth an instant later for I was covered with three rifles and one formidable looking old "pepper box," which, had it been twenty feet away I would have had less fear than a stone in the hand of a fairly good shot. My thoughts went rapidly over my past life as I expected to visit the "Great Unknown," and wondered whether prayer would be effective after so long a service with sin, and would it be just to do so under this stress - when ample time had been given long ago. The explosive exclamation, "Shut up yer mouth!" coupled with the leveled rifles, though they were pointing four different ways, allowing us to see up the barrels to the breech in all of them at the same time, stopped our moralizing. There was no room for argument and mechanically we "shut up," and sat down, though the latter was not a part of the command. You can't imagine what space of time had passed in my mind during those few seconds - childhood to burial. Everything included was pressed into that short space and we were disappointed that we were not killed, though quite agreeable so we assure the reader.

After some backing and filling about the Court House, we were placed in cars and sent forward to Gordonsville. Packed in freight cars like sardines, and only one side door open, was like we had heard of Hades - a veritable sweatbox! How the least wounded suffered with the heat and lack of fresh air; what must have been the agony of those badly

Federal prisoners being marched to the rear by their Confederate captors.

shattered men, without a dressing or anything to stay their suffering, along with the thirst that follows all such injuries!!! The day was one of anguish and heart break to hear the moaning forced from those strong men, and unable to do a thing to relieve them. Thank God! Gordonsville was reached at last and hope was strong that fresh air and water were plenty, and medical aid for the helpless, dejected and sorely wounded. Hope had receded hourly for we were placed in a "Y" of the railroad surrounded by a twenty foot embankment. We thought we had been miserable before, but now, with about 2000 in such a small space - no water, sand for our bed, the sun at nearly 100 degrees in the open and beating down upon us seeming to concentrate its rays upon that triangular spot where the sick, wounded and dying huddled like sheep - it was worse. The "Y" was the death-bed and grave for many of our number. A few yards away, water and shade in plenty was available, comfort for the suffering and dying, yet, we were condemned to this fetid hole, shadeless, water scarce, and no attempt to assist the dying and wounded by medical aid.

While lying there a train stopped and we discovered it to be a train of wounded from the Rebel lines at the Wilderness. Among them was a car provided with a canvas, covering General Longstreet, badly wounded in the fight of May 6th. Two nights and days of this comfort of Hell and then we were moved toward Lynchburg; and near the outskirts of Charlotteville we had a breakdown of our locomotion department. We "Disembarked" and went into bivouac for the night near the track. Just where we made our bed for the night was on the edge of the embankment and on a curve of the railroad, and about thirty feet above a sand lot. During the night, while enjoying a troubled cat nap, and thinking during the waking moments of the home far away, a relief engine came and disturbed our rest, and suddenly awoke us to see what seemed to me a locomotive heading for me direct with the dazzling glare of the headlights full in my face. Without a thought of the sentinel within ten feet of me, or the possibilities of a landing place, or the correct aim of the man behind the gun, we made a leap for life - as we thought it - from the oncoming iron monster of one big luminous eye, and rumbling wheels, noisy and rushing steam, feeling it was to be our "Juggernaut" unless we avoided it. We landed safely on our head and shoulders 30 feet below, followed by the bullets of two rifles of the guards, which fortunately were wide of mark or we should have had more violent shock to the anatomy of a two hundred and twenty-five pound Yankee. Thanks to a stout neck that did not break, but for days and weeks considerably painful, with a very polite way of carrying our head, it may have appeared somewhat dignified, though not intended.

We finally reached Lynchburg after a torturous day and night in cattle cars, cramped and hot, an incident during the night somewhat relieved the monotony of the trip, which at one time looked as though some of the either innocent or guilty would be relieved of all worldly troubles. Sitting in the single opening of the car, (the door) on the side were two "Johnnies," neither of them good-looking or of a social disposition. On the contrary, were most savage of feature with every line of cruelty plainly stamped on their dirty phiz, and very much inclined to abuse the "damn Yanks," trying hard to elicit an answer to the question, "what do youns come down here to fight weuns for?" This they coupled with frequent threats that "They had a notion to blow us all to Hell befo mawnin'!!"

Wednesday, May 11, 1864

Left Lynchburg Va. and enroute for Danville. Cars run 20 miles and we lay all night cooped in the cars.

Thursday, May 12, 1864

    Started again for Danville 60 miles distant and made some 30 miles and lay all night in the cars and received no rations from the Confederates since the 10th making 6 hard tack and 2 oz of bacon in 7 days.

Monday, May 16, 1864

    My birthday! and a very pleasant situation I am to spend it in a Confederate Prison with a prospect of not getting free very soon.
    Destitution stares Virginia in the face.

    One of them was a South Carolinean, the other a Kentucky bred; the first had an ugly scar on his face that awfully disfigured his already ugly countenance, and language that was made much stronger in expletives than the writer could find in his category. The Kentucky bred was not all that "Kentucky bred" means, but he certainly was a thoroughbred in both foul and profane language, with the accompaniment of long hair and beard, both uncombed for a generation, and the genuine "Virgin Leaf" tobacco juice canals from mouth to chin - and evidently his clothing shared the flow. In order to get a breath of air, at long intervals the men confined inside would work their way to his door. The writer had his turn with the rest and while there, our smelling qualities became acute, made so no doubt from the fresh ozone which the slow-moving train made better. Following the "lead" of our nose we made out to locate the "aroma" of meat, and to our utter surprise it hung against the door jamb - right under our nose - and it belonged to the Kentuckian, who was seated in the door way - legs hanging outside, as did his mate. More than one of us thought how easy it would be to push both of them out of the door and try to escape; the thought smacked of possible, deliberate murder, provided either of them or both were killed, and as yet, personally they had done us no harm except abuse us by their filthy tongue, and escape was not assured even though the door was clear, as there were eight men on each car top, and had we escaped their bullets, and not been successful finally, our re-capture would have meant death to some of us, had either guard been killed.
    However, these thoughts abandoned, our sense of smell sharpened by hunger, led us into a new line of thought - how to get some of Kentucky's meat and "pone" from that sack at hand, so invitingly yet so dangerously, without being caught. Cautiously we intruded our not over clean Yankee digits, into the sack, fearing discovery at any moment not know-

ing what might follow, "touched" the grub for a piece of meat, which was ham, and two corn "pone." We thought of taking more but feared that it might be missed before we could dispose of it, and remove all traces of smell, or substance. Once it was in our possession our desire for fresh air was satisfied and we removed to the rear end of the car, where our chum was, and the two of us ate the ham and "pone" - much too quickly to enjoy it, or save a possible attack of indigestion. (I can taste that ham and "pone" yet.) We had only nicely put it out of sight and rubbed our hands and lips with the dirt from the floor of the car, which was composed of the fragrances of tobacco, grain, cotton and stable, combined - and not overclean, we must admit, yet, we did not falter though it was very unpleasant; a stir and loud voices at the door convinced us that we were not a moment too soon as "Kentucky" had missed his grub and was so ungenerous as to make ado about it. This woke up South Carolina to see where he stood for breakfast. They were on equal terms, for other Yanks had followed their sense of smell and had taken all that was to be found in both sacks. Well, I never heard more inconsiderate men in all my life. They actually made things blue by their sulphurous language, and they threatened to kill the whole "damn lot of Yankee thieves." They smelled of every one about the door that they could, without leaving the door - no use, the Yanks had outwitted them!

At daylight the train stopped at a little station just outside of Lynchburg, and those two irate Rebs invited the "damn Yanks" that stole their grub to step to the platform and they would shoot them. Not a Yank was willing to honor the "invite". The "gray-backs" dared, damned, begged and pleaded, but without response. Then they became furious for all their more fortunate comrades laughed at them and goaded them to frenzy by their jeers; and but for their Captain - this man was a real man, not a Fletcher - who was enjoying it hugely, they may have shot some innocent man or men, for, in, in their rage they pointed their rifles at the the door repeatedly, and as often the officer warned them to stop such work. Had Fletcher been in command at this time, we have no doubt that murder would have been done by these men.

At Lynchburg and short on greenbacks - thanks to the brute Fletcher, who had first chance, May 7th, compelled an exchange of gum blanket, haversack and fork knife and spoon combination, and left me penniless, except for the five dollars of Confed received for compulsory sale. The latter now seemed a Godsend, as passing through the city of Lynchburg, on a bridge crossing the North Anna River, a chap came along clad as a baker with a pan of what he called bread, twenty to the pan, and one dollar Confed each. I closed a deal in a wink of an eye. They were called loaves but my term would be biscuit as they were that size - small spongy and light. The twenty biscuit were bought by myself and two others. Everybody near us was hungry and some were of my own Regiment - but that would have made no difference. Seventeen were handed over, three retained for personal consumption; but while eating the first the eyes of those without food were so wistful and appealing that I held my own in my teeth with one in each hand, closed my eyes, put out my arms, and they were gone in an instant, and I had made no choice of the hungry crowd. Alas, all were gone too quickly to derive any satisfaction, and still left the same old "vacuum," I have thought since, had we eaten several hundred of them we might have been satisfied - they being so light and airy that they might have aided us to escape by lifting us up out of our surroundings and soared away, with the hope that the wind might be blowing northward - but then the time for landing would come and we were not master of the situation, and with no experience in the "air line route,"-then what? Yes, those biscuits were airy, they seemed like a dream and left that impression!

We were put to pasture southwest of the city of Lynchburg in a depression of the ground near the river, backed up by a high slope to the west from which frowned several cannon, supported by Infantry. While we overlooked the river in front, we also looked over some 3000 Confederates. With bluffs on the North, the East was protected as on the high slope in our rear - by cannon, loaded with "grape and canister." This of course had a soothing effect; i.e., we made no demonstration or any serious "objection" to this kind of treatment. We were fed here, of course, as the grass was not long enough to crop on, or green in the scorching sun of May in the South. Seven "tack" were issued per man, for forty-eight hours. No sign of covering. "The sun shone for all," and it did shine! Oh, how hot! There was no air to speak of and the shade of night was welcome as it brought coolness and dew that became almost too cool and damp for comfort. Here we met Richard Vincent of my home town for the first since May 5th, and we were indeed glad to meet each other, even under such conditions. Vincent was a man that ought not to have enlisted because of his physical condition, and under size, an asthmatic. With all these defects his intense loyalty would not be put aside, and he gave his life for his Country by a most horrible death which will be explained later on.

But the morrow was to part us again, I being put upon a train for Danville, Va., where after two days and nights in those sweatboxes to swelter and swear, no doubt, there was another incident - one more bright spot in that night's journey and about the proper hour for ghosts and hobgoblins to saunter forth upon their mission. Two guards at the door, and all hands sleepy, the guards did not seem so strenuous as the former unreasonable fellows. In this case the tops of the cars had a larger contingent of "Confeds" ready to fire at anything that looked of "wooden nutmet variety." The grub sacks of the guards hung beside the door and it was evident that they had no word of the Yankee trick done the former guards, a former experience became vivid - the same hunger gnawing at out vitals, the same overcoming perfume of ham, bacon or shoulder was troubling us, nostrils filled with it, mouth watering, and we "fell" and followed the line of procedure, carefully removed such as we could and not disturb the owner in his "reveries," as he no doubt was thinking of home and feasting. We were our thoughts of feasting as we could not live on "reverie" much longer, and we were not long, for when my hand went down the second time, there was another hand there and both quickly and quietly removed them - each thinking the other was the owner, but instantly learned better, as no remonstrance came from any source. The same careful disposition was made after I removed from the door with my "game" secure, and for "obvious" reasons. One of the guards was lacking an eye, and not very handsome at best; the other was just the ordinary, uncouth looking "Cracker;" both had the misfortune to lose their grub. In this case, after hastily eating our "catch" we rubbed our hands and lips with plug tobacco, in any form, is disliked by me, sickening me every time I used it, but it was more welcome in this case than to be caught in such justifiable "Kleptomania." I say "justifiable" - you may say no, but we shall not argue the case now as the limit is outlawed. That ham and pone to me were as enticing as ham or turkey is to "Brer Johnson" on his tour of "inspection" after all honest people are asleep. In the morning, at an hour that the guard thought seemly to indulge in breakfast, he was somewhat disappointed at finding that his breakfast eluded him. He said some very uncomplimentary things about "Thieving Yanks," and the one-eyed monster was exceedingly wroth, and he actually swore and tried to persuade those who had offended to come to the front with an acknowledgment. All were so unkind and obdurate as to refuse this chivalrous invitation - not knowing his real intention - whether to compliment or reprimand them. There were fitful outbreaks from time to time, and every Yank silent as though dead.

Two long hours had passed; the train stopped; the guards were changed. A few hours later we reached Danville. We left the cars and viewed the muddy "Dan River." We crossed it went into quarters at tobacco house, Number one, erstwhile prison close by the river. Our room was assigned us and we were sent, under the guard, to the third "flo" to find that some two hundred others had taken quarters there; but we made no objection of course as they had the "precedence" and we selected the only places left, the plank was not a soft one as the Confeds were economic people, as we did not accept the exciting "skirmishes" we had about possession of own person, they felt that too much food or too often would be a menace to good health. Besides, they themselves were having outside exercise so they required the bulk of the supply. This, we had learned by experience; wounded, sick and dying were all served alike, and it was pitiful to hear the stifled moans during every hour of day or night, and no way to aid them. Dawn of day would find the suffers still in death - a relief to them! They were removed and taken out for burial - not as human being, but as an animal. All places vacated by death were filled by a new arrival.

The "menu" at Danville was not an elaborate one - soup, as they burned it, was served in cups, a chunk of black bread of a sort not known in the North, that was the full course of the "menu." I have many times eaten thrice as much of a quality that had a name, and then was not overloaded. The water was in a barrel at the stair landing. Everybody helped himself; some would wash their cups in it; other set their hands and managed to remove some of the "accumulations" of the past month or two. (As the water came from the Dan River, it did not seem to change the color much, though the flavor was more varied.) Those having no towels - and ninety-nine and nine-tenths had none - were compelled to use some part of their clothing to wipe upon, and this usually was the part most used in sitting position. How clothes were washed I never learned - though there a week I never saw any vermin in the process; but the "still" hunt was a daily pastime and was a real necessity in order to maintain a personal ownership. That floor had many men as lodgers and every person had close neighbors in plenty. I found some while there, in fact, had made their acquaintance before under less adverse circumstances, close friends, yet not on speaking terms. I spent my birthday here May 16, 1864, and not much elated over the return of that birthday. Little thought had I, that six more days would find me in the prototype of Dantes Inferno - Andersonville!

Tuesday, May 17, 1864

Ah Yes, I am freed to day from Danville Prison but only to journey to Georgia a distance of 500 miles. The train ran 50 miles and now stops for the night. Paid $5.00 for one lb. of bacon in scrip. North Carolina is some better looking than Va. but poverty looks upon the Confederacy I think.

Wednesday, May 18, 1864

On the road to Salisbury at 7 O'Clock. Distance 50 miles. No food since the eve of the 17th. Arrived at S. about 6 O'Clock PM. recd. Bread & bacon for one day. Moved on some thirteen miles and halted. Bivouacked in the woods aside the road.

CHAPTER THREE
THE HELL OF HELLS

Thursday, May 19, 1864

In cars again for Columbia Junction where we arrived at early next morning. Drew rations bread & bacon.

We left the muddy Dan and its ville; marched, those who could, some twelve miles in charge of one Captain Beauchamp, (Bo-chong to be true French) and his men who had seen service and had some human sympathy for us. Beauchamp was an ideal soldier and a gentleman of course. We fared well under this charge, but his charge was all too short. His sympathy, no doubt, was the greater because he knew where we were going and we did not. His expression, at times, when halted for rest he passed among us, seemed sad and quite depressed.

Our day's march ended. We were put upon a train and reached Columbia Junction; "disembarked" and were made as comfortable as possible - as to shade and water (no feather beds,) divided into squads, and ham and wheat flour were issued to us; four ounces of ham and one quart of flour. What a treat that was, though, we had to cook it as best we could. Wood and water in plenty, close at hand, and the Captain and his men made everything pleasant by aiding us in every way. No stringent guard over us - he depended on our honor, in exchange for good treatment, and it was evident that no one dishonored his genorosity for no complaint was heard in the count-up in the morning. What a medley of methods and designs in the art of baking! The Captain enjoyed the scene to the fullest extent, being both laughable and pathetic. Those who made their dough too thin and had no more flour to thicken it with had to make "slapjacks" some had not the art of mixing properly - dough too stiff and lumps of flour through it; some wrapped about a green pine stick, and after peeling the bark held it over the fire and turned it constantly to prevent burning; nevertheless it burnt on the outside and was covered with pitchpine soot, while the inside was entirely raw and flavored with pine sap; others patted the dough down on a piece of board, "a la mode planked shad," turned it up to the fire, baked and burned it also, but it was fairly good; others used flat stone and partly succeeded; but the most practical made turnovers and placed them in the hot ashes where they baked most perfectly provided they were not left too long - which some did only to find their "dream" a charred mass and the prospect of supper gone. But generosity prevailed and comrades shared what they had. All these things were quite funny then; but shortly would have been a serious matter had they occurred. We all kept up our spirits, even the wounded that came with us, as we were ignorant of our destination.

There were rumors all the time that Savannah, Georgia, was our destination for parole or exchange, and the thought on our part was not abandoned until we passed Savannah the next day reached Augusta where the gallant Beauchamp left us, and we noticed that here our guard was doubled and it made us uneasy. Many were thinking that this move meant ill for us and that hateful name of the Golgotha - Andersonville - would not down, and some be proud of, otherwise we should have heard of some injuries or deaths as about all were retaken in a short time by the Confed troops located near there, and the help of a pack of hounds that were kept plentiful in that section.

Friday, May 20, 1864

Again on the cars for Augusta Ga. Arrived at that place 3 O'Clock on Saturday. Drew crackers & bacon.

On reaching a station not far from Savannah the day before, the train stopped and some felt that the rumor about parole or exchange was correct; but disappointment was the result and some of the men secreted themselves under the trains alongside, and we went on and left them, but they failed as they came on after us in the train following.

Our new guards were a very "unsocial" lot and frankly told us that we were on the road to Hell - Andersonville. Many hearts were heavy and despondent and some determined to chance liberty or death. Among those were men who were not easily covered with a rifle, until they made the leap. Five of them I knew as from the Second New Jersey Regiment, but not a man escaped. All were sent into Andersonville at the same time as those on the train! In that part of Georgia troops were all about coast and inland which left but small chance for anyone to get through, provided he did not starve or fall in their hands before starving. We had heard of that awful place to which we were going but knew little of the realities, we soon knew by experience.

While we lay at Augusta we were treated very nicely by the ladies, though very strong in rebel sentiment; they had hearts, they were human, they pitied us but had no love for us, and we really cannot blame them under the circumstances, being women. One elderly lady, who handed me a piece of cake and a cup of milk, (think of it - milk and good cake!) said that she had a son in the Confederate Army and he might perhaps be in our predicament, as she had not heard from him some time and there had been very hard fighting, and if such was the case with her son she hoped some Northern mother would do him a kindness. I assured her that her son would get good treatment. With tears flowing down her cheeks she replied, "I hope you will soon be released!" Ah, did she have some inkling as to what our future was to be? We thanked her very cordially for her kindness and hoped that her son would return to her unscathed by war, to comfort her life for many years. She was a widow, and he, an only child, therefore how much more she needed him!!! When about to leave she proudly said "I do not treat you this way for love of you or your cause. On the contrary I hate your cause, but you are human and of God's image, educated and intelligent! Why should I not be human?"

The train started and again we noticed the increase of the guard to every car, which gave deeper cause for depression, even among those who had been the most optimistic. We were loath to leave Augusta, having fared so well; but the arbiters of our fate were in charge and we had no choice but to bow to the inevitable. The awful stories we had heard about Andersonville were flatly contradicted by the officer in charge at Augusta. This made us feel more cheerful - he proved to be an unmitigated liar. Had we known that which we learned so well later, almost to a man, those who were so swiftly closing the gap with such suffering and death, we would gladly have courted death at Augusta, or any place along the line in order to escape the terrors of that horrible place of torment and starvation.

Saturday, May 21, 1864

Again on the cars, we have been for 10 hours. Drew 10 tack & some bacon. Awaiting for 3 PM.
On the way at 4 PM. for a distance of 70 miles. Arrived at Macon 3 AM.

We passed through Macon where some officers were confined. Our stop was short, closely guarded, and here again the guard was increased. This was the last straw needed - creating a reality, not suspicion, that all was not well with us. Only fifty-five miles between us and a Hell of Hells of the Confederacy. One night and a part of a day we travelled and then on "The Sabbath," May 22, 1864, we found ourselves in our refuge! No, not refuge - but the place of suffering, torture and death, beyond description, to die a death that no language can express. Andersonville! Oh, that name that sears the hearts of mothers, widows and orphans! That chills to the marrow of the living, who once knowing its horrors can never forget them! The name that has gone to the most remote corner of the civilized world as the most inhuman spot on God's footstool! The Apache savage was a cruel tormentor but was not enlightened and death at his hands came quickly; but at Andersonville torment equal to that of any barbarian of the past ages was prolonged!

Under a still stronger guard we left the cars and looked about us in order that we might discover any ray of hope, one bright spot on Nature's face - there was none!!! All that was visible was a ramshackle platform station in very unsafe condition, two houses that defied description, but could not defy the elements in their tumble-down condition - doorless, windowless and almost roofless, barely good enough for cattle shelter. For a God-foresaken place Andersonville tallied the description most perfectly. Woods - from the tall and stately pine down to the starved-to-death scrub oak and bunch pine. Woods, woods, all about us; to the east we got a glimpse of some tents of the troops that guarded the world's greatest "Charnel House;" a winding road through sand led to the "home of the Hopeless," a thin thread of a stream that had found its way from a loathsome-looking swamp of dead pine and cone, Indian grass, that lay south of the railroad, in a tedious, erratic course, led past the rear of the camp of the troops that occupied the slope on the north side of this miserable, puny thread of dirty water that entered the stockade barely depth of water enough to cover a foot half buried in the sandy bottom; yet, it must serve that abode of misery, starvation and death, where 35,000 human beings were crowded at one time - the only water for all purposes, freighted as it was from the sinks of the Confederate Camp. "Tis said that distance lends enchantment to the view. Not so, with the view a scant half mile distant, the silence of death fell upon us who were waiting to enter where so many thousands had and would enter, and so few returned there-from with life still in the form of a once strong, healthy patriot. From our vantage point during the preliminary of "counting off" into the hundreds, really only ninety, selecting the heads for the "messes" we could see in the distance, over the top of the "Stockade" where depressed by the slope of the ground, to us it looked like one great ant hill in perfect working - so continuous and closely were the motions. Stronghearted, brave men who had almost gleefully faced the cannon's mouth, spouting death and wounds in their ranks, here, sank almost in helpless despair - some actually did, and died - yet, the thought was "where others can live, we will not die!" The few only succeeded.

Sunday, May 22, 1864

Enroute for Andersonville the Military Prison of the C.S.A. Arrived at 3 PM and march to said camp (Sumpter). A Bull Pen and such a sight I have never seen. Horrible destitution prevails.

Monday, May 23, 1864

One more squad of prisoners came in (400). Drew our ration at 4 O'Clock. Vermin is quite abundant. So much is that the earth itself is alive almost. 5 PM more prisoners from the Southwest & Potomac Armies.

The counting process over we were assigned to the 27th Detachment. Each Detachment was composed of 270; each Mess was again divided by three and I was in the lower third Mess. Our guards here were bold and sneering, none of them having smelled the battle's smoke, being raw levies of old men and boys that could hardly carry the arms they had, but were backed up by the Florida Artillery. They much enjoyed our despondency and chagrin and mental suffering, and delighted in tormenting us with that saying of that fiend, Winder, that "they would kill more Yanks here than Lee would at the front." We could not, nor would not, then harbor the thought of this truth, or realization of such statement, which was indelibly impressed upon us so soon thereafter as an actual fact. That which we thought impossible in any civilized nation, even a barbarous one, was absolutely possible here. That human beings, civilized could systematically plan a death so horrid and cruel - starved, sick and wounded men, barbarians would disfigure and torture, and thus cause death in their anger; but to coldly calculate and compass the destruction of human life by slowly starving, killing piecemeal as a result of such calculation, was beyond conception by any but those who knew from its contact. The huge gates became more and more distinct as we solemnly marched - as it seemed to our own funeral - and to many thousands it was literally true. We reached the "Stockade." How that name compels a shudder even at this forty-third year of freedom from its deadly embrace. It was here that

The road on which Charles Hopkins walked from the railroad station to the prison. Over 13,000 U prisoners never walked back.

we had our first introduction to that infamous wretch, Henry Wirz, who was to be the arbiter of our fate. One would think, from the thousands he had received and glutted with satisfaction; but not so, he was just as joyful as though we were the first toy he had owned in his boyhood, intolerant, boastful, and profoundly abusive to the "Damn Yanks," "they would not bother Lee again after he was through with them!" And that was to be a verity indeed!

After some delay those big gates yawned before us like the cavernous mouth of some great monster; and we were "lockstepped" in by fifty and sixty at a time, or all the "lock" would hold; the gates in our rear would close and a similar pair of gates would open in our front. Our gaze was riveted to the inside moving thousands, all who got near us as we passed in, crowded that single street - if you can so term it - to a "pack" twenty or more deep, each watcher intent to discover some comrade, brother, father or acquaintance among the incoming "fresh fish," as the prisoners before us termed us. Oh, what misery was there depicted upon so many of those gaunt, hopeless faces, filthy and black from pine smoke; ragged and almost nude with the vermin plainly seen upon the poor apology for clothing! Some begged to know the fate of friends, others to learn of the death or capture of someone close to them by some tie of relationship; some met a brother or friend as unfortunate as themselves, and bemoan their fate. Indeed, this picture in its great Stockade frame was a rival to Dantes picture of Hell. The stories of those who had tasted the bitter realities of this place were enough to chill the swift, warm stream that made the hearts of heroes beat so rapidly now. A beautiful May day, and Sabbath, yet, we could not rejoice while marching into "Hades" with those awful gates creaking a sad requiem behind us, and to so many, forever. Well may the "legend," "He that enters here leaves hope behind" have been placed over the entrance, for truly it was so. The prison was a parallelogram of about two to one as to its length and breadth of about eighteen acres at this time - was enlarged July 1st to about twenty-seven acres - and one third of this not habitable, being a swamp of liquid filth. This was enclosed by wooden walls of hewn pine logs, from eight to ten inches square, four feet buried in the ground, eighteen feet above, braced on the outside, cross-barred to make one log sustain the other, and a small platform making comfortable standing room for the guards, every one hundred feet, with about waist high space below the top of the stockage, reached by a ladder. A sloping roof to protect the men from the sun and rain had been placed over them. Later in 1864 the second line of stockade was built and a third was partly built for protection - it was said if attacked by Federal troops, but we knew it was to discourage us from "tunnelling" - the distance being too great. The Florida Artillery had cannon stationed at each corner of the Stockade, thus commanding a range from any direction, four guns were so placed near the south gate as to command the gate, and over the depressed section of Stockade, which at this point was about forty to fifty feet lower than elsewhere, and at this point the little stream entered the enclosure. The "dead line" so much talked of and feared was a line of pine, four inch boards on posts about three feet high, and seventeen feet from the stockade walls, thus leaving the distance all around the enclosure an open space, and incidentally reducing the acreage inside, and giving the guards a clear view all about the Stockade - or the name given it by its inventor and architect, "Bull Pen". The infamous General John A. Winder, the bosom friend of Jefferson Davis, who named him as a "Christian gentleman," was the architect and builder of this wooden Hell. The "Richmond Enquirer" known as the organ of the Confederacy, said of Winder, when he was removed from command of Libby and other prisons, to make his Headquarters in Georgia and in command of all prisons, "Thank God, that General Winder has been sent from Richmond; but God help those who fall under his care." That was a strong recommendation of Davis's "Christian gentleman," and by a bitter upholder of Davis and the "Cause!" To intrude inside this deadline was instant death, or wounds that would cause death by the rifle of a watchful, ready, willing, murderous guard; provided he did not miss his mark intended and kill or wound someone not aimed at in camp. As to missing some victims, was almost impossible in that crowded place.

On August 17, 1864, Southern photographer A. J. Riddle recorded several panoramic views of Andersonv Prison. These photographs are the undeniable proof of the horrors of Andersonville. (Notice the sentry bo along the wall in the distance.)

Friday, May 27, 1864

The commandant of the Prison or "Bull Pen" sent a squad of men inside to find the tunnels that have been reported to him by some traitor in the camp. They were successful enough to find three tunnels and closed them up. If a break is made they (the Commandants of the fort) plan to open with grape & cannister on the pen.

Inside the camp death stalked on every hand. The death at hands of the guard, though murder in cold blood, was merciful beside the systematic, studied, absolute murder inside, by slow death, inch by inch! As before stated, one third of the original enclosure was swampy - a mud of liquid filth, voidings from the thousands, seething with maggots in full activity. This daily increased by the necessities of the inmates, the only place being accessible for the purpose. Through this mass pollution, passed the only water that found its way through the Bull Pen. It came to us between the two sources of Pollution, the Confederate camp, the cook house; first, the seepage of sinks; second, the dirt and filth emptied by the cook house; then, was our turn to use it for all purposes, until later. Near the deadline all took water for all purposes, and drink being a necessity, hence, other purposes must be limited as to quantity, and the hours which taken. I have known over 3000 men to wait in line to get water, and the line was added to as fast as reduced, from daylight to dark, yes, even into the night; men taking turn of duty with men of their Mess, in order to hold their place in line, as no one man could stand it alone, even if in the "pink" of physical condition; the heat of the sun, blistering him, or the drenching rains soaking him, not a breath of fresh air, and we had no covering but Heaven's canopy. Air-loaded with unbearable, fever-laden stench from that poison sink of putrid mud and water, continually in motion by the activity of the germs of death. We could not get away from it - we ate it, drank it and slept in it (when sleep was possible and exhaustion compelled sleep). What wonder that men died, or were so miserable as to prefer instant death to that which they had seen hourly taking place, and so preferring, deliberately stepping within the deadline and looking their willing murderer in the eye, while the shot was sent crashing through a brain that was yet clear. This I have seen and know; the victim intended to close the door that led to doubt as to how he would die. Others, not mentally balanced because of a starved brain and system, wandered inside the fatal line and were ruthlessly slaughtered. One poor demented comrade, not instantly killed, lay for hours in full view of his comrades - gasping and struggling with death, but no one could go to his rescue for fear of the same kind of a death. Men, who at one time, were lion-hearted, brave in battle, shuddered at the sight, and wept like children, and cursed the murderer. This victim was a demented, starved, one-legged veteran who had lost his leg at Chickamauga; hence, his name by all who spoke to or of him. Very frequently some poor fellow was shot upon one pretext or other, none of them valid among "men." Three, we personally know of, met this fate while getting water - ignorant of the danger of forgetting themselves, touched the deadline and died of their wounds in a short time. The "Silent Reaper" was busy on every hand and in so many ways and some so pitiable, that a heart of stone would relent toward the victims in their loathsome misery and suffering.

A Union prisoner, in this sketch by Gen. Lew Wallace, is killed trying to get a drink of water beyond the dead line.

Thursday, June 2, 1864

Has been very hot and sultry all day today & cloudy too! A man shot today for getting outside of the Dead line. Many amusing incidents taken place in camp. But indeed I think if I could see some of Home more so or at least they would amuse me some.

Saturday, May 28, 1864

Nothing of great interest. only the prices. Beans are 35 cts. (of our currency) a pint. corn meal at 25 cts. per quart, and tobacco at 35 cts. per 7 oz. and everything in proportion with Confederate scrip paper $400 for 100 of our greenbacks. News from the Sgt. today. The Regt. does not claim any organization not even a company. Originally (400) strong (May the 4th) the Brigade is consolidated.

Sunday, May 29, 1864

Sunday indeed! Although there is many in Camp that has made no difference. A few men came in today (1,005) from all parts. A number of the 2d N.J.V. came in today. The Major & Lieut. Colonel are dead. Col. Henry all right after 18 days fighting. John Seitzer alright so I hear.

Monday, May 30, 1864

As usual nothing to say of interest. But camp hears the rumors of paroling or exchanging will take place soon. Rations are being cut short by the thefts. A set of inconsiderate rascals are on duty outside of the works or stockade. More devoid of honesty & principal.

The month of June gave us twenty-seven days of rain - not consecutively, but so frequently that no one was dry in all that time. Everything was soaked - even the sandy soil. Still, this watery month was a blessing in disguise as it gave water plenty which was pure to drink. The boast of Winder was that the selection of this spot for his Bull Pen was the place where disease and death would come more quickly by "natural causes" - when a removal of two hundred feet east would have placed us upon a living, pure, deep and clear stream of water, properly named, "Sweetwater Creek" which had we been allowed to utilize would have saved thousands of lives but "no" that was not the intent of its inventor. To kill by natural causes was made more possible by this location. Woods in front, right, left and rear - deep and shady woods everywhere and not a semblance of shade in this large acreage, all cut down at the time of building. A merciful man in the absence of building would have left shelter enough in shade to have helped keep off the scorching sun. There was a clump of three shoots from one stump, which had no branches for forty or fifty feet, and then had so little foliage that it looked like a baby's parasol on the handle

The creator and his creation. Confederate General John H. Winder (left) in charge of all Federal prisoners at Andersonville.
(Above) A view of the vast misery inside the prison pen. Note the latrine along "Sweetwater Creek."

of a "family" umbrella, and that was the limit of trees or brush - not a blade of grass was there in all this barren "pasture." The nights were cool, at times uncomfortable for men without clothing to speak of and insufficient food in kind and quality to make blood that might warm up the system. As before stated, woods were all about us and we were not allowed enough to warm the sick, or to cook over, the ill-cooked food sent in, or the raw article served at times. The baked food sent in - underdone or overdone, if bread, was sometimes like raw cornmeal dough, or else burnt to a coal. Raw beans, raw rice and raw meal, ground cob and all, unbolted, was served us a great deal of the time. The beans came to us cooked, dirt, hulls, vines, cock-roaches, and weevil bugs that infest the beans, more properly called cow peas, were included. No effort was ever made to bolt or sieve the corn meal, or pick the objectionable substances from the beans or rice. Cleanliness was not a virtue of the cooks at the "hostelry."

Shortly after we went into the Bull Pen there was a gang of ruffians - our own men - who set to robbing anyone whom they could of any kind of valuable from a tin cup to a watch or money, if the victim was so lucky as to have any cash. Our little band of five had preempted a spot that gave just room for us all to get to Mother Earth and not crowd our neighbor. One covering for all, Heaven's canopy, night and day, so all fared alike in that respect. Near us, on the south side, was a party of old prisoners having been taken at Chickamauga in October before, and they had a covering made like a shed roof, thatched with pine tops while green and this kept the sun off until late in the afternoon though not rain proof by any means. These men knew the ways of the Camp Sumpter and informed us to be ready at all times to resist the attack of the "Raiders" who would not stop at murder to obtain any object of value a man might have. Only two hundred feet east of us, and near the clump of trees in the southeast corner, was a coterie of men known as the "raiders," composed of some of the worst element the army had in it, bounty-jumpers, men who took a bounty payment when enlisted, soon as enrolled would desert to some other recruiting station and repeat the operation again and again until caught, getting large sums of money to squander at gambling and worse methods of parting with their ill-gotten gains. This crowd was not the only lot of "bad men." One gang was led by one Collins, nicknamed "Mosby" - of Confederate guerrilla fame - with less honor and manhood however for Mosby attacked his sworn enemy while the "Raiders" robbed and murdered their own Army comrades. Another gang was formed and headed by a man called "Slim Jim," who had been the right hand of Collins in the "raids" of the Camp and they fell out about the "swag" as most thieves and cut-throats do. The Mosby gang attacked us one night soon after our warning, but we put up such a hot fight that they veered away and some other poor devils were the victims.

Saturday, June 11, 1864

Rained all the afternoon and part of the night just enough to make a man miserable. Very often a man killed outright by some of the "Raiders" just for a little sugar or onions or any thing of the type. Rumors of all sorts as usual. May God send us a parole or Exchange.

Wednesday, June 29, 1864

Gloomy morning. Rained last night. Mush for breakfast. A man nearly killed and robbed by the raiders this forenoon. A number of them was "spotted" and taken out. I expect they will be hanged if they get their just dues.

I have not seen John Miller for 2 days.

About this time, June, there was a feeling among the "respectable and honor-loving class that something must be done to protect life and preserve order. Meetings were secretly called and held. No one was permitted to join the movement except those known to be loyal to their comrades' welfare. The genius of a detective was needed and was found in many unexpected men. One Sergeant Keyes was made the leader and so strong a formation was founded that it became very dangerous to raid. This resulted in a change of front on the part of "Slim Jim" - Ellis was his name - who from fear of being made a victim of Keyes' New Law and Order crowd, called "Regulators," that he joined them in order to get square with Mosby's gang who still did some business because of its numbers, and had attempted to rob "Slim Jim" of his ill-gotten funds, said to be $1000 to $1500 which had been smuggled into camp by the owners evading the keen eyes of "Johnny Reb" only to be robbed by his own comrades. The feeling of enmity between Slim Jim and "Mosby" Collins was deadly and each wanted the worthless life of the other and both deserved the gallows. The "Regulators" grew strong because the determination of its members to make this home or abode of the wretched safe against robbery and murder.

One day a new levy of "fresh fish" from Sherman's Army came in, among them a man who seemed a quiet and well-behaved character, of German descent. He had some money and a watch about his person not knowing the danger and he displayed both, not purposely. This was noted by the sneaking spies of Mosby whose job it was to locate the swag and the spot where the "prey" settled. This man, Urban, located near the south gate. Suddenly there was an uproar and shouting and clubs were in play. It was all over in a few minutes and no one knew but those in close proximity that a man had been almost beaten to death. After some time he recovered minus all he had of value which we learned was a gold watch and some two hundred dollars in money. He was badly bruised about the head, but able to tell his story to Wirz, who entered the gates at Urban's request in German language. The result was that Wirz sent guards inside under charge of an officer, and with Urban to recognize any of his assailants, if possible. He did - one of them in particular; and so strong was his statement, his recognition so clear, that it brought about his arrest, and seven others. The one so surely recognized was known as "Philadelphia Jack" who wore a red cap - the fact that helped spot him. The seven were taken outside; placed under guard; and each in turn was taken before Wirz for "Chatechism" and punishment, if the "third degree" did not elicit information needed. All stood the test but this "Red Cap" who, cowardly cur that he was, to the weaker he was cruel. He turned what we call "state's evidence" and saved his neck and only received the ball and chain, and fixed upon the other six the the crimes that none suspected, though many others were

New prisoners arrive inside the Stockade. It was common to greet new arrivals with the jeer "Fresh Fish!".

known. Theft was common, murder was suspected but not actually known outside of the sworn gang of cut-throats. The six were tried by a jury of their comrades through Sergeant Keyes. The trial was conducted as though a real constituted court was in session. Attorneys were a-plenty in that Bull Pen capable of taking almost any case to Court. Judges, Jury, and the whole machinery complete, was chosen from the "ranks" of Yanks. Good, capable attorneys were assigned to culprits. The pleadings of a Bull Pen lawyer were quite as eloquent as any heard elsewhere. While the attorneys of the rascals knew full well they ought be adjudged guilty, their argument was truly eloquent as to their innocence, but the evidence was too strong and convincing, and the "State" won. Those six miserable men had woven a halter for their own necks - two of them "guilty" as accessory to the crimes, the others "guilty in fact." The most exciting day in that "Den of Horrors" was July 11, 1864, long to be remembered by those who saw the simultaneous hanging of six men, and they Union soldiers, though bad ones, and turned into Eternity by their own comrades. Mosby, or Collins, the leader of the gang, a slim, redheaded, sandy-featured, ill-looking specimen of mankind, was nearest the gate - the gallows were continuous - next in line was a small man named Muer, a sailor captured in Albemarle Sound, from the Water Witch; then, Champlin, Patrick Delaney, the only manly one of the six and not guilty of murder, but admitted he was willing and ready to do murder, were it necessary to their success. He made no plea for his life, but declared his innocence of the actual crime of murder. Next in order was Sarsfield; then Curtis, who aided by some of his friends was released at the

A sketch of the hanging of the Andersonville Raiders.

moment that he was to get on the board on barrels, which constituted the "drop" and by some means, obtained a knife; brandishing this, he rushed in the direction of the sinks, and wading and plunging through this horrible mass of filth, to the north side of camp, hoping to expect his well-earned doom, but alas! for such hopes, it could not be - he found a sturdy little "regulator" at hand, ready to meet him and he was compelled to surrender or die in his tracks. While this was going on and he was being brought back to the scaffold, the other five were sent on their journey to meet their Maker and atone for their wrongs, but Mosby, as light as he was, broke the rope as he was "dropped" and lingered awhile as company for Curtis; but respite was short for as soon as he came back to the world he recognized his bitter enemy and his Nemesis at his side "Slim Jim." To him he pleaded and begged, even pledged a cool $1000, if Jim would spare his life, but nothing would move his old Lieutenant in crime. They were separated for all time - on earth - and Jim's reply to all pleadings was most characteristic of such "thugs," once they are at odds. "No, damn you, you were after me for my money at one time. Now, I am after you for your life!" And at the display of a murderous knife he was ordered to get up on the board, which he did with the aid of those about him; the mealsack was once more pulled over his face, the rope again adjusted, the board kicked from under him, and this time life was strangled out of the man who cooly took the life of others. Curtis was delivered just in time to see Mosby drop, and not the gruesome sight of Mosby's struggles, and the limp forms of those who had "passed on" beyond human aid. Crying, begging in the most cowardly way while being pushed and dragged to the gallows that he had deserted for a few moments only, a respite that gave him time to reflect and call up a lifetime in a vivid manner, again to be face to face with his manner of "shuffling off," and the twisting form of Mosby was a horrible example. Weeping, groaning, limp as a rag, he hung on his rope, hoping to break the fall when it came, and it came quick and found him a wriggling, twisting mass of human misery. The "gang" removed the leaders and peace and quiet was the order, so far as the inmates were concerned. The "Regulators" now were in control and the key to the situation was "Keyes."

Monday, July 11, 1864

Breakfast, cornbread & meal coffee. Morning fine & cool. "Aney" gone to the hospital from which he will not return. Prisoners from Sherman & Grant. Some 4,000 have come in the past three days. I saw a gallows (being) erected this morning for to hang "7" men charged with murder of which they are guilty. PM. Dinner was as usual when we can trade meat for beans. Dumplings, bacon & beans and good soup. Only six men were hung. They died the "ignomanious" death at 20 minutes past five. Their names are on another page.

Sullivan, N.Y. 76
Moseby, N.Y. 76
Beuer, N.Y. 76

Curtis 52d
Delancy, 83 PA
Munn

The graves of the Andersonville raiders.

Friday, June 3, 1864

Rained all night last night as I supposed it would. Very warm all day today and towards evening the usual amount of rain must come and trouble us as it most surely does. The wind blows here just as much the rain. It blows in through the shelter tent very severe.

Saturday, June 4, 1864

Rained all night as I predicted. "Very pleasant indeed" "I must say" John Miller of Co. K. came in today. Taken on the 17th at Spottsylvania C.H. Usual rumors in camp of Exchangings. Little did I think to spend the last day of my time of service in a Bullpen.

Sunday, June 5, 1864

Rained during the afternoon and was very likely to continue during the night. No news except the rumor of a number of men being sent to Savannah. All sorts of rumors are rife in Camp of Exchange & parole of which I believe neither is very likely to take place until August or September. Some sick have been sent to our lines so says rumor.

Monday, June 6, 1864

Nothing unusual except that I don't see the 4000 men being sent to Savannah for Exchange. Rumors of the fall of Richmond. The U.S. Government should treat their prisoners as the so called Confederacy does theirs. I would not lift my hand to aid them in any way. Jeff Davis' "little" Confederacy is rotten to the core. Rations today as follows: Bread (corn) bacon & mush. Scurvy is quite prevalent because we get no vegetables of any sort.

Captain Henry Wirz, Commandant of Andersonville Prison.

Tuesday, June 7, 1864

Rained today nearly 3/4 of the time. Prisoners from Richmond arrived today also both old and new rumors of Grant surrounding Richmond and Sheridan cutting seven (7) Bridges between Richmond & Danville. I can see no sight as yet of getting out of this miserable Pen. Dead average 20 a day.

Wednesday, June 8, 1864

Nothing of any great interest except it be that some more prisoners came in from Atlanta & Richmond. A very few rumors favorable to us. The Confeds are down in the mouth about something. Rumor says that Genl. Seymour is to be added to our number in this Pen. Rations quite short today which was bacon. Bread (corn) & rice that a decent man would not feed to his swine. No rain today for a wonder. What is to happen? Oh Dear.

Thursday, June 9, 1864

Again no news today. Only one thing that I feel quite put about. Raw meal & spoiled bacon today for rations. A very few prisoners came in today from Atlanta from Sherman's Army. Rained today nearly all day just to make all miserable. Prices are up. Onions 1.00 apiece (new ones) ginger cake 1.00 apiece. Potatoes 3 for $2.00 meat per ration 25 cts. Money is an object here.

Friday, June 10, 1864

I must state here that I had a good breakfast for a rarity in a "Pen" rank. Bacon and meal & water and meal not for dogs. Oh what a delicacy! But dinner I ordered a different bread. NOTHING! Worse here than in the French Bastille. The commandant of the Prison wishes to play a Yankee trick upon us. They say parole.

Waiting for release, is the title of this sketch of Andersonville prisoners by Walton Taber for *Century Magazine* in July, 1890.

Monday, June 13, 1864

Raining yet and a most cold and dreary one too. Making the night too miserable for any brute to sleep. Rations were bacon & boiled rice not half enough to keep the life in a man. Great talk of Parole tomorrow but I place no credence in the matter. Very cold and dreary rain indeed.

Tuesday, June 14, 1864

Still raining as I thought it would. What misery prevails in this Camp or "Pen". In human devils, the Confederates are and no one can change the fact. Continued the usual amount of rain to fall, characteristic of the "Sunny South".

Wednesday, June 15, 1864

I was much pleased today upon seeing an old friend but very sorry to meet him in this place where I could not receive him as I would. Rations were short today by the rascality of the Segt. drawing for them.

Thursday, June 16, 1864

10 AM. cloudy. I expect Woe be to the "Confeds" for their villany. I sent a letter to my Company & one to Father. I do not expect them to reach their destination. A number of the Regiment came in today. A. Fitzgerald is the man I spoke of in the preceeding page. Corp. Karrington of Co. C is here too.

Friday, June 17, 1864

8 O'Clock Raining and has been all night. Stouts Co. F. and John Voorhees of Co. B are here. I saw F. Owens yesterday and Brogan and Freeman. Rations are bacon and 1/2 bush of cooked rice for thirty for tweny four hours. Shamefull treatment for any "Chivalry" to boast of. A great deal of raiding going on in camp tonight.

Saturday, June 18, 1864

8 AM. Raining is the days duty as Dunn says. And it did all night. A fine thing for a number of Prisoners who are just the same as a flock of sheep turned into a field and no shelter scarcely "indeed". The rain was told to clear up, but no use, it could not, speak out.

Monday, June 20, 1864

8 AM. Cloudy as usual. I feel quite unwell. 11 AM. I feel very bad.
Rained all afternoon and part of the evening. Rumors of an exchange of the Prisoners to commence on the 25th. I would like that the people of the North knew "to a man" the sufferings and hardships that the men had to go through here. No people at "War" ever treated prisoners as does the "Rotten Confederacy".

Tuesday, June 21, 1864

Morning clear and the "Sun" is shining bright but rain is in the clouds and we will have the daily duty before night. I had a poor night last night but feel somewhat better this morning.
John Miller has the fever and was delerious all night last night.

Wednesday, June 22, 1864

Another clear morning indeed. Exchange talked of a great deal to come soon. One whole clear day for a month. John Miller has been delerious with the "fever" all day and is yet. A tunnel discovered today in the opposite side of Camp. I was down to the "Brook" and had a good wash.

Thursday, June 23, 1864

A most beautiful morning for a "wonder". I went to sick call to get some relief from my cold. It took about four hours to get prescribed for the medicine. John Miller has the Typhoid fever and I got him prescribed for. Another tunnel found today on the N.W. corner of the stockade, disclosed by some traitor in camp for corn bread. 400 prisoners came in today.

Saturday, June 25, 1864

Morning fine but the "Sun" intolerable being very warm all day. I had a very good dinner today, also John Seitzer and George Dunn. 25 cts furnished all the ingredients. Rations came early today on our side. Meal. Made very good soup considering the situation. John Miller is in a very bad condition and no relief from the Confederate Doctors. So much for us.

Thursday, June 30, 1864

Morning fine and very hot. Report says Charles Munn is in camp. John Miller came here last night and laid down in the street all night, still sick. English took him to sick call this morning.

A tent belonging to the raiders was dug up, and a number of things were found. Money watches, blankets. I took John Miller to his Sgt. today and told him to attend to him or I would report him.

Friday, July 1, 1864

Morning fine. Talk of a move in the "Pen". John Sietzer scalded his ankle yesterday very bad. For breakfast I had dumplings & beef, not very good. The beef was horrid. Dickie Vincent is in the hospital. 5 O'Clock PM. moved in the new "Pen" crowded in just like sheep. John Miller was on the ground near the gate and in a very bad condition. I pitched a tent over him for the night.

We had moved to the north side of the swamp on July 2nd, and while going along the path we saw a most loathsome looking human being, and having missed one of our men for several days, thinking of course, he had gone the way of the many who became in a demented condition, we thought there was something familiar about him and stooping to examine we found the living body of John Miller of Company "K" of our Regiment, almost naked, worn to skin and bone, nostrils, eyes and mouth alive with maggots -- a horrible sight, yet breathing. He died the night of July 2, 1864, and was then accounted for in our "Mess."

The day before I had met Richard Vincent, Jr., of the same Company, who was in a pitiable condition. He begged me to take a Bible that his mother had given him, and a telescopic pencil that his uncle had given him, and said his uncle was editor of the "Blue Hen and Chickens" at Wilmington, Delaware. How this pencil escaped Wirz's minions is a mystery to me. Richard again pleaded for me to take them, but I had no idea that I would reach home and told him so, and that I would hunt up the Sergeant of his Mess and have him sent out to the hospital -- then his chances would be better than mine of getting home. Yet, I knew this to be a false hope from the condition he was in; but my statement to him was such that he brightened up and I was successful inside of two hours, in getting him outside into the hands of the hospital people. I called on his Sergeant July 3rd to get tidings of him. Report said he was living. On July 5th I again called and this time the Sergeant reported that he had died July 4th. What was the fate of his Bible and pencil? I have never learned!

Sunday, July 3, 1864

Morning fine & very hot. I was on an hour duty last night tunneling. Dicky Vincent is dead. I think it is so. Dame rumor is always in the "quiver," she says Richmond is taken, and that Grant would make it a 4th of July celebration like Vicksburg. My expectations of the war and where I should spend my 4th is somewhat dampened.

The graves of Richard Vincent (left) and John Miller (below). Both were dear friends and comrades of Charles Hopkins. John Miller survived for only 28 days in Andersonville.

Monday, July 4, 1864

    A very hot morning. What a 4th I can spend here. No more notice taken of it by the Confederates than if it was never celebrated. This makes the fourth 4th of July that I have been away from home. One in the D.C., 1 in a transport (& myself wounded) on the James River. One in Baltimore & 1 in a "Bullpen." Raining all through the middle of the day and quite disagreeable. I saw none of my aquaintances since we left the old stockade.

Tuesday, July 5, 1864

    Morning cool and a little breeze is blowing. Breakfast in preparation. Beans & dumplings and soup. Horace Bower & Sam Abel are here also some more of the Baltimore boys. The "Bullpen" appears to catch all of them. Sam Abel was taken on the 12th of May also Bower, and he was wounded. I have not felt good for some two or three days. I was weakened by the effects of the diarreah. I have taken some more of the pills prescribed by the Confeds. I know the composition so they will not harm me.

Wednesday, July 6, 1864

    Morning fine and cool enough for comfort. Breakfast in preparation. Meal cakes & gravy. John Buckley of Co. G is dead. (Died June 27.) For dinner beans and dumplings & soup made of spoiled bacon. Oh what a delicious dish!

Thursday, July 7, 1864

    Morning beautiful. Dame rumor said some time ago that the 7th of July was the day to commence Exchanging & Paroling. I don't see it yet. I done some sewing today on a shirt. Patched the sleeve. Been digging a well close by us 5-8 feet and water made its appearance. Prisoners came in from the Cavalry Dept. They say the 6th Corps is with the Cavalry in the rear of Richmond.

The gravestone of John Buckley, 1st N.J. Infantry.

Jack Fitzpatrick

Another view of the stockade taken by A. J. Riddle in the August heat of 1864.

Tuesday, July 12, 1864

Morning cool and cloudy. Camp was quiet last night. I was on the opposite camp digging a well. Breakfast Johnnycake and gravy. Dinner cake and beans and bacon. Cat in the soup. Light living for a prisoner. Prisoners came from the Army of the Potomac. Biscuits and anything almost in the line of pastry can be had here if the exorbitant price is paid. Biscuits for $1.00.

Wednesday, July 13, 1864

Morning fine and cool. I was at my usual occupation last night. Hope on hope over. A man shot for being outside of the dead line. Southern chivalry to a T. I had not much sleep last night and could not get any for the heat through the day. Rations meal & rice and bacon. Bakeshops are as plenty in here as in any other city of the same population. The Bullpen is an incorporated city.

In the following diary entry, Hopkins contemplates a mass breakout.

Thursday, July 14, 1864

Morning cool and a breeze blowing. Breakfast in preparation. Roll call over. I think that there is 31 thousand of the most cowardly or else very well, contented men in this camp that ever were mustered. It is next to impossible to keep them in the pen if they were a mind to try to get out. Excitement amongst the Rebs for fear of a break being made. A shower in the afternoon.

Friday, July 15, 1864

Morning fine and quite hot. Breakfast coffee and gravy. The excitement for which the Rebs were turned out last eve was because of the Capt. heard that a break was to be made. Two blank shots were fired to alarm the camp and the Rebs were formed in lines diagonal from the northwest and the S.W. corners of the pen. The guards were reacting very bad at the alarm.

Saturday, July 16, 1864

Morning cool. 6 hundred came in and E. English got out on the outside and was caught. Corp. English came in this morn released from the stocks.

Rumors from the war front excited the men.

Sunday, July 17, 1864

Morning fine and cool. Breakfast bacon. Bread and gravy. Rumor says that Ewell's Corps has gone to Pennsylvania to divert Grant's attention. Rumor is always upon the alert for now it says Charleston in possession of U.S. and burnt to the ground. The Rebs are excited about something for they seem ill at ease as ever.

Monday, July 18, 1864

Morning very cool and hearing of rumors said that we are to be moved to Alabama. Charlie Munn was here. I think Aney is dead for rumor of him has reached us that he was admitted to the hosp. 6 O'Clock P.M.

Private Aney of Co. K. died July 15.

Tuesday, July 19, 1864

Morning cool and fine. No breakfast so far on account of the Nonappearance of meat. Rumours of a parole to take place but no credence do I put in it for many reports have been denied. Great excitement about a petition being sent into the General Government by a committee of three.

The headstone of Pvt. C. R. Aney, 1st New Jersey Infantry, at Andersonville National Cemetery.

The nights of July, after sundown, steadily cooled so that before morning it became quite cold for most of us, minus clothes and no covering. In August and September - to the thirteenth - we found ourselves getting up on all fours, gradually stretching out to the rays of the sun, to nearly normal height. Any day now you could see numbers of men wading from knee to waist deep in the liquid, fetid filth of the swampy level -- groping with the hope of finding some roots to dry or wood to cook over the half-cooked stuff sent in -- such was the scarcity of wood inside, with acres and acres of wood about us, only to look at. Woe to him that had the slightest sore or abrasion of the skin which might come in contact with that polluted mass -- gangrenous sores resulted, low fevers of the camp engendered -- the horrible sores the contact produced seem incredible to tell of, but the facts were undeniable. Cancer-like, they eat into the little flesh that the victims had, bared the sinews and bond -- the poor fellows rotted by inches. Starvation, polluted water, exposure to sun and rain, and cold nights and many of them of a truly sleepless night, brought on fevers that were almost surely fatal -- causing delirium of several types.

The cases of insanity were numerous. Men, strong in mentality, heart and hope were in a few short months, yes, often in a few weeks, reduced to imbeciles and maniacs. Today they know you and look upon you as friends and comrades; tomorrow they are peevish, whining, childish creatures, or raving maniacs. Some would beg for something to eat; others asked for wife, mother, children or other relatives; some, in their delirium were home talking to their friends, enjoying the good eating that Mother set before them -- they seemed happy, many forever talking of hunger and a goodly number were furiously wild, and had they been strong they would have been dangerous -- not knowing their closest friend, trusting no one, raving and cursing in fearful language. Happily, may I say it, all such died soon, worn out and exhausted by this emotion. Yet, there was never a time that these terrible scenes were not enacted. It was piteous to see, but compelled as we were it filled every waking moment in that long stay at Winder's Bull Pen. These scenes caused much depression and added to the inward mental note - if not audibly spoken "when shall my turn come and must it be as this?" The mental anguish of those days and months was the slowest torture to him who still had a clear brain -- a cruelty to which the barbarian was a stranger. Just think and imagine, if you can, what your thoughts would be to see a father, son, a brother, or even a comrade, not related, slowly but surely becoming a mere skeleton, a maniac, appealing continuously for something to eat, talk of home, friends, in his delirious spells; knows you not -- you, helpless to do more than endeavor to live yourself, cheer him up when your heart is breaking, and do not believe your promised hopes to him. Under such circumstances was it not wonderful that suicide was little or not known to any except demented ones? These were the hours that tried the mental strength of the "man," and were a hundred times worse than the thoughts of a hundred Gettysburg or Chickamauga battles! One was to die in glory under the folds of that flag which he was sworn to defend, and be among his comrades, dying at post of duty. The other was to rot in misery a degredation among blood of our blood, kin both by blood and Country yet they had forgotten all the ages had praised them for. "Chivalry and Civilization." The average deaths per day for seven and a half months were eighty-five. But during the months of July, August, September and October the average was one hundred per day. One day in August, following the great freshet, I counted 235 corpses lying at the south gate and about it. Many of those had been smothered in their "burrows" made in the side hill in which they crawled to shield themselves from sun and storm, the soil being sandy, became rain-soaked and settled down upon the occupant and became his grave instead of a protection. Others, who had no shelter, in whom life was barely existing were rain-soaked, chilling blood and marrow, life, flitted easily away, and left but little to return to clay. These holes or burrows in both the flats and up the north slope, were counted by thousands, no doubt there were some that never gave up their dead but lay there as buried in their self-made sepulchre. No effort was made to search unless the man was missed by a friend, and of such are these that are "unknown" upon the records for some 12,912 at the "Hell of Winder's."

Natural causes, indeed!! There were murders committed by most "unnatural causes" and methods -- systematic causes! Orders were issued that all should be vaccinated, and yet in all that den of filth, dirt, starvation, polluted water, vermin, flies, reeking with the filth of the open sinks, and polluted swamp mosquitos ever at hand, small pox cut no figure whatever, to October at least. Squads of ninety were ordered up to the gate for their possible death warrant, "Vaccination." Some were fortunate enough not to "take;" others, the moment they were treated and could turn aside, wiped the vaccine off and cleansed the spot by sucking the blood from it in order that no vaccine virus be left to work its destruction; some evaded it by tricks and lies. The writer did his own "scratching" and covered the wound with mucous from his mouth -- which may have been as dangerous had it been left to work its "scurvy" destiny -- and bared his arm for inspection, which was no trouble, as my shirt was armless. After avoiding the operator, the inspector followed and passed me as "done." By this deception we escaped a death perhaps

The open sinks in use at Andersonville.

that hundreds found at the hands of those who had used impure vaccine matter. We are satisfied, as one, as we had the best opportunity to watch the effect upon one or two that were near us. One of them, a black hero of Burnside's Brigade of negroes, had lost a leg and an arm at the Wilderness and had, up to this time, been able to say that he was recovering from both those fearful wounds. Not satisfied with this dusky man's misfortune and suffering, which were self-evident, the authorities could not forget the "exquisite" pleasure it gave them to inject their "system" of death from "natural causes" into the blood of this man they so grudgingly hated because of his color and because he was in Uncle Sam's uniform. That poor fellow died a short month later from this poison that became a part of his wounds and the arm on which he was operated had been amputated half-way between shoulder and elbow and was eaten away as if by cancer, until death came to his relief, at which time the tendons and bone were fully exposed. "Natural causes" -- My God!!!!!

What a record Winder and Wirz took to Hell with them! They must have surprised the Devil by their henious crimes, and Satan must have given them highest rating!

Local citizens view the misery of the prison from a guard's roost.

Andersonville burial detail at work.

The famous Providence Spring, so much read of, was made possible by the great storm and freshet of August 9th, 1864. It broke in the Stockade near the south gate, inside the dead line and swept to the lower side and broke through there also. Near the north gate, some fifty to sixty feet south on the slope, the heavy downpour of rain rushed down the slope inside the dead line and under the strata of sand, found a clay bottom and struck a small thread of pure water and food-famished prisoners feasted their eyes on it for days. It grew a little larger and promised hope to those who might be able to drink of its purity.

Being out of reach, all sorts of devices were invented to get some of it. The coy, little, life-giving stream persistently wriggled its way inside the dead line, though we were glad to welcome it to our side of death's border. Small it was, but to that camp would have been like drinking diamonds -- so precious were its drops to the minds of those that knew not pure water for months. After a time the Yankee devices came into play -- ingenious indeed they were. The Yank that had access to wood, or could beg or buy a mustard cup of the guards, was happy, and lucky. Every contrivance to entice water inside was brought into action, and was much like fishing and losing your bait, or your catch also. Cups, tied to strings, obtained somehow, even to robbing the mealsack of an inch or so, to unravel and make a line, then the "casting" was equally the performe of our expert, as for fish, in order to land the cup, with mouth upstream and on its side in the little water line, where, at best, but a few drops could be obtained at each cast, often all was spilled before landed. The art of recovering the cup with contents was quite a trick. Some were successful; the majority failed to get enough to satisfy the slightest thirst. The fishing process was very dangerous as the fisher dared not reach over or under the dead line. The stream grew a little stronger and to some extent nullified the bad effect of the water obtained at the usual place at the brook, whence it wended its way and its purity with the polluted brook scum, thus spoiling one and improving the other -- not a bad swap! Wirz, the helpmate of the devil, concluded that even those precious drops of Nature's nectar, so hardly and dangerously earned, were entirely too good for the "damned Yankees," and would in a measure defeat his "natural causes" system of death, and right here is where Providence Spring comes to our rescue. Wirz sent a force of negroes into camp to stop the flow of water of this Providence Spring. Their efforts were in vain - fruitless, but Oh! how fruitful to us poor wretches as the stream of life resented the brutal interference of Wirz, and in its wrath burst forth a torrent compared to its original flow. All the curses and demoniacal ravings of Wirz availed him nothing -- he could not stop it or turn it away, being located so that it reached us eventually. We now could get water from near the dead line, by an extra reach -- pure as crystal. Wirz went so far as to lead it out of reach, yet its flow of pure water into the former reekings and seepings for the rebel sink was still a vast improvement, for it purified the stream and increased the flow.

This condition of things stood for a few weeks when a committee of seven were appointed to meet the "Devil" at the South gate to bid him "good day" and induce him to allow the water of Providence Spring to be led into camp by the method of sinking several rice tierces or barrels at intervals with a trough from each to the other, also from each of them inside the dead line to one inside the camp so that the long single line of waiting men could be cut into several lines, thus preventing waste of water and the long tedious wait to get it. By appointment Wirz met the committee. The committee was so arranged that four were chosen to speak. When halted and formed in front of his "Satanic Majesty" the speaker nearest him when the halt came, was to open negotiation for the water supply. When ranged in front, it fell to my lot, being directly in front, face to face, to make known our request, and we thought it a reasonable one under the circumstances; but you can imagine our surprise as well as my colleagues' when Wirz ripped out a sulphurous oath, accompanied by "reinforcements" -- a brace of navy revolvers, aiming them at us, we mean both singular and plural -- for we imagined that we would see the points of each bullet in both guns, though they were aimed in different directions. Then followed this most exquisite language, "No, the water of the creek is good enough for you God-damned Yankee sons of -------" (no, man, gets it) go back, or I will blow your damn brains out and send you to Hell!!! Think of it -- he send us to Hell!!!! We were there now!!! We had reason to believe he could and would accomplish the first, but much doubted that he could do the latter, but we did not tell him so. Here was a case of passing from childhood's first remembrance -- standing at our mother's knee, learning to lisp our little prayer; from that, all through the past life, to that moment, remembering names and faces of loved ones, and the smallest matter long ago forgotten even beyond this moment of the quickening of memory to the "dog" burial I should get over to the acres of the silent dead to the north of camp. We could see all as vivid as a panorama. We have read methods to aid in refreshing of memory and retaining it, but this seemed to be a "lightning" method. We had no chance for an argument, in fact, we were in some of a hurry, and the command was promptly executed, being so peremptory. We "right faced' and quickly moved off without music, and steadily marched away, each mind much concerned about its owner, until we crossed the footbridge over the brook; halted, grouped up to look each other in the eye; then compared notes as to "individual"- experience in those few exciting moments. We all agreed that each of us could count the bullets in those "gatlings," the quickening of memory the same and when we turned our backs on this most cowardly brute we actually could feel the crashing bullet passing through our much disgusted and starved anatomy, and most agreeably disappointed when stopped, took a long breath and found it was only a dream. Some felt like swearing no doubt, yet being unable to do it justice no loud effort was made to do so.

  Providence again came to our rescue. Wirz fell sick and went home to Macon, fifty-five miles away. (We wished the distance might be -- eternity!) He thought he was to die and we hoped he might. Our next "Boss" was Lieutenant Davis, who was not much improvement over Wirz, who had, no doubt, left orders behind to keep up the "natural cause" system. The Committee tried Davis on the water question but he would not work with us. Matters moved on as before, until Wirz recovered and returned to us and we thought his "malady" was "Chirrosis of the heart." We once more met him on the water question. This time it was not our personal lot to be spokesman and our heart was too close to our throat for comfort until the point was passed that would have chosen us and I was anxious to get beyond or fall short of that possiblity. The die cast made a Michigander named Drake, spokesman. I was not sorry, indeed -- we had looked once into those "magazines" of Wirz as long and often as cared to. This success crowned our efforts and it may have been the "speech" of our friend Drake was more musical or magical -- we don't know or care -- it was persuasive at all events. Wirz consented at once and sent some slaves into camp, lumber and other material and the committee was the "Boss" of the work, known as "The Water Works Contractors." There were no millions of money in this, no graft, but there were precious lives and everybody was happy - even the dying, as they could be under such condition, the sick need no longer beg and pray for a long drink of pure water, as they had their wish complied with, once made known.

A post-war albumen card of Andersonville belonging to Charles Hopkins.

This writer, among a number of others, invested his life in operating a tunnel on the south side and had spent many tiresome hours, day and night, "scooping" out sand with a half of a canteen, which was also used to "cook over" the grub. Every kind of an implement was used that had an edge, and the sand was scraped in front of us then drawn up to the knees, while in a stooped, cramped position, in the hole that scarcely allowed the body to pass, then push the sand to our rear between the knees and use our feet to kick it back to the worker behind us, one after the other, until the well was reached, where it fell to the bottom. This "well" was ostensibly a well-its real use was to dispose of the sand dug at night and during the day it was taken out giving the appearance of digging for water.

The removal of the sand in the daytime was curious to look at as it was carried to the low swamp in all kinds of ways-in a shirt, if there was one whole and strong enough; in a pail if you owned one or could borrow or steal one; even the nether garment filled with sand, resembling the lower parts of a man being carried to burial. Our tunnel was done! We imagined that we could almost see Old Glory at some point on the Atlantic coast to which some of us had planned to go. The hour came to make preparations. The writer was the last man out of the tunnel, after a close inspection, gave the word "all is ready." The farewells were said to those too weak to go, but they bid us "Godspeed" and many messages were given that must be remembered to send to home and friends. They were repeated and repeated that they might impress so, that they burned in on the brain, that memory should not fail the hopeless, pitiful. Goodbyes were sent to mothers, wives and children by men who knew they must remain, rot and die and be buried worse than a dog, far from all loving friends. Oh, how sad the choking sob and a prayer of such, though it was not by any means an established fact that we would escape, or even get home if we did escape from this awful sepulchre where living and dead were daily companions! Yet, there was hope in the hearts of many - slim as it was, the chances were ninety-five to five against us. Still, we were willing to give that incessant toil to this end, and take the slight chance, knowing we subjected ourselves to some fearful, devilish punishment at the hands of Wirz should we fail and again be taken. Yet, what could be worse than to rot and die by inches. our party was to a sorry and fearful disappointment. Sergeant English, of our detachment, was to lead the crowd and to assure himself that all was clear, crawled inside to inspect and brought out a piece of a spade blade we had borrowed, and wanted to return. Coming in contact with a root, (and I had warned him not to disturb it as we would pass it safely), he attempted to remove it and succeeded, but with it came tons of sand - fortunately behind him and not on him. Now he was a prisoner in earnest and in a trap of his own planning which obliged him to go to the outside end of the tunnel and make an opening to get air. He made a hole through the crust of pine needles that lay thick on the surface, and remained there until daylight. He made himself heard by the guard - and there was quite a stir among the troops who fell in and surrounded the place. English was taken out and placed under guard. With the rest of us who were waiting in anxiety for his return - for we knew what had happened - being just out of reach of the fall of sand, our mental suffering was unspeakable. We knew he had met with an accident, for the air that followed the fall of sand was driven into our faces and the dull thud we heard. No sound that we could make met with a response from him. We thought him surely buried alive until, as above stated, he was taken from the outside. When rescued by the Rebs from his tomb he was held for the decision of Wirz, and "wonderful" indeed - he got no other punishment than, "You had better not try "him" again or I will kill all the damn Yanks that try to get away.

Wednesday, July 20, 1864

Negroes are fortifying outside. The Rebels stopped demonstration on this place by the cavalry reports and their paper's say that three heavy columns of infantry and cavalry are raiding on this place and Macon. Great reports flying about camp of the Cavalry moving on here. Some 200 men made their escape by tunnel last night.

Friday, July 22, 1864

Morning cool and cloudy. I have the tooth ache this morning. Breakfast of molasses cakes and coffee. More prisoners coming in today. I see them at the station. No dinner and for supper meal cakes and molasses & coffee. Another man from my Regt. of Co. H. came in. Rations meal and bacon. Market very high for as pork gives up high prices fluctuate as in any New York market.

Saturday, July 23, 1864

Morning cool and fine. Breakfast molasses cakes and coffee. I am pestered with the Neuralgia today again and no sleep either night last. A shot was fired into our tent nearly by the murdering thieves. "Rebels". I had a root of a tooth pulled by a good dentist this morning. A rare cure in a Bullpen. Great tales of paroling on first part of next month. We are in a queer place to be here for the Western Army is moving on here.

Sunday, July 24, 1864

Morning cool. Very cold last night. Had no sleep at all with my face it is much worse than it was. My face is much swollen by the neuralgia. I went to sick call and was prescribed for. Dinner rice and bacon made into soup. Very good. Tales of fighting at Atlanta being heavy. Hood in command of the Rebs. "Johnston relieved." Exchange the main topic.

Monday, July 25, 1864

Morning cool unless men all have blankets, they must have nearly frozen last night. No help for me with my face all night. I was to see the dentist today again and got him to lance my gum, and I feel relieved a great deal. My face much swollen yet. Rations bacon, rice & salt for two days. The wretches intend to fill us by some other means. "No salt." Supper rice cakes and coffee. Very good indeed. "Economy".

Wednesday, July 27, 1864

Morning fair and cool. Slept well for the dampness. Prisoners came in this morning. 200 several armies. Hancock & Sherman & Siegel. A man shot or literally murdered being one of the new arrivals. Only just his head under the dead line. "The miserable guards" that constitute CSA authority here. Some 100 doz men came in today. The one shot was one of them. A good job being done in the camp by filling the swamp. An offense to all.

Thursday, July 28, 1864

Morning fine and cool. Aney's death confirmed by Seg't (Rebel) this morning. He died about the 12th or 13th. Could not find the accurate dates. An escapade occurred last night, on the opposite side of camp. Rations were meal & bacon & salt. If the present Administration should receive all the curses that some of the ignorant and impatient men grant them, they would be nonexistant.

Friday, July 29, 1864

Morning fine and cool. Breakfast cakes & coffee and gravy. Two shots fired last night and quite an excitement prevailed last night. "Rebel" account says "Ewell" was in Maryland and that he expected to meet nothing but cavalry but he met some of the infantry as well as cavalry and left "My Maryland" with some trivial cost. Report says Atlanta is being shelled very horribly. Sherman is driving Hood towards Macon.

Saturday, July 30, 1864

Considerable talk this morning of parole.
For dinner today a most rare thing! Nothing! Why? Because we had nothing to make it of: Damn. Rumor says a Seg't Major came in and had this paper from Baltimore, America. Washington Chronicle and Herald all state: Camp parole at Hilton Island and parole to commence the 7 of August.

Sunday, July 31, 1864

Morning cool & cloudy. For breakfast soup & bacon & cakes. Quite palatable. "The Rebs" appear to fear more than ever the safety of the prisoners. Working very hard outside at the works to defend. Rumor says our cavalry is fighting at Macon, a force of 25,000 men all mounted and supposed to be under Stoneman. Rations rice & bacon & salt. Rebels anticipate an attack upon this place for they worked all day.

Monday, August 1st, 1864

Morning cool and cloudy. At 11 O'Clock I arose and went for water and had a good wash and washed my shirt and I feel good. Breakfast rice soup & bacon burnt a little. !Oh! What a shame! Dinner was rice soup & bacon. A change from breakfast! Today distant cannonading was thought to be heard. Rumor paroled 1500 men (sick & wounded) at a place 4 miles from here. Supper rice soup & bacon boiled in it as usual.

Tuesday, August 2, 1864

Morning cool & cloudy. No rain as expected last night but quite cool for the season. Breakfast of rice soup & bacon as usual! For diversion I made a box of green pine. My first trial at carpentry! Rumor says Gen'l Stonemann is a prisoner and his staff and 400 men. He destroyed east Macon and all stores for supplies to Hood!

Wednesday, August 3, 1864

Morning cool and pleasant after a night of rain and some of the heaviest thunder & sharpest lightening that I ever heard. Breakfast rice soup & bacon & rice cakes. For dinner nothing! A great number of sick been going out all day. Some 1500? said to be going to our lines or Hilton Head, South Carolina.

Thursday, August 4, 1864

Morning cool and pleasant. Breakfast meal cakes and juice, bacon, gravy. Very good considering the circumstances. Been sewing all the afternoon on a pair of drawers. No roll call this morning because so many sick are going out. Good news of victories by Sherman's army by the prisoners from him.

Saturday, August 6, 1864

Morning cool and cloudy. Today is the day for the reported exchange or parole to commence. Some of Stonemann's raiders came in thoroughly beaten and nearly nude.

August 8, 1864

Morning cool and cloudy. The Q Mstr told in my presence yesterday that paroling was going on and the Sentry confirms the statement. For breakfast rice soup & cake and a small piece of boiled beef. Prisoner says some 3000 men are going out today. We sold our beef and bought some Bermuda onions. Dinner of course was beans, soup & beef & dumplings & rice rations fresh beef & meal & salt & wood. Sold three rations of beef for 50 cts and now we can get beans or any thing. Supper rice & cakes.

Thursday, August 11, 1864

Morning cool & cloudy rain must come I suppose around in the afternoon. Breakfast beans & soup & molassas & boiled beef. All in all it was a splendid meal. Talk of statements in papers that a general exchange to take place on the 15th of the month. But I do not know what or when it will be done. Dinner comes under a different head nothing on account of the rain. Rations are bread & beans (very small at that) and beef rather strong in smell too. Supper beans & soup & bread. Negro gang been working for the past three days and 100 white men would do the work. The time repairing the stockade.

Friday, August 12, 1864

Morning cool & cloudy. I look for rain again today about noon or ration time. Breakfast beans & soup & beef (tainted) some beef (cooked) came in this morning and issued to men that was "literally" written. Shame for the brave "Rebs". Rumor says Fort Gaines & Morgan and Mobile are lost, a statement in the Rebel papers. For dinner molassas & gravy. I was to see Chas. Munn. He is very sick with the chronic diarreah and giving way too much. No people about him he is too discouraged. I wrote him a letter to his wife. Rations beef & meal & salt & beans. Supper rice, meal cakes & meal coffee. No rain today for a wonder to be sure.

Saturday, August 13, 1864

Morning cool and clear. Roll call. Breakfast beans & rice & soup & beef. Very good. John Litzer brought boards enough to floor his tent and a large stump. For dinner we took a skip! Rather a fat way of living. Great talk of exchange on the 15th. It has gotten to be most reliable thing that our officers are exchanged and going away. Rations breakfast bacon and beans & no salt. Some of the men draw cooked beef and it is often very bad. For supper meal cakes & bacon & meal coffee and beans.

At that time Wirz thought it a real joke for a Yank to imagine that he could get away from him. Tunnels by the score were dug and started - a few only were successful in the matter of escape, and fewer still made good an escape after digging out. After moving from the south of Jordan - as the boys termed the creek, rather the Styx of pestilence - into the new part on the north side, we again engaged in a tunnel scheme to liberty, if possible, making the third enterprise of the kind. We, the writer, was getting beautifully thin, and had "we" had to wait a little longer, a worm hole would have answered for a tunnel. We thought the quality known as "cheek" was good at times and had served us to good advantage before while dealing with the Rebs, and if we intended making further use of ours it must be soon while we had it. It may have been a fact that it was getting harder, yet true that it was growing smaller. So one day I got the loan of a bean bag jacket and pants of one of the fortunate ones who had access to the meal room at the Cook House outside and he took - did not stoop to stealing - bags enough to make himself a "nigger suit" and the writer, as the fashionable tailor in our section, cut and made them - to fit of course - hence, having received no pay for services, made claim for same as a lien in advance of other pay for the use of them at times, he being broke to a "stand still," made no dispute whatever, though there was a possibility that he might never see them again - or me. I togged up as a Johnnie, and borrowing a hard-looking slouch hat, "we" were declared to resemble the Rebel Sergeant that counted our Mess, who formerly came from New York. Whether this resemblance claimed was a compliment to him or me I don't know, and will not discuss now. I set out to personate him and succeeded in a fair measure.

One morning after the count had been made I supposed this fellow had other duties in camp and I made bold and leisurely moved toward the south gate with head held a little low over a small pass book, with pencil in hand, as I had seen him do. I passed the deadline mark, with "our" nerves strung to a high tension, as momentary detection was possible,

The South gate where Hopkins strolled out.

107

and might easily mean instant death. I passed the first wicket through the big inside gate guarded by an officer and posse of men - "we" did not count them - "our" mind was busy in another direction. On to the last wicket, fifty feet distant, and Rebs rubbing close to me. Once I raised my head and looked them casually over. I took this chance for fear that I might be acting too coy - with bated breath and thumping heart, (so loud did it seem to beat that feared it might be heard by the man I passed). What little blood "we" had in "our" veins was making race horse speed, and almost choked me. The wicket was safely passed and I breathed once more God's pure air with a silent prayer that I might be on my way to real liberty. The pure air was like wine to me - what a thrill coursed through my frame - almost faint with joy; but the thought "you are not out of danger" brought me to my senses. I passed slowly on towards Wirz's Head-Quarters as the only road in that direction, unfortunately. Had I gone north and to the Station, our woods beyond the Cemetery I may have fared better, no one knew. "Our" stride was increased, breath abated almost, in passing headquarters only thirty feet away when out of the corner of my eye I noticed standing at the open window the very man "we" were impersonating, while I thought him safe in camp. I noticed he looked curiously puzzled and interested and moved steadily on, hoping against hope. Soon I heard, "hey, there, you Jersey; Stop!"

Just then I was quite deaf and my name was Hopkins - why should I notice such a salutation! He followed and finally placed his hand on my shoulder lightly; I turned and said "Hello" and he repeated it, both minus the "o" I think. However, he convinced me - against my will - that I was headed in the wrong direction to reach camp - the sarcasm of it! I said I was not looking for the camp just then, but was more interested in getting away from it. We parleyed a little good-naturedly; and he thought I deserved better success for so bold an effort. I told him if he would attend to his own business and leave me alone, I would attend to the matter of success and take my chances - slim they might be, but I would gratefully thank him. He demurred, talked of the rights and merits of the matter. He wasn't a bad fellow at heart, but his duty was paramount with him and his position, and preferred duty here, rather in front, making himself a target for careless Yanks. He wanted to exact a promise from me to make no other efforts to escape and promised that he would get me into camp without punishment, and to make it very clear, he most fluently described the punishment that Wirz meted out to Yankees for attempts to escape, as so many reports were coming in, of late, of such efforts. He also stated that my attempt had been so bold and fearless of consequences that it would infuriate the Captain. Well, his "word painted picture" almost took my breath and for sake of getting a few more draughts of pure air, I offered to sit down on the roadside and argue the case, and we did, and I know that while his argument to return inside the stockade, was backed up with eight cannons within call of his voice almost, my argument was long and strong enough to give me inspiration and prove to him that it was wrong for him to turn me over to the "tender" mercy of Wirz for such punishment as he could devise, for the results would be quite as effective as if handed over to the wild Apache Indian. My final answer was "it is my privilege to escape Hell in any way possible, and your privilege and duty

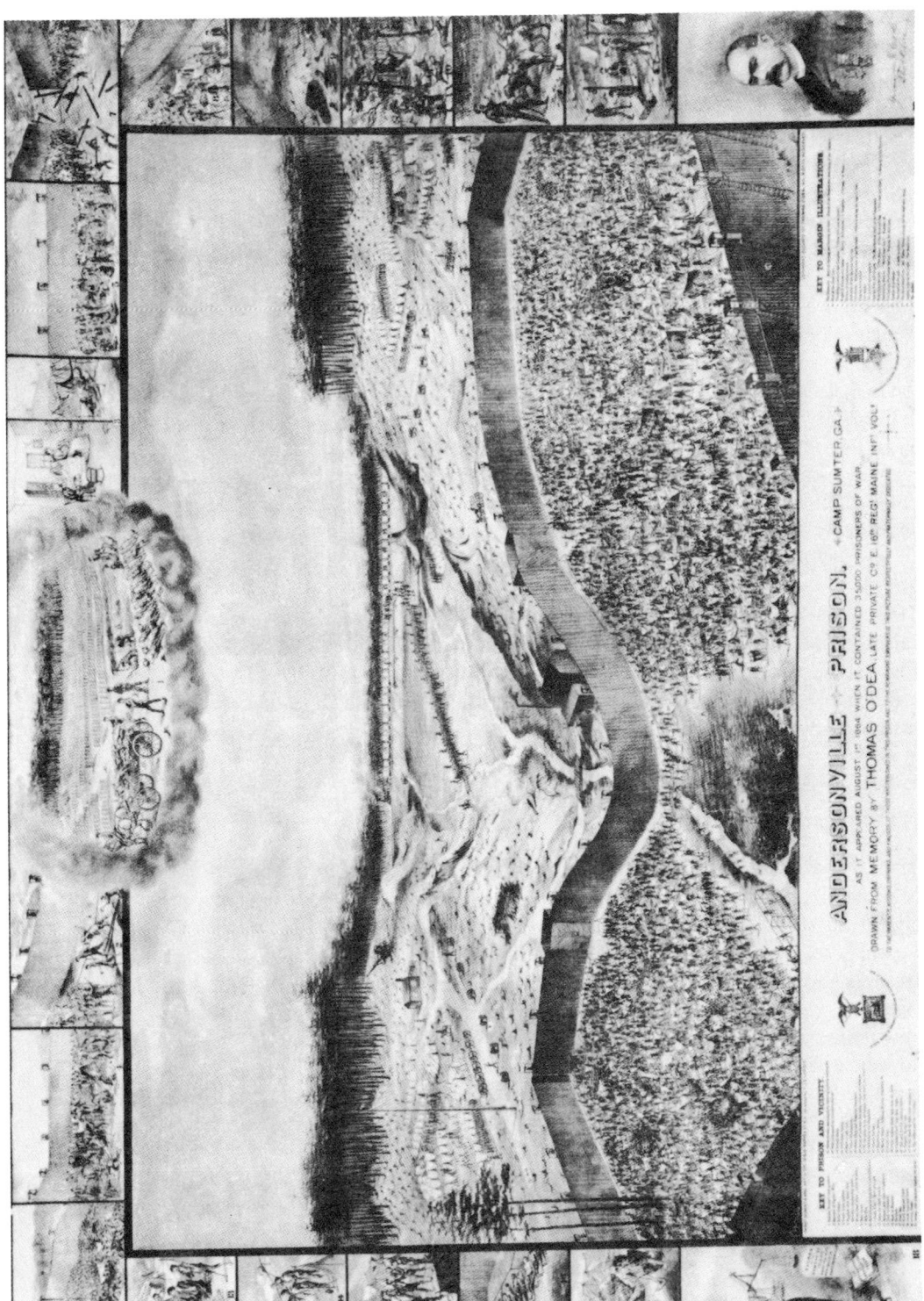

A post-war lithograph by a former prisoner at Andersonville.

as an attendant of this "Military Academy" to catch me. He looked good naturedly puzzled for a moment, and said "Well, you damned Yankees are smart, and I like your grit, and will take you in the stockade this time; but if you ever get caught again, I know you will go to the "collar" or "stocks." I rested my case with satisfaction and gratification to this man. I thanked him and we shook hands cordially - I know I did - and I could afford to. We were good friends after that as long as I was in that camp.

Allotting squad rations by number, is the name of this sketch by Walton Taber.

Tuesday, August 16, 1864

Morning cool & clear. The 15th passed much the same as any other day and no sign yet of the much wished for parole to take place. Wednesday is the noted day now. I am not sure of any particular day. It must soon come. Breakfast beans & soup, beef & meal & rice. No dinner. Barracks being built in the Camp by our men. Our men are worse than the genuine Rebs in almost any respect where they have any authority. Hence the name "Yankee Rebels". Rations beans & bread. For supper beans, bread & soups & a little beef. Some rain fell and then the eve was fine.

Wednesday, August 17, 1864

Morning cool & foggy but never the less the sun is out in all her glory. Breakfast beans, beef & soup minus the bread this morning as we only got 1/2 rations of bread and no meal at all. Managed to get some meal & had meal cakes for dinner. Very hot all day. John was out again and got some more wood. The average deaths are 130 per day in Camp and hospital so says the "grave diggers". Rations beef & beans, salt & bread. A mistake was made in 29th or 2nd and they drew 2 rations. Supper beans & beef & soup, bread.

Thursday, August 18, 1864

Morning cool & clear but the sun is getting almost intolerable through the day for the last four. Breakfast beans & soup & bread & beef. No dinner today because we had no meat to cook with the beans. Made a chicken board & crib board & a puzzle. Rations came early boiled beef & beans & salt. The beans were unusually clean to day. Heretofore there were more bugs than beans. Some of the most filthy victuals issued to the prisoners that was ever issued to any being. For our supper meal & salt & bread and some wicked beef.

Friday, August 19, 1864

Morning cool & clear but getting warm as the day advances. Breakfast beans & molassas, soup & beef. Roll call passed as usual but fresh beef came soon after which was never done before. Small rations of beef, "very". Day very warm indeed and sultry. A small shower came and made the air cool and started a slight breeze in Camp. No dinner today but we made out to fast one meal a day anyhow by pastime in garnish. Rations for the day bread & beef & beans & salt. For our evenings meal we had beef & beans & soup which was extra good because we had a good bone. Got a bone for breakfast by trading a little wood.

Saturday, August 20, 1864

Morning cool & was cloudy but as the sun has strived for the mastery for the past hour has at last shined for a short time at last. Breakfast beef & beans & meal cakes & soup. Beef came in early as usual. No dinner again. Some men came in from Sherman's army. Atlanta not taken as report has stated all along. It has been raining all the day and makes it quite disagreeable. Rations beans & bread & salt. For supper (which was also dinner) we had beans & beef & bread & soup. New rumors are rife that the exchange is not in progress for a surety. Sold 2 cups & 1/2 canteen for $2.00 bought a cup for 35 cts.

After some time in camp, feeling my system that which indicated illness ere long, having contracted scurvy and other camp diseases, that waste the strength and flesh rapidly, aided by the slow stages of starvation, for lack of nutritious food in quantity and quality. "We" felt that "We" could not expect to survive what men, who were as rugged or more so, than I had ever been, had succumbed to. "We" were one of the "always hopeful" kind - and had a right to be because my birthplace was Hope, New Jersey, but the many horrible deaths we had seen and hourly witnessed, knowing our infirmities to be the same that caused the greater percent of deaths, led "us" to thinking and "our" mind was fast settling to the prospects of the final result. In this desperate mood, with yet a clear brain, "we" thought "we" could not wait the slow progress of our tunnel, then under way, and once more "we" togged up in borrowed plumes, and determined to walk out and die if discovered. To stray was death - to die in the effort to escape was possibly a quicker death and "we" were as unconcerned as though it was not "I". "We" chose the north gate this time, with the hope of reaching the woods near the Cemetery and then the good services of some black friend would come to "our" aid - the negro was, without question, our friend when possible to avoid detection. "We" reached the outer wicket and had hope beg within us, when about to step away, the officer bent a little to get a view of "our phiz," as I may have been more bashful than our first trial, and he may have been more careful than other officers. He peered under my hat. I boldly faced him and coldly looked him in the eye - he knew I was no Reb and said "You are a Yankee!" I stiffly replied, "I am, why!" I had started, knowing discovery might mean death, and would, had it been known by Wirz that I had been out before in the same bold way. The reply of the officer, though I was prepared for the worst, as I thought, chilled me to the marrow. "I must take you to Captain Wirz!: I replied, "you may as well let me inside, I have met the Captain and need no introduction!" Suiting my action to my wish, I moved to step inside of the wicket, but he stopped me. I thought to flatter him and said "Colonel, I shall be better satisfied, and thank you for your kindness.' (He was not a Colonel nor had he any kindness.) "No, you must go and see the old Captain!"

Well, thought I, I suppose I must meet the devil, and really I did not want to, for in my former experience about the water question, it had not been very pleasant. What could this be - now, that he was mad whenever he heard of an attempt to escape and this attempt so open and bold, and the first to be tried in this way up to that time! You may guess how I felt - my memory was again sharpened. I felt as though I were already condemned and on my way to a quick death. I was also busy in thought of the nice diplomatic things I might say to him, that my life not be taken on the spot. How nicely particular I was when starting out - that if death must come that it be quick. Was I now quibbling over a "nicety?" No, not so much as to a quick death, as to the one who was to do the job. "Our" reverie was soon over! "We" awoke, and there stood his satanic highness in the flesh before me. I saluted and said "Colonel Wirz (they like to be exalted in rank) I am brought to you for an attempt to escape, not by a stealthy, tunnel route, but boldly walked out of the gate and have thus far given you no trouble as the tunnellers do. I deem it my privilege, as long as not under parole, to make my escape, whenever possible." "You do, eh, you damn Yankee. Valk out, eh? Vell, you von't walk out again soon, for I fix you so you von't vant to valk soon! He raved and cursed like a madman. In fact, he was all the way through. He said many uncomplimentary things that I took no heed of, for my thoughts were much "inward" and "northward." After quick retrospect of the past, I came to the conviction that my time was short at best and what matters now, so long as the end was quick and painless as possible and shooting was my choice if well done. I had given up hope and became calm and cool as one could while looking the Grim Reaper in the face, but I did begrudge this fiend incarnate, the privilege and satisfaction of pointing me the way to Eternity. I would rather he went ahead, I noticed in the crowd standing about me, the man who first caught me and allowed me to go back. He gave me a pitiful look of recognition and with my eyes I thanked him. Wirz continued to fume, swear and laugh in his sardonic way. I expected the shot at an instant and had steeled myself to meet him defiantly in anything he might conjure up as punishment or death - I preferred death instantly!!! Really, I had no fear of it and felt so unusually calm about the matter, that I wondered at it. He finally turned to me with "Vot shall I do mit you, you damn Yank? You Yanks makes me troubles all the time! Shall I hang you, shoot you, or kill you?!

As he left me little choice, I replied calmly, and was just as cool as though it were not a choice of the kind of a death, "Colonel Wirz, put yourself in my place and let me ask you your question, and as you would decide, so will I. Now, to hang or shoot you mean to kill me - if you don't make a mistake, and if you intend to kill do so by placing your pistol to my temple and you will have my thanks. Now Colonel, your question, "What shall I do with you," leaves room for a doubt in your mind as to what you will do, and leads me to believe - (what a whopper) that you want me to suggest something. I prefer to live and you will be kind enough to permit my wish to be gratified, we can agree quite readily, I am sure!!" "Vell, ve agree, but you must promise not to make escape effort again." Now, for another one-sided argument and feared I had not guns enough for this tough customer. Encouraged by my former good luck, as I thought it, I set in. "Colonel Wirz, you know that life has little worth without liberty, and it is clear to me that you would try to escape in any way you could were you in my predicament. I have violated no rule of war - no rule of your camp even, for you have not prohibited attempts to escape; and if you had it would avail but little, for liberty, next to life, is sweetest and self-preservation is the first law of Nature, and to remain passive inside that stockade and not take advantage of any means to save one's life by escape from a sure and horrible death, would be most unnatural in a human being." This was a long speech for me and I wondered at myself. "You are too smart a Yankee and can talk just like a Yankee lawyer. Anyway, I was going to hang or shoot you, but you must be some punished for you make example for others to run away, and I make example of you!" I tried to argue this point of punishment, for I had some slight idea of what his methods were, or thought I had, up to that time and until had tasted of some of his most "exquisite," but now his "Dutch" was up and argument was in vain. What I had heard of his stretching methods, made me shudder, but I was to know what the "stand-up collar" was, in reality. I have worn them since, but there was a vast difference in the method of wearing, I learned to my regret. To describe the appliance, imagine two posts set firmly in the ground, of sufficient height to accomodate the loftiest Yankee; at about four and half feet from the ground holes were bored in a winding course through the posts, that a pin could be put in at about every inch. Over these posts were slipped two planks with holes at ends to take the posts; the plank at bottom was about twelve inches wide and two inches thick. In this, there were two holes about a foot apart, near the center of the plank, large enough to put the Yankee foot in, with a movable piece to close up about the ankle and pin it to that position in order to hold the feet of the victim securely. The upper plank was wider and cut in the middle to pass the neck of the victim from one side to the hole in the middle and a similar sliding device to close up on the neck, as well as to strengthen the plank at the point of its weakness, by the hole and cut to get in. Now, all is ready. The victim steps into the shambles below, is locked fast, his neck passed into the collar, the sliding pieces closed and pinned fast.

The corners that came into contact with the flesh were not rounded off - in this beautiful device of torture. I suppose it was overlooked. Had it been more comfortable and the "collar" worn with the more grace, or if it had been padded some, the victim would have felt more grateful. Now comes the real punishment. Hands are bound out full length of arm, useless to aid as support in any way, the upper plank is now raised at each end, inch by inch until the large toe can scarcely touch the ground, when the body relaxes the least, by the stretched neck or all parts of the body, the "pinning" up process is continued until both planks are sprung almost to breaking, either the neck of the poor devil in the toils, or the plank. This may have been a "gymnastic" cure for some of our ailments, but is for the purpose of elongating the body or neck, it was a perfect contrivance invented by a demon, which inflicted the most horrible pain and torture. After hanging at both ends in the boiling hot sun, pouring its blistering rays upon the bare head and face for about an hour or less, although it seemed like Eternity, the victim was relaxed, examined and if living, and your body had allowed you to stand on a toe, you were elevated another inch though the previous "stretch" seemed all the poor anatomy could stand. I now realized what Wirz meant by hanging - indeed, it was most "exquisite" punishment and my thought was "why I did not beg to be instantly killed," (but at present writing I am not quarreling with myself for not asking that boon.) Hanging would end sometime - this seemed to last a lifetime and will for me. To describe the pain that racked body and brain is beyond my power of expression. Within the first half hour, I was wishing that I might be killed at once, twisting the head continuously from one position to another to rest the spot most pressed upon by the hard and not smooth edges of the "collar" until at last the neck was girdled, raw, bleeding, feeling like a hot band of iron about the neck, and jaws and chin in the same condition. What more could I hope but to die soon - that punishment lasted eight long hours; but after the first hour a semi-consciousness in a measure gave relief, as to time. Why my brains were not cooked or destroyed is a wonder - in the emaciated condition by starvation. How I suffered that day and for weeks to follow. I cursed myself for thanking Wirz for my life at the outset. Had I known that which I was to experience, nothing would have daunted me from exasperating Wirz to the point of killing me at once, even though it was to attack him personally. After getting over the effects of that torture, my mind was still on liberty, regardless of what might follow, realizing I was fast breaking in strength and preferred to die alone in a swamp of anywhere but in Andersonville Bull Pen, even if home and friends be not reached and final resting place be "unknown." Hope of ever seeing home and friends again had about died within me, but escape I would, dead or alive!

Jack Fitzpatrick

A modern view of an escape tunnel or a well dug by Union prisoners at Andersonville.

CHAPTER FOUR
ESCAPE

The tunnel that I was a party to digging, when I had strength, was nearing completion, though much more of a contract than the "failure," having to project one hundred feet farther to be beyond the second stockade, which was built to prevent or discourage tunneling, as well as a barrier against attack from Sherman's raiders, in an effort to release the prisoners. We heard from some newcomers that Stoneman and Kilpatrick were on the way to release us. At all events, history proved this to be true, and Stoneman was worsted in the attempt, and made prisoner. With August came death, dealing heavy strokes daily. Nearly three thousand of the flower of the youth of the north were silent - they had answered to the call of the Reaper, and passed form torture and misery. The projected tunnel was located some seventy feet from the north gate, and north of it. August furnished the foggy night acceptable to our party and between twelve midnight and two in the morning fifteen men crawled through the long stuffy hole - like rats - to the end and opening. Now the greatest caution must be observed and it required the stoutest hearts to face it. All could not go at once. Each man must move like a snake and as silent - none to follow until the preceding man was at fairly safe distance in matter of time. They were to have five in each party as near as possible for mutual comfort and protection.

Prisoners at Andersonville gather for distribution of rations.

Crawl, crawl through weeds and briars, until the brook was reached, then the crawl was a horror-through mud and filth to the railroad, under that to the site of an old sawmill up the flume, or the remains of it, slimy and dank, to the intake and lastly into the water, covered with frogspawn, briars and rushes - simply a nasty, shallow mudhole backed by a swamp reeking with the seepings through dead vegetation of generations. Wading, crawling, and striving in all ways to place as much distance between us and the Hell behind us, before the daylight gave our trail to the Rebs, and to find some safe place where the tired, starved, almost bloodless frames could rest. Blood was oozing from countless wounds from briars crawled through, and the dead pine and gum branches that met us at every move in the dark. Among our five were two that needed help and received it from the rest of us in every way possible - not caring alone for ourselves. Though pressed by them to make good our own escape, they felt the time had come for them to give way and starve in the swamp. Their plea fell upon deaf ears. Chilly, smothered with mud, weeds, dead pine needles, that had been rotting for years, feeling our way breaking a path or trail for the weaker ones, stepping into holes deeper than the general surface, plunging neck - deep into the slimy mess, even head first into some of them, praying for daylight - at least a little, that we could see our surroundings! Daylight came and found us yet in a swamp - not knowing whether we were nearer or farther from the Bull Pen. We had been unable to guide by the stars, as none shone, as the fog did not lift during our leavetaking. The sun moved it after daylight. Exhausted from lack of food, pressing labor of escape, the condition of body, the rags upon us, wet, clammy and cold, we had used some water in our mode of transportation, we were not clean. The month of August, in a southern clime, and yet we shivered, though not from fear. We found a little piece of rising ground, carefully surveyed it, painfully dragged ourselves to the high point and lay down to rest - or die - either, was welcome. We had placed as we thought, at least five or six miles between a cruel death and liberty - as we were the first five to leave the tunnel. While resting in this uncertain prospect of success, our thoughts reverted to those behind us, hoping they had succeeded, at least as well as our party, though it was certain they had not made the breach very wide for the progress was slow, nerve-racking crawling to liberty, not knowing at what moment detection would come to them. Our little party rested and slept as circumstances would permit - the sleep of exhaustion. Two of our party should not have made the attempt. One, we felt sure could not last long in this struggle; but he was determined not to go back alive. The other was so much of a cripple that he was helped when one could hardly help oneself, yet, true to each other in peril, willing to do all that could be done to assist one so determined to live or die - at liberty. A third one was not strong by any means. The night struggle had told very much on his nerves, as he feared recapture and its possible results. Each tried to cheer the other by some funny story, but the eyes never lied, though the lips spoke encouragement. Another of our party was a member of Company "B" of my Regiment. He had lost an eye but the other never failed him, with a nose that was acute in sense of smell, ordinarily of a jovial and devil-may-care disposition - but now, quite subdued! While taking the much needed rest, if I may term it such, tattered and torn as to clothing and flesh, the first insufficient to cover our nakedness, the latter much out of place by the briars and thorn-like, dead spikes of dead pine, covered with black ooze, and blood from the injuries - mingled, - as we all, certainly, had a streaked look. Waiting events, or the darkness of night to cover other miles of misery and torture form hunger, our hearts upon that sweet born liberty. Our comrade of Company "B" was a little excited, sniffing and looking about. He said, "I smell onions." None of us saw anything about us that would indicate a habitable spot other than our own small island in this great swamp. Our Company "B" insisted that his nose was no liar, and wanted to forage. Being the acknowledged leader of this party of five, I objected on the grounds that where onions grew, enemies might also be found.

All were in desperate want of something to eat and the eyes of all pleaded as no voice could. Objection was useless - he pleaded as well as the others that it might be a negro hut and they were our friends. Company "B" started cautiously, following his nose with high hope that he would find something to eat and no enemies. We waited, perhaps twenty minutes, with the little breath in us abated in the act of listening. Soon we heard a dog's bark and instinctively we knew that we were caught - or saved for awhile - which would it be? With hearts beating that could almost be heard by each of us, and faces covered with the slime and dirty water - that were evidently touched with a pallor not easily seen, whispered conversation among us four, the decision to escape or die, if our captors would kill us. The bark of that dog continued (I can hear it distinctly today!!) Soon came our comrade, arms full of what are called "leek," a species of the onion family, and he was unconcerned as though no danger was at hand, his whole mind was on his burden, though but a single article of diet they were very nutritious. He most sacredly divided them, each man his actual share. The dog quieted down and we felt more secure.

After a short delay to munch the vegetable we started with the hope of getting farther on in the swamp to avoid being hunted out by bloodhounds. We knew if we had been discovered that the alarm would soon be given and the manhunt would soon follow. Though no one had been seen at or near where the onions were taken, yet the bark of the dog meant to the owner that something unusual had caused him to bark. We had made only a hundred yards perhaps when we were stopped by the sudden breakdown of one of the party. He urged us on - to leave him and save ourselves, but we could not and our progress was slow now, and very laborious on all. Suddenly we heard the bay of hounds some distance away. They had found our trail! We did not know which party they were following, and hoped not ours - which was something selfish, but natural. The sound grew nearer and nearer and hope died within us. We realized it was our trail they were on. Either by the sense of smell to the hounds or intuition as to the direction we had taken, at all events we were being closely hunted. We lifted our comrade to his feet and again started with the desperation that small hope of escape engendered - while the savage baying of the hounds seemed to nerve up all of us. We reached a strip of swamp and entered but a short distance when the weak comrade sank helplessly down and died, while we waited, hoping to be missed by the hounds. Making sure that our comrade was dead, we left him sorrowfully, while each of us really hoped that our turn would come before recapture and left among the "unknown" as none of us knew the full name of the comrades except two of us, and that was company "B" and of my regiment by the name of Buckalew, of Trenton, New Jersey. Hurrying along through the brush, briars and cone of pines, now stopping to listen intently for that dreadful bay of the hounds, so near that it seemed our death warrant. The sound stopped and we were encouraged and for several hours felt safe - night would help us, we parleyed in stifled voices, as to direction. I had made observation before day, and felt that we were going northwest and must soon strike a road leading from Oglethorpe; others argued that I was wrong. Three of us parted with the most obstinate one, he going south and would not be convinced of the fact that we three were moving northwest. Along toward sundown, hearing no sounds of hounds, we thought that we were safe and halted to reconnoiter our position before resting for the night march intended.

   A few moments later came an awful suprise - the baying of hounds and on our track! We moved to a rising ground and not a moment too soon. We took to some small trees in the opening - two of us were fortunate in having strength enough to swing up clear of the ground and the teeth of the savage brutes at our feet, but the sight that met our gaze when we had recovered from the fright of being hamstrung by the dogs, was one that time could never efface from memory. Frightful dreams we have had, but this was no dream. The other poor emaciated comrade, who had exhausted all his strength to keep up with us thus far toward home and liberty, had no power left to lift himself out of reach of those hellish brutes. They tore him, limb, muscle and flesh - such as there was - so that he prayed his captors to shoot him. He could not stand or move himself from his position, and they did a merciful act, unintentionally - shot him to death; and another "unknown" rested while some fond mother, or other loved one would wait in vain for him or record of his death. Buckalew and I were ordered to come down from our roost. We came down of course, and looked about for our fourth man, whom we had not heard from since he left us, and thought that he may be trapped. When convinced that we were not to be dog meat, otherwise we preferred the death just witnessed, and did not hesitate to say so.

Escaped Union prisoners being set upon by dogs.

What a sharpener of memory was this incident, not the first. But the question, mentally, "What next?" We moved on but a few yards, when we reached a road, and were bound each to a horse, rather saddle by a tether rope. We were waiting for something - I judged, and rested while I could, during which time kept up an "awful" thinking. Why were we made fast to the horses? I thought of everything from hanging to being dragged to death - and this seemed the most suggestive from the preparation. Buckalew and I conversed with each other without notice from our captors - this seemed ominous to us, we concluded to ask the privilege of being shot like a soldier. We discussed the matter as if we were not to be the victims. Why we were waiting was soon answered when a party came up the road, and with them was our comrade who had gone south but did quite as well as we had. He was broken down with his tiresome march, exposure, fright and disappointment. We were soon to know why we were bound to the horses! I, to the one of the left, Buckalew to the right, the returned comrade in the middle, who was fast giving way, being bound by the wrist at right and left to the rope attached to the saddle, and to each other in the same way. The horses moved on quite briskly and the pace was almost too much for Buckalew and me, as the pull on our wrists by the lagging body of our comrade, which made it very painful, the pulling of the muscles, tension on our frames, this became torture to us, what must it have been to the comrade between us? A halt came, which was merciful.

The middle comrade sank to the ground and begged to be shot, as the pace and pain of pulling at arms length was torture to him and was killing his comrades. Our wrists and hands were swollen by the pinch of the rope, to a bursting point, it seemed. Our bodies wrenched by the sidewise pull at the helpless victim in the middle was giving us. Argument availed not, though all three of us were suffering so that our eyes almost popped out of our heads. We move on; our broken comrade fainted and sank to the ground but the horsemen only laughed and ordered him to his feet. He was unable to do so but we dragged him to his knees, they spurred on their horses and he is dragged at length over the sandy road and the little so called bridges, composed of two or three poles so the water could percolate through, the poles were rough and knotty. Not a sound from the fallen hero, and we two straining every nerve to keep up and drag his weight, though not much, was likely to kill us by that sidewise drag which made travel very difficult, even to a strong man. Again we halted, after dragging his limp body nearly a mile - it seemed a thousand - the skin was ground from knees to toe - tips of our dying comrade. He could scarcely speak to be heard, but the bloodshot eyes he turned to his tormentors and gasped, "Shoot me! Do please shoot me!" He was untied from us and we two were lashed together with a good-bye to our comrade so soon to find release. We move on slowly. A few moments pass; the horsemen ride up; we know that "unknown" has passed out of life and is free from torture. We gladly, devoutly, say, "Amen."

Being near dusk, and our salvation, we were taken into a plantation house, in charge of two soldiers, and five or six children and as many "civilians." We were not dead, nor yet, not quite alive, but the human hearted woman gave us milk and bread with some "powk." i.e. some part of a swine. We lived rapidly then, in the course of two hours. We had eaten twice, and slept once. Sweet potatoes were baked in the ashes of the old-fashioned open hearth fireplace. After we had finished our second nap we were given a chance to wash and change our "rainment," so very scant and dirty, and brief at both that we blushed when in the presence of the lady, but the blush may not have been noticed through the accumulations of the past thirty-six hours. After the wash, which was delightful, having had real soap to use, and a good rubbing given us by a colored friend, some "nigger" clothes, they termed them, were handed us so that we might be presentable to the "lady folks." The "nigger" costume was of some coarse cotton goods and some better than those we had shed, much cleaner and "immune" from those friends that had annoyed us, and stuck close to us through our mudbath and all other adversities. The "Ladies Circle" was not augmented by the new comers, and they sat up late with us; baked sweets and urged us to eat all we wanted; talked and ate with us; wanted to know of the fashions and prices at the "Nawth;" their general conversation proved them to be only some of the low "crackers" and not of the "F.F.V's" of the South. Of course, neither of us knew the slightest about such matters as hats and women's wear, etc., but, dear me, didn't my comrade pride himself on a full knowledge of such matters, beyond Mason and Dixon Line. I was thinking of graver things, he taxing his imagination to be able to reply to the many questions on the many subjects that he was an entire stranger to. The hours wanted. We were left alone in the care of the guards. While the conversation was going on and the eating ditto, we noticed that we were hiding a goodly quantity of the toothsome sweets.

    Left to ourselves we found in a short time that there was danger in eating. The potatoes were eaten without salt, salt being very scarce. It was very dry eating. We drank much water, as the water was good; the result being a "fullness" quite a stranger to us for several months; so much fullness that it caused pain, which food would have given us, and for the rest of the night we both gulped and retched in misery and severe pains. After awhile we became worn out and actually slept, and morning came all too soon for us. Our relief from pain, with sleep to follow, was due to the kindness of a colored lady, who concocted a dose of hot water and wood ashes mixed, not so palatable but gave comfort in an hour. She knew her business on home remedies. When we awoke, the first topic of conversation was "What will be done with us when we reach camp?" My last experience was not pleasant to think of and we preferred death in some other way. We were ordered out after our host had given us a square meal of the "Inevitable" salt pork and corn pone, but which was delicious to us. At the door was a wagon and team, to our surprise. We wondered if this was for us or some of "fambly." The team was typical Georgia style, two very aged and sleepy mules, looking as of stone, and quite immovable, but they were alive as they moved when the whip cracked and from the cavernous throat of the driver was something smoky, and the sound lifted, lifted the long, drooping ears to near perpendicular - of course the team understood while we did not. The dogs and extra men had gone into camp or elsewhere, we did not care - which left two guards and the driver to look after us; but that was enough in our condition and no arms. We rode all the way "home" in the wagon with some sweet potatoes and a few onions, beside them there were two small sacks of potatoes. We wondered why they were separate from the general lot and it worried us, we could not study it out, but when camp was reached we learned to our surprise that they were the "compliments" of the hostess of the night. God bless her, while we enjoyed her hospitality, though we did suffer from excess of sweets! The gifts no doubt, were for the very accurate information that my comrade had so freely given on things he knew as little of, as he knew of Heaven.

We bid our coachman good-bye, sending our heart-felt thanks to our hostess for her kindness; but the coachman's tip was not extended, for the most obvious reasons that we were "short of change." Waiting under guard, we thought "what, oh, what, will be done to us this time, as I would surely be recognized!" We had no use for the "necklace", we had worn once and still have the scars on my neck and jaws. to be instantly killed would be charity and mercy rather than again endure that suffering which we felt must end all for us. Sure, swift death was preferable to the slim hope of surviving once more from that awful torture - we certainly could not look for any mitigation of the same at the hands of Wirz when recognized. This soliloquy ended abruptly. "Eyer, you Yanks, who you-uns as been run away, git up in line! We will take you-uns to see Captain Wirz!" Great God, how that name was burned into my brain! I had told my comrade of that torture and how both of us were facing that - or worse, if possible. My comrade says, "I will follow your lead, wherever it may be." I replied, "I have only one life to sacrifice and do not want yours to account for." He says, "Never mind, I will go with you." We slowly picked up the little sack of potatoes - I don't know why - I suppose it was mechanical - it seemed just then that I should never want for more of anything in this world, for I was convinced that I was on the last lap of life; if Wirz was to pass on my punishment. Just at this time there were some new prisoners at the South gate in line to march in, and had just commenced to move, we were close both to gate and the moving line, there was some confusion among the guards, and I saw at a glance our only hope. I softly spoke to my comrade, "Step in line and I will follow a file or two back." He hesitated and wanted me to go first. I looked him in the eye, and signed for him to be quick; he did so reluctantly. I flanked in a few files back and passed to the other side; moved up to his file; and beckoned him to come with me. We passed well up to the front before the gate closed and the inner gate opened, both of us now free to move as fast as we could. We pushed along until inside the dead line, aided by those new men to whom I quietly told in a hurried manner why were so anxious to get in front before discovered, and two of them did crowd us up front in a jiffy. Once past the dead line we were safe to move anywhere and hurried to our old "home." We had not been missed by the guards until we had made good our escape "inward" this time. Reaching our old place we found it preempted by others, but we were given a hearty welcome by those who knew us before we had taken our French leave. We made close inquiry as to the return of those who had also started. It was then that we got the full information that fifteen had left by that tunnel and thus far eleven had been returned. We could account for all but one - where was he? What an ending for all that hard fight for life and liberty! This was not the only case, for tunnels were prevalent in camp. Our welcome to this place was cordial in the sense that we were alive and you can imagine how grateful I was to escape the guards and evade a parley with that human devil, Wirz! An attempt was made to ferret us out, and take us outside, but my name was not "Hopkins" now, and the sergeant that knew me was sent to Macon for duty. And I hoped he would never return, for the thought of that "collar" made me shudder.

Monday, August 22, 1864

Morning cool & very cloudy. Rain is expected at any moment. Breakfast rice soup & a small bit of meat & bread of the same quantity. Considerate excitement in Camp about raising a police force who all in all are a pack of thieves or as bad nearly. Extorters. One party wants to rule the Camp and make it what it once was (a den of murderers & thieves) and the other party wants to reign supreme. Charles Munn very low and will die in a short time. Rations bacon & rice & molasses & bread. Very good for a change. For supper meat & meal & coffee & bacon & bread. A most sumptuous meal.

Tuesday, August 23, 1864

Morning cool and clear but the heat is getting greater and will continue to be some what tolerable until the sun comes up and then oh then. Breakfast rice, molasses, soup & bacon a small amount. Sgt. W. H. Howell or "Barnum" as we call him was admitted to the hospital this morning in good spirits. I am detailed to draw rations today. For dinner we had beans, soup & bacon. Made Howell a soup of rice for his dinner. Rations beef, bacon, bread & beans and salt. For supper, coffee, bread & beans & some meat. Mosquitos rather more plenty than is agreeable.

Wednesday, August 24, 1864

Morning cool & clear but getting very warm as the day goes on.
Made some mush and sold it this morning for 55 cts. Breakfast rice, soup & beef. Bought some meal for 50 cts this morning and will save for a while as we have only stayed for some wealth. Dinner beans & soup. Ration of beef came in a small bit, not enough for a bite. Two of the large Sutlers bought themselves out of this Camp and are to be passed off as officers upon our exchange agent. Rations of meal & beans & salt. For our supper coffee, meal cakes & bread and beef. Had a good wash to go to bed on.

Saturday, August 27, 1864

Morning cool & clear but as usual gets extremely hot ere noon and from after to 4 PM. Breakfast, rice (boiled) and molasses quite a meal indeed. A small shower we had about noon. Samuel Nixon visited in our tent today from the center of Camp. Rations rice (cooked) beef & bread. We had a 1/2 of a beef's head and boiled it and made a good stew and plenty of meat. For supper beef, bread, rice & soup. Charles Munn is dead. He was taken prisoner on the 13th of June.

Sunday, August 28, 1864

Morning cool & clear. For our breakfast, beans & soup, bread & beef. Spent the day in mending a shirt for Samuel J. Nixon. It was a considerable of a job too. Bought some thread for 20 cts that would have cost 5 cts at the North. Also a part of the mornings work was the straightening up the accounts of Charles Munn for the sake of his wife & child so that they or she might collect it if possible. Rations beans, bread & beef & a very small ration of salt. Supper of beef & bread & coffee.

Pvt. Charles Munn, 1st New Jersey Infantry.

Wednesday, August 31, 1864

Morning cool & cloudy. I expect rain. Breakfast, rice soup & beef & bread. One of the guards stated voluntarily that he thought an exchange would soon take place for there was talk of it outside and their papers full of it. No dinner and an early breakfast --- very good in here. But supper was ordered.

Our beef fried & bread & beans & gravy & pepper. Rations of bread & beef & beans & salt. Business in Camp appears as lively as ever except at the Camp Sutlers.

Thursday, September 1, 1864

Morning cool & clear. The night was very cool last night. So much so that I caught a cold in my legs. I have the diarreah quite bad but I hope soon to be better. Breakfast beans & beef & bread & soup. The whole Camp are living altogether on the issues of this month for an Exchange. My entire hopes are centered on it and I would not despair even if it did not occur this month. Despair is out of my line. Rations beef, bread, rice. For supper boiled rice & bread & beef. I have a very sore mouth caused by the failing of my teeth.

Friday, September 2, 1864

Morning cool & clear. I had a miserable night. I could not sleep. Breakfast beans, bread, beef & soup. The Belle Island prisoners are being set apart from the rest of the prisoners again. I suppose to send them first which is before they die. Belief stronger than ever all thought of the anticipated Exchange. I have a very sore mouth yet and can get nothing for it. Rations cooked beans, bread, beef, bacon. Supper beans, bread & beef a small piece of bacon & coffee.

Saturday, September 3, 1864

Morning cool & cloudy. Rain is ready to descend almost. Breakfast beans, beef, bread & soup. Rumor says that the authorities have ordered the prisoners to do all the business they have to do by the railroad between now and the 10th for then the CSA (or USA?) will take charge of all the transfer of rations for the prisoners. But we have no way of knowing ourselves of such things. Genl. Winder is relieved, and the next item is he goes to Richmond. Rations beef, bread, beans. For supper beans, beef, bread & coffee. My face is getting very sore on the inside.

Sometime before we took leave the Raiders had been very open in their work, but after the hanging became very secretive - but they were yet in business. A comrade of my Regiment, by name of Samuel J. Nixon, had a watch and wanted me to trade it for something better to eat. I took it and was "dogged" daily and shadowed at all times by some one of those cut-throats--being unsuccessful in making a trade, handed it back to him--glad indeed for the silent shadowing ceased. Two nights after Nixon was awakened by the cold touch of a knife at his throat, and a command, "Shut up, or your life will pay the forfeit!" Of course he shut up and handed the murderers his watch to save his life from a throat-cut, as this was sure, and this was the man who on the scaffold said that he had not taken life but was willing to, and this was the attempt. Delaney felt a package in his breast pocket of the remains of his coat and demanded it, he told him that it was a Bible given to him by his mother and they had no use for it, but pleading was in vain, they cut it out and took it away. The old "adage" and some Scripture, I think, blessed be they that have nothing, in this case it was good logic in here, so far as the raiders' work proved it. Several men of my Regiment died in this Bull Pen in a short time and just now I was on the wane and had been almost ready to let go the lifeline in despair, but I still insisted that where others could live I ought to try to do so. One day I saw a strong, sturdy man come into camp. I think form Sherman's forces, and in a dazed manner, made his way to the north side. Listlessly, he looked about him - no place to go, he asked no question, nor would he answer any, always with that same far-away look in his eyes; hopeless, speechless, horror-stricken at what he saw. He sat down on the ground, drew his knees up, arms across his knees and head resting on his arms and never to our knowledge, or of the others near him, by word or act, did he recognize anyone. I peered under his arms, raised his head, his eyes wide open but they saw nothing. When I appealed to have a drink of water, no effort was made to accept it, though sitting in the broiling sun at 95 to 100 degrees, no shade here, all day, all night in cold dew, for four days from time of entrance. We discovered him dead as he sat, no change of position. Among the unnatural things to happen was an incident of brute cruelty of one of our troops to his comrade in arms. There were other cases and many of them, but none compared to the action of this brute Stanton, by name, Irish by extraction, a bulldog face and build, hair, strange in such men was short and kinky - so much so that he was named the "Irish nigger" being very dark complexioned, and really this was an insult to the meanest Irishman I ever knew, and no compliment to even a tough negro. That he had no human instincts, was clear from his actions. Stanton was one of the kind that managed to get on the parole list of those who secured some employment outside, and could get some graft of extras in the way of food, though it cost some of us poor devils inside a smaller portion of his "stipend."

One day, while Stanton was employed on the wagon that made delivery of rations to camp - in the afternoon, after having been used in the forenoon, to cart the dead Yanks to the Cemetery. Standing near the wagon was one of the ever-present "shadows." (So called, because starved to the limit of parchment and bones). This man appealed most piteously to Stanton for a bone! You may wonder why a bone, instead of meat, but there was more nourishment in the "cracked bone soup" than in the quantity of meat given and much healthier often, because of the quality of the meat. Stanton's reply was "Yes, step up to the wagon and you will get a bunch of them." With Stanton standing in the wagon, the poor deluded fellow knew not his meaning, but confided in his word and stepped forward in a feeble effort to the rear of the wagon. Towering over him was the cowardly Stanton. The poor soul received a kick full in his mouth with the boot-shod foot, which not only cut the lips of the poor victim, but knocked out eight or ten teeth from the two jaws. Hundreds saw, hooted, cursed and vented their full vocabulary of invective, but none dared touch him for fear of results from the Confederates. Of all the number who made protests, one had called him a coward, and other uncomplimentary names, hardly fit to mention here. To this one Stanton gave invitation to step forward and he could have some of the same treatment. I refused to accept. Stanton jumped to the ground and said "You will fight me for this and God damn you , I will kill you, fight or not!!!" Here again comes the almost daily acts of his cruelty, and tyranny over weaker men. However, in this case his brute strength and bluff courage was of no avail, as fair play was instantly vouched for from every side. The battle was for my life, I knew, cool of head with cat-like swiftness of movement, skillful as to my hands, I soon placed the strong brute in darkness with a bloody face, before my strength was gone, and of course the winner was a hero in camp, but if he had lost, he would have been almost murdered and no one cared, beyond his close comrades. Twice more, later, did the "Irish nigger" make the attempt, and twice failed. Had he succeeded at any time, the offender of his pride would have undoubtedly been beaten to death, or death would soon have followed and no questions asked how he died. Such were the conditions - that human life was the cheapest thing one could think of.

Prisoners' shebangs along the Dead Line.

One other side to the horrors is, the pathetic incidents that occur in this place. While fresh in my memory I will relate one of them, which no doubt has many parallel. In this case where three brothers who were nearby residents, i.e., lying on the ground near us. We made their acquaintance through a humane streak in our anatomy. Their names respectively, as aged, were William, Stephen and James, all three members of the 112th Regiment, Illinois Vols. They were from the southern border of the state and they were most affectionate to each other, showing every sign of good bringing up under the training of a good Christian mother and father. They were very kindly spoken to us and seemed to want congenial company. William was not well, having rheumatism and other troubles; Stephen had contracted scurvy and the chronic complaint of the camp, and not by any means well; James was taken with a fever, which brought him a mild form of insanity, and was a pitiful sight, naked almost absolute, no covering for the three but a piece of blanket, arranged on two small poles like a cat boat sail, that was shifted with the sun to give even a slight shade, at night used to cover them or some of them, as it was not large enough to cover a good sized man, and was as porous as a sieve to cold, dew or rain. James in his delirium, talked of home, mother and good things to eat. Begged continuously and would not eat when offered him. He grew thinner daily and more childish.

Stephan rapidly grew worse, hideous, loathsome sores all over his body, eating into the tissue, like cancer, starved himself the more that his brothers might live the longer - intelligent, brave, manly fellow! How he prayed that his brothers might live, knowing that he, himself, must soon die, though release or relief came at once. No one was better prepared to meet his Maker than he, or his brothers, whose mother had taught them, and they retained her lesson to the last conscious moment. It was pleasant to hear them talk of their home and parents. Mother was the idol, though all were spoken of in endearing terms, but what a mockery it seemed when life was short to them and to close in the manner it did. After a short time James died, knowing not even his brother. Stephen and William, neither of them able to stand; Stephen was one mass of putrid sores, disgusting to look upon even for those so used to seeing so much suffering and horrors. We carried water for them, and did all things for their comfort, and they being entirely helpless. The death of James quite unmanned the two others, he being the youngest, and their sorrow was that James should be buried like a dog. We were requested by Stephen to try and get a man who had been preaching and holding prayer meetings near us in camp, to come and say a few words over the body of James; saying with scalding tears coursing down his wan, then, careworn and grimy cheeks, "Oh, I can't bear the thought of James being buried like an animal! What would our dear mother say?" We consented to find the man, and did at a meeting being held at the "Coliseum" - the name would indicate a pretentious place of meeting, but it was only a hole in the ground, made possible by digging the "tap root" of a pine stump to its very end, making a hole about twelve feet deep by twenty feet across the surface, the slope being used for seating or standing room, by digging escarpments, like steps. At the bottom was the "pulpit" - a pail bottom, or just the ground, "really" a lifting up of the voice, that the audience might hear. We heard this man before, but now his voice seemed to strike us as familiar, more so than before. When he was through with his discourse I waited on him and made my request. His reply came promptly, "Yes". Both of us moved toward our destination, conversing matters in general. His voice now seemed to stir my thoughts. I asked him where he was from. "Kentucky" was the reply. I felt easier, but our conversation led to the fact that he was not "Kentucky" bred, but was from Illinois - to this time I do not know the family name of the brothers. I stopped at once and asked if he had any friends in the Army. He replied, "yes, I have five brothers I believe in the 112th Illinois Vols. some of whom I have never seen." I asked him to name some of them by given name. He at once named three that I knew were in Andersonville with him. I now concluded why his voice troubled me - for I had been hearing a similar voice almost daily in that of William. I remarked that I might be leading him to an unpleasant duty, but he replied, "I will do it." I then conducted him to the spot - one dead, one dying, one hopeless of living long. He recognized Stephen. I turned from, them to allow them as much possible in that crowded place, to privately express both their joy and sorrow. What a sound of mingled joy and sorrow, at the grave, as it were, never shall I forget the frantic joy and heartbroken sobs in one breath as it seemed. The "Kentuckian" did preach a sermon over his brother James, who he had not seen since an infant, and on the spot where he died. The text was, "Two men were in a field, one was taken, the other left!" Such a flow of eloquence, and feeling - tears trickling down his cheeks - such a sermon was never heard in any place or occasion known to those who heard it. The audience, made up of several thousands of all denominations, creeds and no creeds, stood near enough to hear it and hundreds that could only hear, now and then a word or sentence, being so far away, yet every man was moved to most respectful silence, and interest. Thousands in tears, that scalded their way through the grime of the camp and pine smoke, leaving a striped cheek on many a veteran, who had faced death many times without a tremor of a muscle or wink of an eye. Yet there was the saddest of deaths under most harrowing circumstances, and many, if not every one of those thousands were asking themselves, "When shall my turn come?" The body of James was carried out to exchange for wood brought in. The Kentucky brother was named Henry, and was the eldest child and had gone to Kentucky a long time before the war. He gained consent of the Sergeant of his Detachment to remain with his brothers, to care for them. He did all he could to comfort them and was a real comfort in their condition. Stephen died, Henry performing the funeral service. William rallied a little, but was a marked victim. To continue this incident of those brothers, I will need to pass on ahead of my sketch somewhat.

In September, with a lot of others, I was moved to Florence, South Carolina, under the promise of being paroled and exchanged at Charleston. That broken promise proved the saying "hope deferred maketh the heart sick;" indeed, it was too true. The prospect of a winter in an open stockade, even in South Carolina, was not a hopeful outlook for men starved, diseased, without flesh or blood to warm the gaunt frames. Reaching Florence after a long and tedious ride for several days and nights in cattle cars, we were taken to a so-called camp, about a mile from the cross-roads at Florence - the Cheraw and Darlington, and the Charleston and Columbia railroads, made a right angle crossing here, in an old cornfield, with furrows still visible, a guard placed about us, no stockade as yet. To continue the story of those brothers - they remained through the six bitter months at Florence until sent to Wilmington for exchange or to give us up. William seemed to have improved some, until the middle of January when he began to fail and grew worse up to the last day of February, 1865, the day he was released by the enemy and from his sufferings - by death! On that day the train that bore him to our lines was the last to leave the prison. The train stopped at a road crossing; on one side of the train were Confederates, on the other were the boys in Blue, and just over the tops of the trees and about a half mile away we could see floating proudly, that which was to all of us as dear as life itself, "Old Glory!" Streaming eyes and feeble hearts were anxious to once more see its loveliness before dying for its honor. Many in the car had passed the "invisible" line before resting their glazing eyes upon its beautiful folds, and scarcely a man in that car was able to sit up alone, much less help himself to rise up long enough to look at it. Henry and William were close to the side of the car. The boards of the siding had at some time been stripped part way down. Henry was one of our number that could stand, able to help himself and others. William had been in a condition, that indicated early dissolution, and when our car was drawn at the crossing, for the purpose of our removal, there were several Generals, Colonels and other officers near. General Schofield and Terry I recognized from the photos of them. I had noticed a Colonel among the group who bore on his cap, "112th, Ill." At once I called Henry's attention to it. William had heard me, roused up and with his last display of strength of body and voice, almost alone raised himself and looking toward the group, recognized his Colonel. In a voice as strong as natural, he cried out, "Colonel Churchill, do you not know me? Come to me Colonel!" which he did instantly by riding his horse alongside the car, taking the wasted, grimy hand thrust toward him, in a last desperate effort. "No, my good boy, I do not know you." Hardly able to speak because of his former effort, William, in a whisper, gave him name, company, etc.; Colonel Churchill quickly sprang from his saddle and ordered a man into it, and said "Ride to Camp as you never rode before! Have Lieutenant - and his brother mount this horse at once and come to this point at the best speed in the horse!"

Instantly, man and horse were gone. The Colonel and some men gently assisted Henry to get his brother from the car; carefully and most tenderly they seated him on a log, sustained between the Colonel and Henry. Bystanders, in tears they were not ashamed of, stood silent as the grave, intently watching the fast-passing William, whose every breath was an effort, only, in the softest whisper, speaking to Henry and the Colonel, who cheered him and urged him to keep up, that his other brothers were coming; but it was an effort to do so with all the joy it might bring to his last moments. He struggled manfully, and won for no horse with a double burden was doing better service, taxed to his utmost, carrying to the dying one the last joyous moment, noble brute you were!!! Sliding from the foaming horse to the ground and reaching the dying brother took but a second. After the greetings, such as they were, not a dry eye in all the crowd, the Lieutenant took the place of Colonel and it was then that the younger of all, who rode at Death's command, stood a few feet in front of the dying William and became fixed as stone in his gaze, which never for an instant left the face of his brother William. Physicians from the Regiment and Division for that matter, and they were numerous, had done all they could for the dying hero and simply awaited the dread summons. In a low, feeble whisper William was intermittently speaking the names of dear ones, and the last gasp was with "Mother's" name on his lips; a shudder, a slight lift of the head, a last look, sinking into the arms of his brothers - death found him released. At this instant the stocky form of the standing brother swayed and with a heavy groan doubled forward and sank to the ground before noticed. The physicians attended him on the instant. Too late however, he and William, side by side, went to meet James and Stephen. Thus, did the Hells and hellions of Andersonville and Florence compass the death of four out of six of one family.

The Hell of Andersonville.

The "natural" causes of Davis, Winder and Wirz - the two first were intelligent, educated men and professed Christians - the last - a tool, and a willing one. I want to feel in this case that "the devil cares for his own," and has this goodly company.

Now, to return to the Florence field. In October, the new stockade was ready for occupation, but we were still in the field. Our rations were of a better quality, but some diminished in quantity. Water was good and in plenty. The camp seemed to improve some, as in our case of scurvy, seemed to get better, though my legs had begun to twist wrongside out, and feet to change front, and troublesome otherways, my gums swollen and rotting, sloughing off, leaving the teeth almost ready to fall out. My limbs, from the knees to toes, were swollen nearly to bursting, black purple in color, holes in which the finger could be inserted over an inch, putrid, disgusting to look at, while from the knees, torso to head, the body was skin and bone - the skin drawn like parchment on a frame. The vegetables sold by the farmers, as sweet potatoes, onions, peppers, leek, etc. to those who had money, or something to barter, did us much good and the dead line in this case was an imaginary one, being a path trampled in the sand. The same good air breathed by the guards, we also had the privilege of inhaling. One day several hundred took advantage of a good chance while appearing to be in quest of wood, which was all about us in plenty. They began by spreading out from all parts of camp into the fields, swamp and woods.

The guards were all new levies and no one was thought as seriously trying to escape, inasmuch as some returned with rails and other wood. The scheme expanded. Then there was a scampering to corral the boys again. Many had shortlived escape; others, never to be again heard of, having decided to die free, became exhausted and the quagmire, quicksand of the swamp had claimed them forever. A very few may have made their way to our lines and they the most hardy. Daniel S. Farrand of my old home at one time, Powerville, New Jersey, was a member of the Excelsior Brigade of New York Vols. under that fearless Daniel E. Sickles, had by some means managed to keep from Rebel confiscation all through his Andersonville visit, his watch and a pair of uniform pants of fine texture - gray, with a black stripe down the leg. I judge they were N.Y. Militia uniform. He and I were both very bad scurvy victims - he the worse, as he could not even crawl; I was so that I could get along with help to steady me, one leg partly straight, the left leg was inclined to cross the right in the rear and remain there to obstruct its motion. Farrand was only a short distance from me. I called on him one day and he said, "Charley, trade those pants for something to eat and save our lives, if we can." I took them. Next morning, with help of my comrades, I went to the line and called the Lieutenant of the guard. He came and seemed a decent fellow - intelligent, also - I asked him if he would like to buy a pair of fine grey, cloth pants - he must have wondered why I did not replace my abbreviated costume with them. He replied that he would and I said to him, "Lieutenant, you of course mean to deal squarely and not get the pants and leave me to settle with the owner?" He said, "You get the pants, and you will be treated all right!" I sent back to my quarters for them; he asked me outside the guard line and to his tent to make the "dicker." I felt just a little streaked, but went with him. He helped me to a seat and I had a good square look at his face before negotiations were entered into. I concluded that he had a good face - I would trust it. "How much do you want for the pants in Confed. money?" I noticed that they pleased him and asked, "What would they cost you in Charleston?" He replied that such goods came through the blockade and were very expensive. I said five hundred dollars, Confed. He did not faze a particle, nor did I. At once he pulled out of his inside coat "skirt" pocket, what looked much like a small suitcase, and produced therefrom a five hundred dollar Confed. note. I said, "The money is no good unless we can use it. The smaller bills would be better." (He could have taken the pants, and told me to "git" and of course I would have "got" as I always "strictly" obey orders.) But he took the "newspaper" and gave me smaller "promises to pay" in Confed. "script." I told him I wanted to buy some potatoes, onions, anything to eat in the vegetable line and hope he would kindly help me do so, as the farmers would demand "Greenbacks," and I had none. He agreed, and fixed next morning or afternoon, as I desired for me to come to the line and he would pass me out to trade. I was there on time, the farmer also, with just what I wanted - onions, one peck "sweets," twenty bushel tobacco, twenty-five plugs (never used tobacco) and a quart of salt. The Lieutenant gave me an "Escort" of two Confeds to help me. I had a bonanza, as another fellow at the line had greenbacks - I had none - (where he got them or how he kept from the ferret-eyed Confed, I don't know) - he could have bought where I could not. I bargained for the whole lot, the farmer expecting pay in greenbacks, though nothing was said to that effect. He backed up when offered Confederate money, and the price must be more if paid in "Greybacks." The Lieutenant told him that he must sell to the Yankees at the same price as to Confederate Army, or what he had would be confiscated, and given to the prisoners, and he would be refused the privilege of coming into Camp to sell. My stock was delivered and unloaded and what a time to watch - and eat it. I soon had greenbacks - for those who had them came to me to buy. I had the "cinch" on them. That deal was a life saver of more than seven of us, in all stages of scurvy. Farrand was among the number, as well as his chums. What a feast we had, and how we enjoyed, none can tell but the participants. We were generous while we had to give, and many a poor fellow, that was in bad shape, who asked for a sweet potato, and had no money, was given without question. We had been in his condition and were not so far from it then, and could appreciate the term of Dickens, "put yourself in his place." Comrade Farrand had a Waltham watch he had hidden from very covetous eyes. He wished me to deal away, after his supply had given out of the former deal, as he had half of the dicker, and like myself, had chums who had to live from the supply. I first bargained with his for a half interest in the watch - he offered it to me for my part in the deal - and I gave him an order on my father, for thirty-five dollars which would be honored, should he get home and I not. The "order" was honored by myself, as I reached home but a few days later than he. I took the watch, a silver, hunting cased-Waltham, which at that time was deemed the best on the market. I feared reprisal, injury or murder from some "raiders," who knew of my former success, and though I had money from disposal of some of my stock, or something valuable or I would not go to the line for trading. If I could only retain it long enough to trade away, all would be well and the coming winter might be lived through by most of us, from the good effects of the vegetables. An attempt was made to rob me while trying to trade it on the line, but it failed and my assailant fell - his partners closed on me. I stepped or crutched over the line with the help of a comrade taking the chances of the guard knowing me as one who had been taken over the dead line by the Lieutenant. We called for Corporal of the Guard #1. My comrade stepped back inside instantly, when he knew I was safe. The Corporal came; I was taken to the quarters of the Lieutenant, and was all right after an explanation; and as he was anxious to have the watch, we bargained "negotiated," he paid me $2500 of paper "promises to pay after the close of the War" by the Confederate States. He wanted me to get him some greenbacks on the quiet. I agreed, if he would so arrange matters as to get me some farm truck as Confederate money would not buy greenbacks in camp. He made good his word.

Well, we just lived while that Lieutenant was in charge, but when we moved into the stockade, matters changed very much in the next two months. A "stringency" in the market became a bar to more trading as the Confederates were taking all the supplies for their own uses, that were useful to us, the "graduated" and "attenuated" ration were once more in vogue. I had made money in all my deals and had greenbacks and lived good while they lasted, but my mess of five still lived - all had mouths, stomachs and an appetite that clamored for good things as could be obtained - hence my bank could not stand the run and all deposits, balances, stock included, passed into the capacious maws of five receivers.

PRISONERS RECEIVING RATIONS.

The month of December brought many ills and cold weather, scant food, and Lieutenant Barrett, with his frozen heart - or none whatever. Suffering became intense in this colder climate, made colder by thin blood and less clothing - thinner in texture - with a diminished ration of better quality than at Andersonville. Deaths were frequent. A new disease prevailed, "Gangrene," that killed both flesh and bone - blood failed to circulate flesh dry and skin would shrivel to a leather-like appearance - the parts affected of the effects of this stage of the disease I will relate one I knew of, a stripling youth by the strange and uncommon name of John January, who had been attacked with the "swamp fever" as known in camp. Circulation had receded in both feet and legs, from toes to halfway to knees. The toes became black, dry, shriveled, and brittle so that he could - and did - break them off like clay pipes. The "Confed" Doctors refused to amputate his legs saying lightly and laughing, "You will die soon enough without cutting off your feet!" January replied "well, I won't die here!! And I will take them off if you don't." That caused a hilarious laugh from the Doctors. To tell the truth, not a man that knew January's condition, but doubted his word when he said he would not die here. But John January was brought back to camp to die, and refused to, and in a day or so after he had thought the matter all out, and concluded, "I can't live long this way, and it is to die but once, I will try it and take my chances - slim as they seem." With the assistance of a friend or two, who doubting his hopes, but willing to help him, secured some cotton sacking for bandages. January produced a knife that had one large blade that had been possibly four inches in length, but had been broken off at about two and a half inches - the edge very much nicked and much more of a saw than a knife - deliberately set to work and severed the feet at the ankle joint. No blood flowed from the amputation whatever, just a serum of the color of weak vinegar and sticky in consistency. Clay was made in plastic state and with bandages reached to the knees, made wet and plastered smoothly. This kept the flies and vermin from the wounds and possibly absorbed the poison of gangrene from the legs; at all events everybody thought that he must die, and soon. Imagine my surprise in 1894, at an Encampment of the National G.A.R. in the city of Pittsburgh, Pennsylvania,

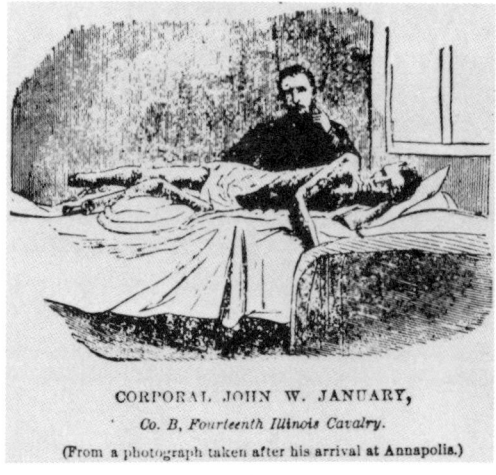

(Above) A sketch from *Andersonville: A Story of Rebel Military Prisons,* by John McElroy.
(Right) Corporal John W. January in later years.

while in attendance at a Union Ex-Prisoners of War Camp Fire, I hear a man repeat from the stage or platform this incident, and announced his name. I called the Chairman to my seat, only a few steps from the platform, and told him that I knew this man and of all the facts as stated by him. I was recognized by him when my "Camp name" was given "Jersey".

The strange part of this man's life was that he was a long time in Bellevue Hospital, New York City, and his case is on record at the U.S. Surgeon General Office, as a special and unusual recovery from what seemed hopeless from the best point of view. After being in Bellevue Hospital for three months, he only weighed forty-five pounds and when I saw him at Pittsburgh he weighed one hundred and ninety pounds and at no time had a Surgeon's knife been used on those stumps, or any other instrument than his own knife at time of amputation. He showed me two as finely healed stumps as one could wish. He used cork feet and walked as steadily as most men with both natural feet.

After they were reunited at a G.A.R. Convention in 1894, John January gave Charles Hopkins this albumen card photograph of himself.

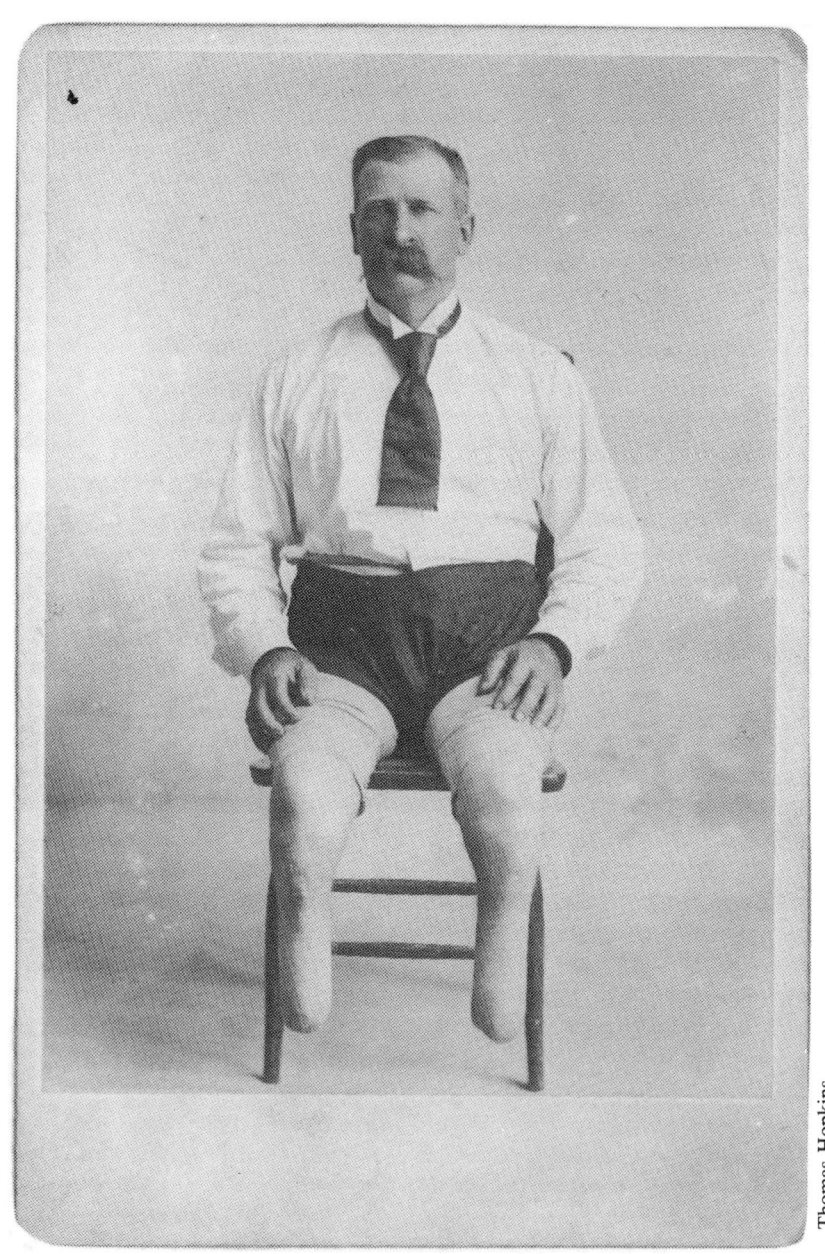

This remarkable image of John January was a souvenier card given by him to friends and comrades to tell of his remarkable story.

On the reverse side of the John January albumen card, there was printed this biography.

Biography

I was born in Clinton county, Ohio, November 29, 1847; emigrated to Illinois in 1852, and located near Henry, on a farm. In the spring of 1861 removed to Minonk, Illinois, where I have resided since, except while in the army. In the fall of 1862 the 14th Illinois Cavalry organized in Peoria, and I enlisted in Co. B; served until captured on Stoneman's Raid, in July, 1864, upon retreat from Macon. I was captured by six rebel soldiers, sent to Andersonville, and there kept until the fall of Atlanta made it necessary for us to be removed to prevent falling in the hands of the Union forces. I was taken to Charleston, S.C., with others, and placed by the enemy under fire of our soldiers and gun boats; remained there ten days and was taken to Florence, S.C., where we passed the winter of 1864-5, and on or about February 15th I was stricken down by an attack of "swamp fever," and for three weeks I remained in a delirious condition; the fever abated and reason returned. I soon learned from the surgeon, after a hasty examination, that I was a victim of scurvy and gangrene and was removed to the gangrene hospital. My feet and ankes, five inches above the joints presented a livid, lifeless appearance, and soon the flesh began to slough off, and the surgeon, with a brutal oath, said I would soon die. But I was determined to live, and begged him to cut my feet off; telling him if he would do that I could live. He still refused, and believing that my life depended on the removal of my feet, I secured an old pocket-knife (I have it now in my possession) and cut through the decaying flesh and severed the tendons. The feet were unjointed, leaving the bones protruding without a covering of flesh for five inches. At the close of the war I was taken by the rebs to our lines at Wilmington, N.C., in April, 1865, and when weighed, learned that I had been reduced from 165 pounds (my weight when captured) to forty-five pounds. Every one of the Union surgeons who saw me then said I could not live; but, contrary to this belief, I did, and improved. Six weeks after release, while on a boat enroute to New York, the bones of my right limb broke off at the end of the flesh. Six weeks later, while in the hospital on David's Island, those of my left had become necrosid and broke off similarly. One year after my release I was just able to sit up in bed, and was discharged. Twelve years after my release my limbs healed over, and strange to relate, no amputation has ever been performed upon them save the one I performed in prison. There is no record of any case in the world similar to mine. My own theory of the cause is this: While delirious I was so weak that the pulsations of my heart were too feeble to throw the blood to the extremities, and below the point of circulation death took place.

Yours Truly,
J.W. JANUARY

Monday, September 5, 1864

 Morning cool & clear. A man shot last night by mistake by a sick man being out of his tent a stumbling about and the guard shot at him and missed him and shot a man that was asleep. Blowed a part of his head off. Breakfast beans & bread & beef. Considerable excitement about this Exchange. Rumour says boats are in the Harbour of Charleston with prisoners aboard.

Tuesday, September 6, 1864

 Morning cool & clear but the sun has made its appearance and with intolerable heat. Breakfast rice & bread. Rumour says Sherman has defeated Hood and completely demoralized his army. James W. H. Howell is dead. He died on the 4th instantly of Epitetas a species of Dropsy.

Jack Fitzpatrick

The grave of Pvt. James W. Howell. The seven-thousand eight-hundred and seventieth grave at Andersonville.

Wednesday, September 7, 1864

Morning cool & clear very hot as usual the sun rises to scorch. A great excitement last night and this morning about some 5,000 men going for Exchange. Breakfast beans. The excitement still rubs up about the men leaving here. More are ordered to be ready. Some 5 trains have just been sent here. Some thinks that we are being sent to another camp for safety But I am inclined to believe that it is an Exchange without doubt.

Unfortunately for Hopkins, the prison authorities, fearing the approaching Union Army, decided to relocate the prisoners to another location.

Sunday, September 11, 1864

Morning cool & clear and a prospect of 29th Detatchment going out today for the point of Exchange. Dunn has been admitted in the Hospital. We are ready for to leave the Camp. We are all ready at once and at 3½ O'Clock we are off for the gate. But we lay all this afternoon "awaiting our liberty". But it does not come. Ration beef & rice & meal but we did not take. We expect to get out tonight. Supper beans & boiled rice.

Tuesday, September 13, 1864

Morning cool very. We ran all night to get to Augusta arrived this morning at daylight. Rebel wounded are here in hospital. Slept well last night. Left Augustas for Charleston on the road a mile or two from Augusta. E. English & J. Lowe jumped off and were caught and put on the top of the cars. Bonebert & Haggard reached Charleston at 2 O'Clock AM after riding all night cramped up in the worst way imaginable. Rations are running short and not hopeful of getting any. We do not discover where we are going or have any settled opinion.

Wednesday, September 14, 1864

Left Charleston at 3 AM bound for Florence or Wilmington. No one knows which. Exchange begins to look dim to the men. We are being carried to another prison. Arrived at Florence at 3 O'Clock and lay all the afternoon & night in the cars without any rations for 3 days. The men look famished and thirst famished. Never did I feel so near death of starvation before. Men sick & emaciated almost to skeletons. Some number of men are sick and lame with the Scurvy and are being put in barns. We are hardly allowed water!

Thursday, September 22, 1864

Morning cool & clear. My man came in with the potatoes this morning and I have them in Camp and for Dan Forrands watch. Breakfast beans & sweet potatoes boiled and bacon. Sold potatoes to the amount of 18.00 and better. Rained most beautiful at intervals all day long. I begin to feel good and somewhat stronger since some time ago. I have a cold in my face again which makes it very disagreeable and unhealthy for me. Rations bacon, rice, meal, salt & flour. Supper rice and potatoes after a hard job to cook them.

Wednesday, September 28, 1864

Morning cool & clear. Not so cool last night as usual. I could make no trade yesterday. Breakfast is now ready cakes & gravy & beef fried. I wish I could see some lights of getting out of the hands of the Confederates. Hope is still bright and unquenched yet. I will soon be five months a prisoner. For dinner we had beans & corncake. Our ration of wood is too small for our use. The rations are getting smaller every day. Rained a smart shower this afternoon. I bought a bushel of potatoes for 500 today. Rations meal, 1/2 pt beans, 1 gill salt 1/2 oz. No meat and a very little wood.

Thursday, September 29, 1864

Morning cool & cloudy. Yesterday was very warm during the night. Some men ran out last night. Our treatment is shameful and I do not know whether they mean to starve us or not. Breakfast sweet potatoes. A large number of men took the oath of allegiance to the cursed Confederacy and a recruiting officer was put in Camp and I am ashamed to say I heard of one Jersey man being one of the 800 men that took the oath. Dinner mush & molassas. Rations rice, meal & salt & molassas. Supper could not be allowed for the stint of rations.

Friday, September 30, 1864

Morning cool & clear. Gen. Ben. Butler's letter is in the Charleston Mercury. Also Gen. Grant's & Sherman's & Hood's correspondence. I look for an exchange soon or a great number of famished men to take anything to get out misery. Breakfast rice. As for their oath them & it may sink to the lowest depths of hell and me in my grave ere I take it. Dinner bacon, beef & sweet potatoes & corncake. Rations beef, beans, rice & meal. Supper sweet potatoes alone. Considerable excitement about Jeff Davis's speech at Macon.

CHAPTER FIVE
FLORENCE PRISON

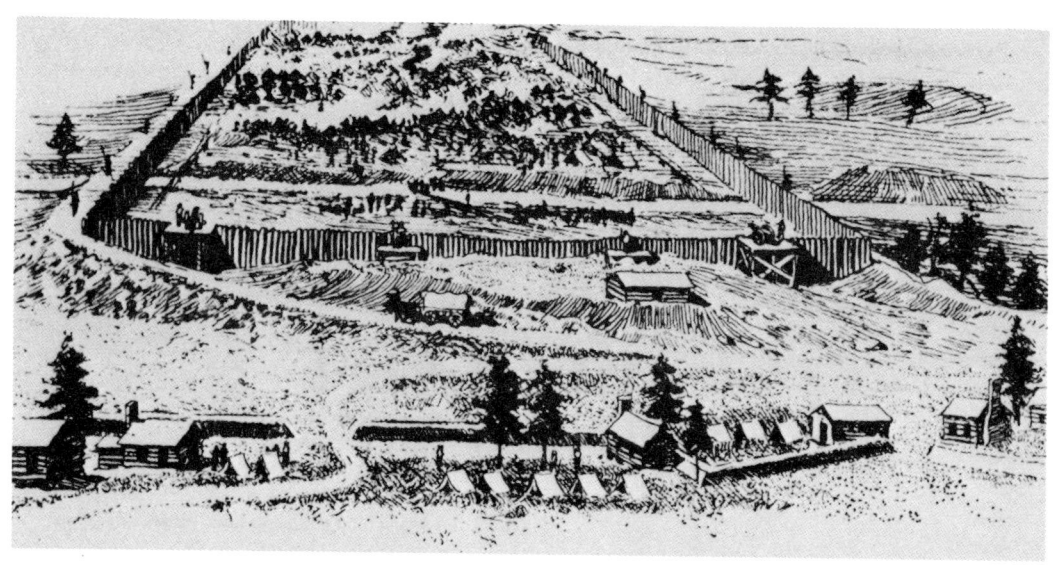

A sketch of the prison pen at Florence, South Carolina.

In Florence Prison, while one Colonel Iverson was in command, I fared quite well, but failed in health, and was looking beyond the "River" daily, wondering how I might defer the "last moment" much longer, still hoped with little grounds to base it on, had said the "good-bye" to my comrades each night, believing my soul would pass in the quiet of the night, and awoke each morning, surprised, as well were my comrades, at my tenacity of life. Sometime before this and when just able to walk with assistance, I had been sought out by the Confederate officers who wanted skilled saddlers and harnessmakers. I could fill both wants - that being my trade - thoroughly learned at home to make anything a horse or horseman needed for the wants in that line. The confederacy needed men badly as English goods were scarce under the strict blockade of "Uncle Samuel," and they had searched every prison for "Yankee" mechanics of this nature.

Colonel Iverson was a gentleman. He appeared one day with some other officers. I was called - they kept a record of all prisoners and their occupation or trade - upon; at this time my condition was indeed pitiable. Colonel Iverson suggested that I accept the situation and take oath of Parole; go to Columbia, South Carolina and teach negroes and others - (Note, I placed negro first) - how to draw rawhide and leather on riding saddles, harnessmake, etc. not to do any work myself, simply oversee others and thus save my life and return home. Iverson was very kind and sympathetic, but my reply to his nicely drawn picture was "Colonel Iverson, I cannot do it, though I die!" My comrades also urged me to accept, holding that I would be justified in saving my life. "No, no, my comrades, you do not mean it. I have sworn fealty to my Country and my flag, included in that oath is life and all if need be, and that sacrifice now seems ready for redemption, and I am willing, ready and glad to make it!" Still urged by comrades, and the offers of $500 per month - Confed - good quarters and good living, clothing and hope for the home return by the Confederate officers. Still refusing, and assured them farther persuasion was useless, the officers - not including Iverson - then threatened to take me to Columbia and if I would not take the Parole oath and give them my experienced service which they expected of me, they would treat me very much worse. Turning to my comrades with the calmest and yet most feeling moment of my life, said, "Comrades, why persuade me to do so dishonorable an act, even though life be saved. You, yourselves, in after years would point the finger of scorn and disown my comradeship and you would be sacredly right. What would life be to a man without a country? Without a name, that was not a reproach and despised - and should be - even by the parent that gave him to the world. No, no, no, comrades, rather let me die among you that are loyal and true. It must be so, for I will not move an eyelash to assist the enemy, to save the little life within me, nor would I do it for life at its best. Speaking now to you of the Confederacy, Colonel Iverson, you would not do otherwise if we exchanged places! You have some respect for a man who will not be bullied into saving a life that would be worthless to its owner at such a sacrifice! I thank you for your good intentions and kindness. To you, Colonel O'Neil and companions, who have deemed it manly to threaten a defenseless, and as you feel, a dying man, I have this to say - the Parole oath, you and your damned Confederacy may sink to the lowest depths of Hell, and I, to an honorable, though an inhospitable grave, before moving a finger to assist your short lived and despicable Confederacy. You, of Irish blood, would not do what you ask of me and you know it! You speak of worse treatment to me upon my refusal! You have my final answer and you may do your worst - worse treatment might be more merciful in death! Worse is hardly conceivable, but you people are masters at this art. I absolutely refuse to aid you in any way - do your worst, I am no better to die in this hell, than my loyal comrades and I prefer their company while living - do your worst to the best of your ability, and do it quickly if you expect my thanks!" I was approached again, but not threatened and I still refused, though life was at low ebb now. About this time Colonel Iverson was ordered to the Southwest and we since learned that he became a Division General and lost his life and almost his whole command at Allatoona Pass, in the State of Georgia, at the hands of the gallant General Corse, who promised Sherman that he would "hold the fort until hell froze over."

Command at Florence passed into the hands of a Lieutenant Barrett and Mosely; the former a blustering bravado, the latter a young and gentlemanly fellow, but not warm-blooded toward the Yankees. Barrett was fond of starting at the gate, with a brace of revolvers stuck out before him; in front were hundreds of famished, starving skeletons, who had congregated at the gate - or as near as possible - walking thus, the awed crowd made haste to get from the range of the revolvers, injuring the helpless and crippled by crowding. But this was a course of pleasure to Barrett to see the Yankees flee from his threatening "battery" which he sometimes shot over their heads. Barrett was a coward. Mosely never did such things. During my stay at Florence, several incidents occurred that may be of interest and I will try and put them in shape as remembered. Florence, like Andersonville, had its native courts, established trial court, Police Court, Chief of Police, Judges and lawyers. Many things of a serious nature were thrashed out here, all of course, of a criminal nature - such as robbing, petty thefts and other less serious, as charges of abuse.

Sunday, October 2, 1864

Morning cool & cloudy. I've had an early breakfast. Beans & dumplings. 9 O'Clock, we are about to move to the stockade. 10 minutes we are on the go. 3/4 of an hour we are in it. A miserable stream of water runs through it. No rations yet & a bright prospect of going without. Men gathering wood and no ax to cut with, nor will be allowed any.

Monday, October 3, 1864

Morning cool & cloudy & rainy. Roll call 8 AM., breakfast mush alone, talk of arranging the camp and will talk about it long enough to talk us out of our rations until night. Snakes (moccasins) are quite numerous.

Tuesday, October 4, 1864

Morning cool & clear. Breakfast flour gruel is what I call a "fat breakfast". I made a bargain for some potatoes with a Reb but he did not come in the stockade. Men are fishing in the brook that runs through Camp and are successful in catching catfish & calico. Some fun, no dinner and am waiting most patiently for the rations to come for nearly famished indeed. Rations came in at 5 O'Clock consisting of flour 1/2 pt per man for twenty four hours & rice 1/2 pt & molasses 5 tablespoonsful & salt not enough to salt anything.

Wednesday, October 5, 1864

Morning cool & clear. Breakfast rice & flour boiled together. A man shot this morning while getting water by stepping on the Dead Line. So ready are the Rebels to shoot a "Yankee". The miserable hounds. Some prisoners came in from Charleston. Some 1500. I didn't see John Seitzer among them. Rations came in beef & beans, meal & salt. Starve we will if such is the certainty.

Thursday, October 6, 1864

Morning cool & cloudy rained last night and of course made it comfortable for us. Breakfast beans boiled & meal to thicken the soup. No dinner. Order in camp to move again. Towards evening we moved. Near the left centre of the stockade on a St. marked out for us. Tent put up just in good time for the rations to come and have supper before a shower came up. Ration, beans meal & salt with the promise of more meal & molasses in the morning. Promises I don't like.

Friday, October 7, 1864

Morning cool & cloudy & looking for the continuation of last night's rain. Five months ago this morning was the first morning I saw as a prisoner. Breakfast beans & soup. Jon Seitzer & Thomas Carrigan come in today with the prisoners from Charleston. They lived well but not here. Our men are shelling the city pretty rapid. Some 2000 came in. We have some 12,000 in here. The yellow fever broke out in Charleston. Rations flour 1 pt per man. Come supper, flour gruel.

Sunday, October 9, 1864

Morning cool and raw. The wind still blowing. No sleep last night for the cold. My feet were all that troubled me. Everything plenty in Camp but high in price. Prices fluctuate here as in all markets. Monetary affairs are much the same also. Confederate scrip is quoted at 20 cts making $500 for 200 dollars.

The Chief of Police was a big Canadian Frenchman, called "big Pete" because of his giant frame - not a bad fellow, but was surrounded by bad men, such as Stanton, the "Irish Nigger," who was Assistant Chief and assumed the whole business. Men under any petty charge - such as taking a cup - which was a serious matter in that prison, as the loser was without means to cook raw meal, when issued as was often done - a cup was in general use, as a means to get water, to keep water in, or cook in. Big Pete was not well and Stanton took command. Three incidents took place in October and November that made a stir in camp. One day a poor fellow of a Pennsylvania Regiment, who had been robbed of everything he had in the line of cooking utensils, including his cup, and used one belonging to his neighbor without asking, and returned it to its place when done with it, but the owner was not satisfied. He wanted him punished and made complaint to Police Headquarters. The poor devil was arrested, taken to Court, convicted and sentenced to be tied to the whipping post and whipped. The day of execution came on October 18th, and Stanton would not allow the man selected to apply the last to perform this service, but out of his own murderous heart - if he had such - came the desire to do it and he did it, to the time of 150 lashes and left the victim unconscious and bleeding - shreds of skin hanging! This aroused the camp to action and men who were not usually caring for more than to be left alone to die, as may be, were stirred to life action. A hasty, secret call was made of some of the men who feared nothing in the form of death, but were appalled at the idea of such treatment to any human being, and no doubt their recollections of slavery and slave treatment were once more revived, for the last applied to the human race was abhorrent to all of us.

To divert a little, some week or so before this whipping occurred, the Sergeant in charge of our mess of 90 men, by name of Edmund English - though an Irishman - while at the gate looking after our rations issued to us, became involved in some trouble with the brute Stanton; and was accused by Stanton of terming him as an "Irish Nigger," being an Irishman with hair that was only a little less knotty than Topsy's. At all events, notwithstanding flat denial by English, Stanton made his charges and placed English under arrest. Trial at the Bull Pen Court was denied him by Stanton, though that made little difference to Stanton as he intended to whip this man most brutally. While this case was pending another case came up where a man by name of Joseph Hopson of Paterson, New Jersey, and a member of my company was placed under arrest upon the charge of theft from one Brannon of Company "F" of our Regiment. He was tried, ordered to receive fifty lashes.

In my acquaintance with both men I knew the charges to be false, and actuated by malice only, and Hopson made appeal to me to save him from this disgrace. I knew that Brannon was guilty of theft himself and went to him and charged him with concealing the paper which he charged Hopson with stealing; and I did not stop at that, but searched him and found it. I demanded that he go to Police headquarters with me at once, and acknowledge the wrong and have Hopson released, or I would make charges against him for theft. He knew it could easily be proven and had only been quiet to save himself the lash, condoned the theft to avoid the brutal treatment which all of us hated. He complied and lied, but that did not disturb his mind - but Hopson escaped.

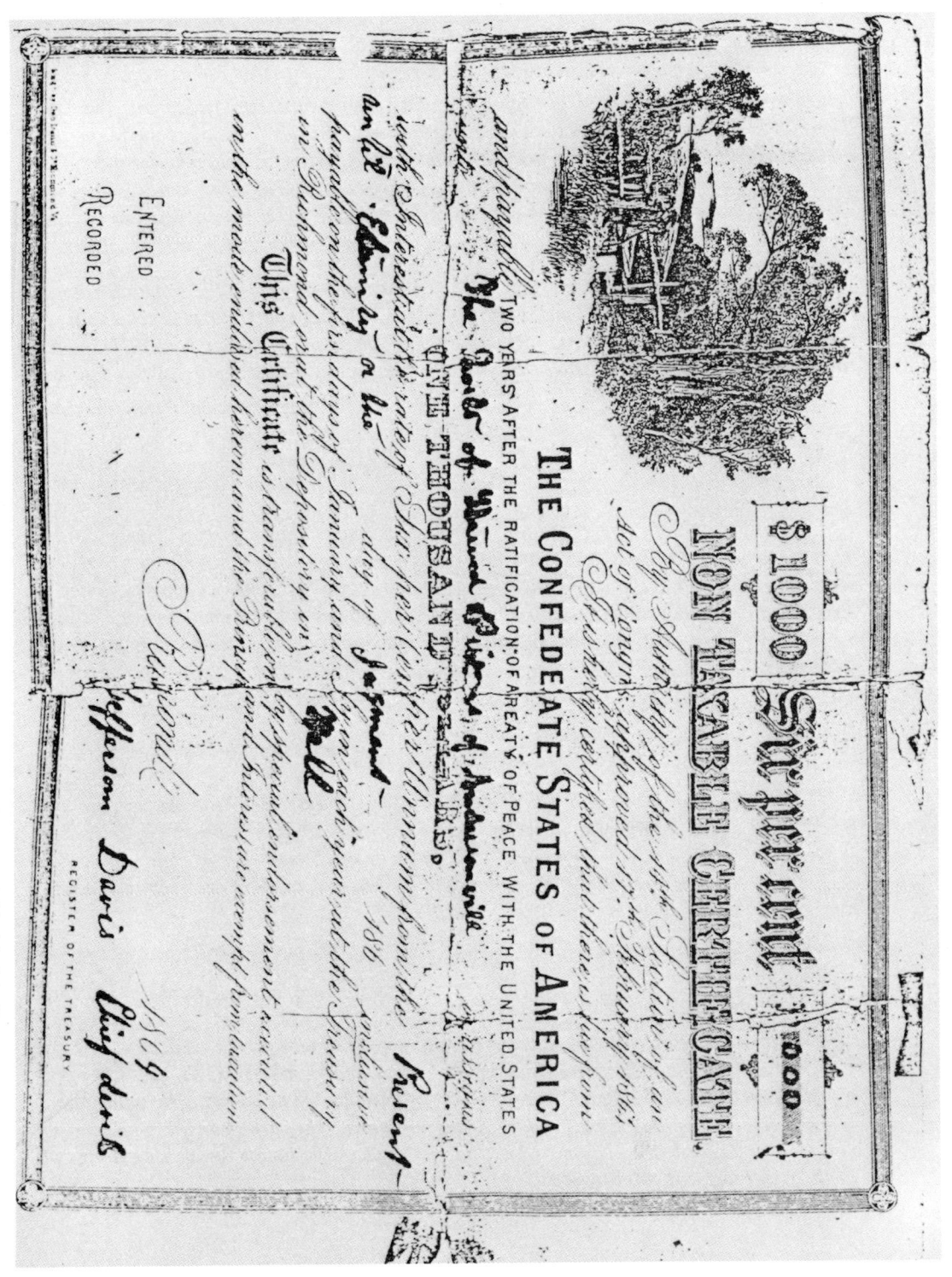

Charles Hopkins saved this Confederate "Non-Taxable Certificate," folded in his diary. Hopkins made it out to "The Ghosts of Starved Prisoners of Andersonville." He sign-

Monday, October 10, 1864

    Morning cold and clear. Last night still colder than before. Breakfast flour gruel and dumplings. We are forced to cut wood with spikes and wedges. The day is warm and the nights are cold and make it so much the colder for us. Heavy dews bring on the colds.

Tuesday, October 11, 1864

    Morning cool and clear and frosty. No sign of roll call & also the same of rations. Report says that a break was made by the men at Columbia and 5000 were tried and arrested by the Rebs. No dinner no roll call either. Some talk of rations now 12M. 1 PM. rations came in. The delay caused by the men taking the oath. Rumors of the Sanitary Commission being here. I hope so for the men need the help of someone.

Wednesday, October 12, 1864

    Morning cool and clear. Night last was cold as usual. Many a person feel spry in the morning to get warm. Breakfast beans and soup. Baked some cakes this morning and very soon got rid of them. The camp has been changed in the respect of commanders and it has caused the change of almost everything and the most important is provision. It is drawn by one man for a thousand and divided in 10 parts and by such means it is cut down materially.

Thursday, October 13, 1864

    Morning cool & windy & clear. I spent my all by getting a kettle to cook in yesterday $4.50. Roll call at 6 O'Clock. Breakfast beans barley & soup thickened with flour. Salt is scarce in camp and sells for the exhorbitant price of 15 cents per pt. per man & salt & molasses 6 tablespoonsful for 24 hours. Scant living indeed. Men are every day taking the oath. What do they think of.

Friday, October 14, 1864

    Morning cold & clear, frost also. A sleepless night almost for the cold. God help the men who are without shelter and clothing. Breakfast meat & molasses. Niggers are working at the stockade and sing all the time a sort of an Indian song as not to be understood. Work is light or so they seem to make lazing. Rations today are beans & meal and no salt for two days. A fine prospect of getting none also. The police are getting things all in their own control. Mob control.

Wednesday, October 19, 1864

Morning cold and the night was so also last night. I slept very uncomfortable. Roll call 6 O'Clock. Breakfast beans & soup. Great, told of special exchange of 5,000 but it can not be. Sutlering is not carried on so large a scale as it was. Men are dying of cold here. Dinner rice boiled. I saw 2 men lashed by the so called police today "brutally". Rations today are better than usual flour 1 pt, meal 1 pt, grit 1/2 pt, molassas 1/2 pt, beans 2 1/2 bushels for a 1,000 men salt. Supper beans & meal worked together.

Thursday, October 20, 1864

Morning cool & clear. I sent a letter for a box but I fear it will not be sent home. Breakfast pancakes and flour gravy and molassas. Blankets are being issued to the Camp from the U.S.S. Commission 5 to a 200 men. The men have to draw lots for them. To make rations go the farther a person has to make wine or gruel or soup. Consequently it does a person harm to be without some bread stuff. Dinner mush & molassas. Rations beans, flour, meal, salt & molassas. Supper beans & dumplings & soup.

Friday, October 21, 1864

Morning cool & clear. Cooler last night than before. Breakfast pancakes & flour & molasses. Henry Ring of my Co. is quite sick with the diarreah. Charleston paper says that returned prisoners state that Lincoln's election is sure. "Poor show" for them then. I hope it is so. Albert Fitzgerald has gone to the hospital it is said he is very low. Issac Vangusin of Paterson is very sick also. Dinner mush and molassas. Rations beans very musty 1/2 pt. flour 1/8 pt. meal 1 pt. no salt molassas 1/2 pt. Supper mush & molassas. It is growing cold here. Matters in Camp are getting worse as to police force.

Saturday, October 22, 1864

Morning cold & clear. Some excitement in Camp about Sgt. English to be lashed by one of the well called "muledrivers" for calling him a "nigger". But he was released and acquitted of any crime. To the rescue would have been the cry if it should have gone on. Breakfast beans & meal & dumplings. I called on Van Guden and found him in a dying condition. Rations beans & meal & salt & rice. Supper beans & mush. We are trying to get brush to make a dirt hut to make ourselves comfortable while we stay in the Confederacy.

On the 21st of October the hearing of English was to take place before Lieutenant Barrett. After a last appeal to the Court, and denial, our appeal was made to Barrett and was successful, and yet did not know how it would end as few of us had no confidence in Barrett. A dozen more men were mustered who had agreed to do their best to save English, though it cost their lives and the life of Stanton was to be taken, at the first stroke of the lash. We harbored murder in our hearts. The day and hour was at hand. The Court that had, at the behest of Stanton, found English "guilty" on no evidence, from no witness, but Stanton, sentenced him to be whipped, and no limit fixed. He was brought to the post and tied, with Stanton standing close by, his fiendish eyes feasting upon the form he thought he had in his power and would kill, if he was allowed, and the victim failed to survive the ordeal. No man was better to bear the name, "The Irish Nigger Butcher" than he. He could hardly await the result of the hearing, so sure was he of his victim. The brave, defiant English, with flashing eyes stood and answered the charges of his tormentor. When Barrett said "We will now hear the prisoner in his own behalf." Without a tremor of fear, in a clear, plain but thrilling, convincing argument, did English state his case; and while doing so, was struck by the end of Stanton's club in the mouth, accompanied with vile epithets. Further outrage was stopped by Barrett. Pointing his revolver close to the face of Stanton, he said, "Another move, and I'll blow your damn brains out!" Barrett stock rose in our esteem, slightly-English was not ordered free. Stanton foamed and gnashed his ugly teeth, and made most awful threats until Barrett closed his tirade by a movement of his pistol to the very mouth of the brute - so close it left its imprint, and the cowardly murderer turned ashy pale and staggered. From that date, Stanton was a broken man. No one feared him, and his power waned quickly. He was taken out for "Exchange" in December and sent to Camp Parole, Annapolis, Maryland; was stricken with disease; made a partial recovery and met in this Camp the man from Pennsylvania whom he had so unmercifully whipped. His victim had his revenge in full. He shot him dead, while no one saw, and never was found. No one shed tears over the "Irish Nigger."

After the English trial, Stanton made a third attempt to get revenge for his two defeats at Andersonville and failed, after getting a good drubbing, which ended the matter. While at Florence, the election for President was on in the North - between Lincoln and McClellan. The Confederates supposed that under the circumstances, and bad treatment by the Yankee Government, in not having us released under the unfair demand of the Confed. Commissioners of Exchange of prisoners, that the Yanks in the stockades in the south would give the Democratic nominee a big majority. We were allowed, on election day, to hold the Polls at the gate, under a supervision of our own choice of officials of election. The process was - on one side of the gate entrance was hung a bag of colored beans, representing ballots; on the opposite side, a bag of white beans, under the eyes of a man of each party. The black or colored beans represented Republican ballots; the white beans, Democratic ballots. While some 20,000 or more men were imprisoned here, very many could not be gotten to the polls; but, with a very exciting day and a very good vote, the Little Napoleon, McClellan, was defeated by nearly five to one. The loyalty of those men was superior to "Copperhead" principles and "Peace, at any price", slogan announced by the Party supporting a distinguished and highly esteemed soldier, and one of our comrades, (much admired and loved by very many) as against the patriot, the much maligned "Lincoln." This was another proof of loyalty vehemently expressed by those who suffered daily the pangs of hunger, the longing for home, and willingness to die, if must be, that Liberty and Equality before the Law, should survive, rather than Slavery, Tyranny and Rebellion should continue.

President Abraham Lincoln.

At one time in Andersonville, and again at Florence, an effort was made to have men take the oath of Parole and serve the confederates by taunting us with the fact (as they stated) that our Government had no care or use for us, in our condition and had now abandoned us to our fate. At Florence, time and disease had made us very good subjects to do anything to alleviate our sufferings and it was thought a good time by the Confederates, to apply bait. Officers came into Camp and made all kinds of overtures to break down loyalty among us - even to men they knew must die shortly, could be no possible use for their cause; it was the principle they were after, and not the men. Wistful eyes, tear-stained faced denoted how strong was the desire to love, Hundreds broke down and wept like children; some prayed for light to guide them; others used language too strong for print, (we justified them); some groaned and muttered in the desperate fight with the spirit of inclination to do that which was right and loyal. The first was strong, as was the desire to live, and loyalty won, once settled, forever settled! Some wondered why they should have given the tempting offer for life, at such a cost, an instant of sober thought; Noble, loyal hearts throbbed with pride and exaltation at the great defeat of the treasonable temptation set before them, and those who had the strength to cheer, sent up such a cheering, that all felt good, at the result thought some died with loyal sound in their ears; others, soon after, and all peacefully acquiesced in the decision, by giving up their "all" to the Nation they had sworn to defend! Who says, they died in vain though death was of the most horrible nature?

A case came under my notice of an alien - German who landed in New York City on the nineteenth day of April, 1864 - a young, well-educated, handsome fellow, who was inspired by the thought that he could help the Cause of Liberty, be enlisting in the U. S. Army. He, therefore, left his home without consent of his parents, nor of his Government (as he was of the Landwehr) and made a short cut to the front, enlisted, the day he landed, in the N. Y. Artillery; was sent to Washington on the 21st of April; reached the front and fought at Spotsylvania on May 12th; was captured; reached Andersonville June 22nd and was the worst looking corpse I ever saw on the 23rd of August - starved to bone and sinew, lying in the sun at the edge of the filthy swamp - bare as when born - his long locks of bright, curly hair, tangled and full of vermin, his fine, blue eyes, wide open, mouth, nose and ears alive with maggots, and he just breathing his last with feeble effort clutched a letter in one hand, though much soiled and dirty. My comrade a German named "Dutch John", took it, read it to all of us of our mess, and kept it until his release and answered it. That was the first news that the fond mother had from her fair-haired, blue-eyed idol. The letter he died with in his hand, had only been received a day or so before his capture. This, he had stated to John, as they soon made acquaintance after he came to the prison - both being Germans. This letter was read and re-read many times by him, while he was near us. He suddenly went away, and we missed him. The hour he died was the first seen of him after leaving us. The contents of that letter, read and interpreted by John, were not forgotten by us. At home, he had all to make life happy, as he was of regal blood - himself a Count - a young soldier on vacation, a mother, who doted on him as an only son. What wonder he read and re-read her loving letter, in his so quickly changed circumstances, and swiftly failing health! Yet, so late an alien, knew for what he enlisted, and expressed himself to my comrade in his talks, as loyal as any who had enlisted in the Cause. He landed an alien, but died a citizen of this Country, though he had never cast a vote, nor could he have done so for two years, being but nineteen years old the month after his landing.

HANGING BY THE THUMBS.

Sunday, October 23, 1864

Morning cold and last night was extremely so. Roll call over we went to the gate to get out for brush. Issac Van Gusin dead. We are going to carry him out to the dead house. Breakfast mush "alone." 4 of us went out with the body and brought in plenty brush and wood. So much for a start. The Rebs admit a great loss at Richmond in the late battle there. Some 10,000 killed on the field. Rations beans, meal & salt, molasses. Dinner mush & molasses. Supper beans & meal boiled together & molasses. A very Dutch diet but we live.

Monday, October 24, 1864

Morning cold & clear. I went out with another "body" this morning but unfortunately I could get no wood. Breakfast beans boiled with meal. Working on the frame of my hut. Wood was issued for the first time today a very small stick. Rations rice, meal & salt & beans. No dinner except a little mush & molasses. Great talk of exchange now and it has caused more excitement than ever before. Supper rice & meal boiled together & molasses. Cloudy looking and look for rain.

Sunday, October 30, 1864

Morning cold and clear. Breakfast beans & meal & soup. Bad as usual and I am ashamed to own it on Sunday, too, but circumstances drive us to it. I have felt quite unwell all day and sick almost into a fainting feeling. Rations all used up & no dinner.

Monday, October 31, 1864

Morning cold and cloudy. Breakfast mush & beans & soup, very thin. The Lieut. in command of Camp or post has left so says Camp rumor, a good riddance, too. Abe Lincoln will carry the day in this Camp if put to vote I am sure. I hope he does at the coming elections. It was put to a vote in 900 men and all but few went for Abe. Such would go through Camp. Rations meal & grit & molasses. No salt! No meat! No beans! Nothing but a bit of meal & bit of grit issued for 24 hours.

Wednesday, November 2, 1864

Morning cold & wet and a little rainy. Our hut leaks badly. Breakfast meal & peas and very few at that. Shivering in our shoes today. Raining yet. 2 O'Clock, some talk of rations. All sorts of supposition of what it is. 4 O'clock, rations come in beef, salt, meal.

Tuesday, November 8, 1864

Morning cold & cloudy. The great day is at hand at last and as much excitement is here as in any town North. Polling white beans for McClellan & black beans for Abraham Lincoln. Lincoln is ahead at 11 pm. Breakfast beans. Dinner boiled beans & soup.

Wednesday, November 9, 1864

Morning clear & cool. Last night was excedingly warm. Well election is over and satiated. Must be the successful candidate, Abe of Illinois.

Monday, November 14, 1864

Morning cold (extremely) last night was the coldest of the cold weather here. Many died of the extreme cold last night in the hospital.

Tuesday, November 15, 1864

Morning cold and last night ditto. If the weather gets any colder here than last night and before I am afraid there will be many frozen limbs in Camp. Breakfast rice soup & beef. I must here state that I had a wash with soap this morning for the first time in a month nearly. What a treat to get a poor wash all in all for once with soap. Rations meal & grit & molasses no salt. We get salt every alternate day. For supper mush & molasses. Evening cool but not as much so as for the past few days. Raiding goes on in Camp also issueing Sunday clothes.

Wednesday, November 16, 1864

Morning cold and clear. I witnessed one of the most beautiful sunrises that I ever saw. Breakfast meal cake and coffee and molasses. Pants shoes & shirts & blouses are being issued to the very men that need them the least. Henry Ring gone to the hospital and was admitted immediately. He will do better there than here in the tent. Rebel paper states that 10,000 have been exchanged and that 20,000 more are to be immediately. So much for Rebel news, I hope so.

Thursday, November 17, 1864

Morning cold & clear but the day is going to be a nice and warm one. Breakfast dumplings & beef soup & rice. A good substantial meal. A number of the Yankee Rebs or men that took the oath have been sent back in Camp and they are all to be sent out back!

Friday, November 18, 1864

A great number of men are out on parole of honor and working upon breastworks around the stockade. Shameful. It is well enough as long as what they do is for the benefit of Camp and the inmates.

Monday, November 21, 1864

Morning cold and wet, raining along just as if something great depended upon it. Tent leaks and of course makes it very uncomfortable. Still raining and looks to continue for the day. Ration time and no sign of them. Some talk of not issueing to Camp today on the account of a tunnel. I begin to believe that no rations are to come in. Sleep is the only alternative. So be it. It is not the first time in the Confederacy.

Tuesday, November 22, 1864

Morning very cold and windy and the ground is damp. Slept very well last night only for cold feet. Very hungry after no supper last night. No chance of getting anything. We have been quest of meal but no sign yet. Scouts returned. Dark looks. Every prospect of going without our daily allowance today again. Wood carried in for to keep warm. Thanks for that. Nothing to come in Camp until some tunnel is found. Sold my pocket book for some raw pumpkin and 1 qt of beans and 6 oz. We had supper of such.

Wednesday, November 23, 1864

Morning cold (bitter). Turned out to roll call. We were counted off by a Rebel this morning. I guess we will get rations. 11 O'Clock and nothing sent in Camp to eat since 3 days ago.

Thursday, November 24, 1864

Morning very cold and frosty. Many poor men are the sufferers in this Pen. Some of the poor deluded fellows that took the oath are the extreme sufferers. Breakfast mush & rice boiled, all in all a good meal for hungry men. I should like to get on one of the working squads in Camp for the exercise and the extra rations. The Rebs appear to be out of provisions. No molassas, no beef for us.

Thursday, December 1, 1864

Morning rather cool and clear. The sun very warm and a cold breeze blowing. Breakfast beans. Another Rebel move on fort. Rations meal ⅔ of qt. per man and salt. For our supper we had mush. And the pot on for to cook for morning. Bed time 11 O'Clock PM.

Friday, December 2, 1864

Morning cool and clear. Rain fell last night. None to harm though. Breakfast cold mush and it was the best since my stay here. Roll call at 12 PM and wood issued soon after. Considerable talk of Exchange and the "point" of it. Rumor says Burnside is in N.C., Wilmington. Rations are coming in - flour & salt. 1 qt. flour per man. For our supper we had mush and dumplings and put the pot on for morning to have it cold.

Saturday, December 3, 1864

Morning cool and clear. Partly stiff this morning. The men from the 2nd 1000 came back from Charleston and state that the railroad is cut.

The 1st 1000 got through safely. Detailed for rations today. John lost a large gold pin on the street. Wood is not on call for today. Rations came in 13 qts. of meal for 1000 & sack of salt for 1000.

For supper we had meal cakes & mush and at 9 PM put the pot on for cold mush for the morning.

Sunday, December 4, 1864

Morning moderate and clear. Last night was quite warm in our hut. Breakfast - mush cold, very good too. We are going to be turned over to some other Commandant I guess. Wood coming in for us. Considerable talk of the resumption of the Parole tomorrow. Some say Charleston and some say Richmond. Rations coming in. Rice & Salt. Supper boiled rice with a little meal put in it.

Monday, December 5, 1864

Morning cold and clear last night, it was somewhat cold. For breakfast boiled rice.

All of the men paroled, that have come back, have gone back out again. Bound for our lines. Davis made a proclamation stating that all prisoners are to be paroled. Wood came in at 5 O'Clock. Rations are ready for the Camp. 1 sack of meal for 100. For supper we had mush, no salt today again.

Tuesday, December 6, 1864

Morning cold and clear. Breakfast mush cold. Report says Gen. Winder is here. The Parole for a time is stopped. All parole working men are being sent in again. Wood came in for the Camp. Great talk of the 3rd 1000 being ordered to ready at 7 O'Clock AM. for to be paroled.

Some say the Confedertes to go in 10 days. Rations came in - meal. Quantity very small too.

Wednesday, December 7, 1864

Morning cool and clear & windy. Breakfast was cold mush. Our 1000 was called this morning and the 4th 1000 also. James Buckalew went out in the 4th. Stout out of my hut also went. I am doomed to stay.

The boys are missed very much by all of us.

Thursday, December 8, 1864

Morning cool and wet. Rained during the night. Breakfast, rice boiled over night & cold for breakfast. Tent unusual lonesome. The 8th & 9th 1000, 10th & 11th 1000 have been examined today. The report says that the 1st 1000 are ordered tomorrow again. I would love to get out of this by the Holidays if possible. Wood came in. Rations today - potatoes and corn meal, 3 small potatoes and a small pint of meal. For supper we had mush & potatoes. Boiled the rest of the mush for morning.

Friday, December 9, 1864

Morning cold and very windy. One of the coldest days we have had. Breakfast mush. The 1st & 2nd 1000 were called over again this morning to get the compliment of 10,000 sick and wounded. 2 PM all over with. Report says Parole and Exchange are all "played out." I am undecided on how to think. Raitons of wood are coming. Getting some warmer than this morning. We will get rain if it gets any warmer. Rations today - potatoes & meal. Supper mush & potatoes. 10 O'Clock it is raining some.

Saturday, December 10, 1864

Morning cold and wet and looks much like rain for today. Breakfast was cold mush for a change! Some talk of 25,000 to be paroled on each side. Some think it is all not true. Those men that went out the two days past are still at the Depot. Some 60 men came in today from Salisbury, N.C. where some 5000 are in a "Pen." They are prisoners since August. Rations meal & beans. Not enough all put together for one meal. Supper beans & mush.

Sunday, December 11, 1864

Morning cold and wet as needed. Rained very hard during the night and some of the sharpest lightening & loudest thunder that I've heard for many a day. For breakfast nothing. Such a pleasant matter for men wet and hungry.

Monday, December 12, 1864

Morning very cold and clear. Last night the wind blew very hard indeed! Cold feet and no sleep from that cause. Breakfast rice boiled. Those men that were taken out did not get off until today and were out in all that storm and Rebel says 8 of them froze to death last night.

Tuesday, December 13, 1864

Morning very cold and clear. Very little sleep last night for the cold feet. I have saw as cold weather here as I ever saw North.

Sunday, December 18, 1864

I had the first shave that I have had for nearly 10 months. Look better & feel better.

Friday, December 23, 1864

Morning cold and clear. Ice froze in the pails last night. But still I slept comfortable and warm. Breakfast beef, rice boiled with potatoes and burnt very bad at that. I have been at work at my shirt today to make it last me through this winter and Heaven only knows where the next comes from.

Saturday, December 24, 1864

Morning cool and clear. Most beautiful night last night for to hold the Christmas parties. I heard something that sounded much like cannonading this morning at 3 O'Clock. Rumor says that Jeff Davis is dead but I quite think is no such good luck. Rumor says that Lieut. Barrett & Capt. Wirtz & Gen'l. Winder are prisoners in our hands. False stories.

My stay at Florence, after Colonel Iverson left, was not so pleasant. During December, some were taken out for Exchange. My condition getting more desperate, when the lines were formed for inspection, I felt my turn to go had come, as the Surgeon promised me on December 6th that I should go next time. On either side of me in line, were married men who had about given up all hope. One of them begged me to help him if I could, as it was known that I was promised my release, and this man was older, and in an awfully crippled condition, and if he reached home alive it would be a miracle. However, against the wishes of my comrades, I listened to his pathetic pleadings. I gave him my promise that, if the doctors would take him in my stead, I would consent. I felt gloomy over doing so, but he being a married man with a family and he pleaded so strongly for them, I thought perhaps I could persuade the Doctors to take me then, or at the next time, ten days later.

The party to inspect, came in composed of an extra Doctor. The man on my right was chosen - and not near as bad as the one on my left or myself - the Doctor spoke to me so kindly that I felt sure of my ground. I stated the case of the man on my left, after asking me if I meant what I said, I replied "Yes". The other Doctor examined me by pounding my chest, looking at my mouth, like a horse trader, pinching my arms to find muscles, and said "You're pretty good yet, and can stand it until January date." Twenty days more! I was left and my old friend in tears and sobs of joy that choked him shook my hand and said, "God bless you!", which made me feel good for the moment with the hope that January might find me still in line and then get my release. I returned to my lonely spot with others, and my comrades were not pleased at my decision, but plainly said, "Hopkins, you are one in a hundred thousand." In reply, I said "Comrades, I should dislike to believe that statement." I thought a good deal about it that night - about generosity and at a cost of possible death.

A sad and dejected Charles Hopkins records in his diary the entry for Christmas, 1864.

Sunday, December 25, 1864

A Merry Christmas indeed. Morning cold and cloudy and prospect of rain. Breakfast beans, boiled rice, beef & cabbage leaves & peppers. A big dish for Christmas.

January came, but so slowly. It found me still alive - steadily growing worse. The fifteenth came, and with it the weeding out process of my friend, the Doctor, absent! Consequence, I was again left, while much abler men were taken from my side. There was some deep thinking done, you may be assured, but the solution remained the same. I rapidly grew worse - whether from increase of disease or partly from sad disappointment, is a question. This, I do know - that the slight hope that I at one time felt now was absent, and home and friends were my day and night thoughts and dreams, if dream I could. I was losing in mentality, and realized it. I became sick with fever and was at times lost in delirium; and on February second (1865), my mates took me to the hospital, located in the southwest corner of the stockade, which was built of rived pine slabs for roof and siding; the rain could get in the roof almost anywhere. The beds were built-up crotches of wood driven into the ground, side rails and bottom of wood, ticks, raw cotton in course sacks, coverlets made of same material ticks filled with pine needles from the cone pine trees, those who filled them neglected to take all the boughs from the filling and these made an "impression" on the patient; provided, he was conscious.

Wednesday, January 4, 1865

Morning moderate rain yesterday. Breakfast of beef & soup & dumplings. Something in the wind wrong with roll call. A man shot today for speaking to the guard.

Tuesday, January 10, 1865

Morning cool & clear. Breakfast of gruel. No supper. Raining all day. Rations meal & salt & potatoes.

Wednesday, January 11, 1865

Morning cold & clear. Breakfast mush & molasses. Rumors of the Kilpatrick Raid. Anticipation is extensive. Rations potatoes & mush.

Friday, January 15, 1865

I must see about Mother's tombstone as soon as I get out of the service. I am to acquaint Amey's father of his death on my arrival. Also John Miller's parents of his death also. Richard Vincent's wife of his death. I must drop a few lines to Wm. B. Linsdith, Co. H., 4th NJV.

Sunday, January 22, 1865

Morning cold & rainy and miserable all day. Breakfast mush & dumplings. Very disenjoyable in a hut that leaks. Raining very hard. Rations wood & meal & salt & beans. Supper mush.

Monday, January 23, 1865

Morning cold & wet. Rained all day. For breakfast nothing. No news. Rumors of Lee were stopped. U.S. Grant 40 miles from Richmond. Trying to believe it. Rations wood & meal & salt & beans. On diet and lousy. Supper beans & a cake of cornpone.

Wednesday, January 25, 1865

Morning cold & clear. Breakfast nothing. Rations wood & salt, beans & meal. The confirmation of the capture of Wilmington here in Camp. Very cold and quite blustery. One of the colder of days here in all the cold weather.

Friday, January 27, 1865

Morning cold and clear. Breakfast beans duff. Lay under the covers until roll call and then on detail for wood. All that does nothing. So cold. But wait with anxious eyes for rations which were meal & beans & salt. For supper dumplings and gruel. All we cooked. The breakfast for the morning beans & mush. Night very sharp & cold.

Saturday, January 28, 1865

Morning cold and very windy. Frost. Breakfast bean duff. I was on the wood squad again today. Worked rather hard. The wind chilled me through. Rations beef, meal & salt & molasses. No wood squad. In Camp meal & beans & salt. Supper dumplings & mush. I feel rather old about 50 yrs.

Sunday, January 29, 1865

Morning cold and frosty. Breakfast beans & mush & beef. News of an Armistace to be got up for 40 days. A proposition for peace.

In the following diary entries, Hopkins is beginning his near-fatal illness:

Thursday, February 2, 1865

Morning cold and clear. Breakfast beans & corn cake. Considerable talk of going to Columbia, S.C. I am not well today at all. I have a slight touch of the chills. Rations to Camp wood at 4½ then meal & beans & salt at 5½. Supper dumplings & mush. Day cloudy and look for rain. Night damp air.

Friday, February 3, 1865

Morning cold and cloudy. Breakfast beans & soup & mush. Exchange news springs up again. Rain for 1 day. I have felt terrible all day with a fever and chills severe headache. Rations arrived at 5 P.M. Meal & beans and salt at 6 P.M. For our supper we are to have dumplings of corn meal.

Saturday, February 4, 1865

Sick. Typhoid Fever.

The interval from February 4th to 24th, I do not know a thing that took place. I was unconscious. I only know from what a comrade related to me after, he being an attendant. He said I was delirious for twenty-two days and nights, and that, with two exceptions, besides myself, every morning, every bed in that hospital was re-filled with a new patient - the others dying, except one man who lived three days, next bed to me; another, who lived two days. There were thirty-two beds in that place. After becoming conscious, the Doctor was at my side, as I looked up at him, he said, "By God, you will get well!" I wasn't sure that he meant that I should have died under his treatment, (of corn whiskey, oak bark and Dover powders), or whether he was surprised at my staying powers. I found out it was my vitality that he admired. He stroked me on the chest, and said, "You will live to get home, you have a constitution that few are blessed with. I wish I had such a one." He was a man not over thirty-six but looked seventy. Rheumatism had made a wreck of him - very lame, stooped, gnarled fingers emaciated form and features, and hair white. With all these ailments of his own, he was a man. He had some nourishing soup sent into me from his table, saying to me one morning "You seem like a real patient, staying so long. The others I hardly see more than once."

I improved a little, and could crawl on all fours if placed on the ground, as that was the only carpet, and that alive with vermin of several species. Complaining of my feet and a spot on the back of my head, also on my right hip, Baker looked me over and found there a round, block of wood. The "chambermaid" had failed to notice the short knob on it, was not upholstered, which had pressed a hole into the base of the skull, on the scalp which remained there for some months. The hip had the same kind of defect. My feet were much swollen, and purple, - the size of one foot was equal to two normal ones. Where the waist of my only garment (which were my drawers amputated at the half thigh, only trunk left, my shirt minus all texture, except the seam frame) was gird about the waist, the close friend of the soldier had congregated and colonized, by getting under the skin, making a home for their progeny. Baker was a New Jersey boy and he said, "I will bring soap tomorrow, and give you a good wash. Wash your trunks, and get you a "Nigger shirt." Next morning, Baker did not appear. His reason was a good one too. He was to be paroled and sent to Federal lines, so I was told, but the Confederates expected to quietly run them up to Goldsboro, North Carolina.

The bad news, next to Baker's non-appearance, was that which the Doctor announced after an examination. He emphatically declared that to live, I must have my feet amputated. I strongly objected, and argued that the operation was sure death, from gangrene, even though my weakened system stood the shock. He admitted that my argument as a probability. I said "Doctor, you have no particular interest in my life, have you? And if not, then allow me to be the one to decide." His reply was, "Well, damn it, I hate to see you die after such a hard and plucky struggle, even if you are a Yankee. And yet, you must die before long, whether we amputate your feet or not. You might escape gangrene and live; but you will always be a very, bad cripple." After another consultation with a colleague in surgery, it was decided to perform the amputation. Next morning was to be the hour. They came, stated the case to me,.and I asked them if they could state with any accuracy that I had one chance in ten thousand to survive the operation and avoid gangrene. I appealed to both of them, that I was a single man and was my own owner at this time, and unless they were intent upon experimenting on me, I would gratefully thank them to leave me die intact - if die I must - as I had no desire to live, even with both feet absent, and I knew that death would follow the operation, in a few days only, if not during it. I appealed strongly to the Doctor, who was first to greet me in coming out of unconsciousness, a short time prior. I assured him that I greatly appreciated his friendly and humane remark to me, that, he hated to see me die, after so gallant a struggle, that if he would let me die - if I must - let it be with an unmutilated body. They left me after telling me that I had some grit. I never saw either of them after, for the day following, the camp was almost depleted by sending the men away in trains intended for Goldsboro.

The next day, February 27th, and all men were taken out of Camp but twenty-four, who were in the Hospital, and I was one of them - all said to be too ill for removal, and of course, all were expected to die there. About the middle of the forenoon, I crawled out of the charnel house, as no one was in attendance, nor, could I hear a sound in there.

The men next to me on either side were stiff in death. I crawled down to the gate after some effort, and out on the frosty ground. I could see in the distance, the smoke of a locomotive, and heard its "toot-toot", concluded to make that attempt to reach there, while life lasted, for to stay, was a lonely death. By dint of the hardest work, I crawled to a low spot, that contained about an inch and a half of water at the deepest, and five or six yards wide, covered with an egg shell of ice. To crawl to the point where the rest crossed, was too far and no better as to water. I came to a conclusion at once, to cross though I felt that the chill would be my end, as the little blood in my system would be so chilled as to stop flowing. The method of locomotion was sapping my strength fast, as placing the arms at full length in front and use my hand and forearm to drag the body forward inch by inch, hard work indeed. However, I pulled through the water and ice, chilled to the bone, shivering, that wrenched the body. Several times, after almost complete exhaustion, I was willing to give up, yet, hope had not deserted me. I persevered and fought off despair that was creeping into my heart. I shut my eyes, saw home and friends and the past of life in that struggle, may it not have been, that the vision gave inspiration for another effort. I tried. The distance was too great for me to make it in my condition. I had thought it out, and about to cease the hopeless task - exhausted, breathless, slowly waiting for strength for one more last effort, the railroad seemed farther away - miles, so far as my ability to reach it, I was not seeing objects, the hearing almost gone, was I fainting, or dying!! I came out of the spell, recognized a voice, and near me I faintly saw forms, felt a touch, but saw no more until I awoke at the railroad, wrapped up, and near a fire.

INTERIOR VIEW OF THE HOSPITAL.

During the night, fires were kept up all about us - the sick and disabled - waiting for the single train of five or six cars "locomoted" by the only engine, which was in the last state of asthma - that would not accomodate many, thereby, making several trips to Wilmington, rather to a point seven miles above the city to the Junction of the North East Branch of the Cape Fear River, the distance was about twenty-two miles. The object of the fires about us, was first; to keep the guards and prisoners warm; second to note any escapes; third, to possibly keep life in those whom they wanted to pass to other hands. The intention to send us to Goldsboro, being frustrated by the burning of bridges above Wilmington, by Schofield, and Sherman was passing that way, Wilmington being now in our possession with Schofield holding all communications on the West.

The Confederates were forced to make terms for parole, or taking the results of a fight, with us on their hands, with sure defeat in sight. They chose to deliver us up to our Army, at above stated point. Up to this time, many had been sent up on the single track and train. While waiting for morning, taking such sleep as possible in our condition, two of us wrapped in a cotton covering, were very rudely wakened by the howl he gave. He was burned by the fire catching the covering, both of us were quickly rolled over together fire put out and order restored. Sleep was again wooed, but in vain, as my comrade was burned painfully and no remedies.

With daylight, came the train - and a train of horrors! The ground occupied by the waiting men who expect soon to be at home with friends in comfort and happiness, a very large number lay still in death, that came to them in the silent night. This made lighter work for the train hands, but more for the grave diggers. After a long wait for the train to get ready, we were finally put aboard. I was in the last car of the last train that left the camp, with prisoners and I, and the two remaining brothers, spoken of heretofore.

On the last trip at the expense of the defunct Confederacy, there were some novel railroadings. The engine had very little grade to climb at any time, and not a great load to pull, but it coughed and groaned and spit fire and made slow progress, yet to us, it was better than walking. Some of the boys said it took twenty-two hours to make the twenty-two miles. However, they stopped twice to wood up and water. The water was passed up to tender in pails by negroes, taken from a ditch alongside the railroad. Wood was passed in same hands. The steam came slowly, no matter who was fireman. After many hitches, we got under way, leaving Florence - the time seemed forever, as we left the sight of the last hell about ten o'clock A.M. and reached the Crossing, the point of negotiations about 2:30 P.M. a trifle over five miles an hour by "steam". At this point were Generals Schofield and Terry, with other officers galore. When the unloading of our car was taking place, General Schofield, after seeing so much misery and suffering from the former cars, was overcome by the sights that came from the last car - ours - with tears streaming down his cheeks - cheeks that never blanched in battle, though thousands died and were wounded badly. Yet the humane heart within him was weakened at such horrid looking, and unsightly objects of suffering. He called General Terry, and placed him in command, and left the scene. General Terry, fresh from his hard won Fort Fisher fight, that gave him Wilmington, was no exception to the piteous and heart-rending sights, for his tears flowed as freely as those of a child, as did those of every person present. Terry had instructions that, not a man should be returned to Confederate captivity, regardless of any defect in the program of parole. What a scene! Every man that greeted us, was wanting to aid us in every possible way. The dead were carefully removed and tenderly cared for by the comrades; the living were given every medical aid and made comfortable in a grove nearby - well sheltered, everyone covered warmly and given warm drinks and food, where it was safe to let them have it, fed to them, not allowed to gorge themselves. We were held here until we could be taken down to Wilmington; but alas many among us, who at last were released from the horrible past and had high hopes of reaching home and loved ones, had once more looked upon ''Old Glory'' but to die, sleeping peacefully away, feeling safe under the folds of the flag he loved and died for. Pitiful sights of friends from Northern homes had, by some means come to Wilmington to claim some loved one, and to take them home, but to find them not - or a corpse, in the latter case, they expressed sorrow at his death and joyful in the fact that they had the privilege of taking his remains to the home among friends - those he loved and that loved him.

    I finally reached the City of Wilmington, N. C. by the little toy steamer that seemed to be searching its way down a brook, so narrow was the stream that led up to where

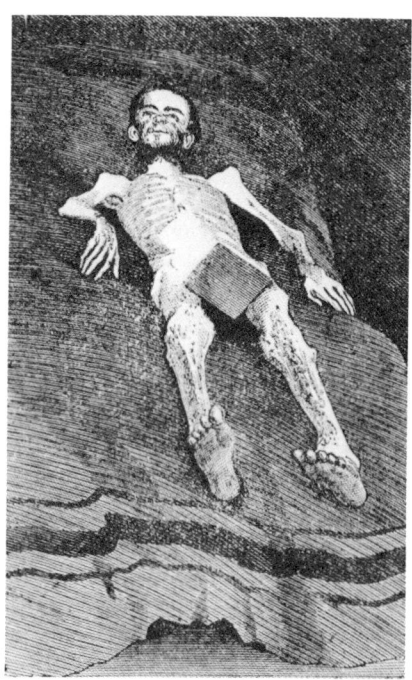
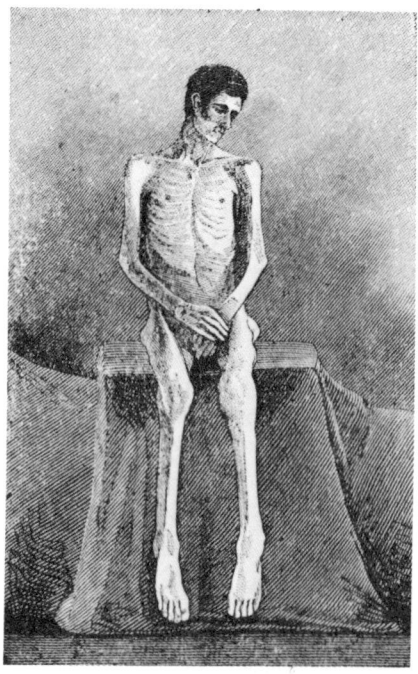

Engravings made of Union soldiers upon their return from Confederate prisons.

we embarked. At Wilmington, we thought our troubles at an end, plenty to eat - if you dared to - good water and comfortable lodgings. The two former, we enjoyed very much, but with so much good, came some unpleasant results. The Army Commissary had issued bread, meat, potatoes, onions and all such provision. Those who could masticate the solids were better off than those whose teeth had parted company with them, or the gums so swollen that anything harder than soup was the same as if out of reach.

While lying in a house near the street, and just off the wharf, seven of us had our meals prepared by a colored "Aunty", and we were doing very well, as she carefully cautioned us not to eat too much at a time as the food would sicken us. Some of the hungry ones wanted a taste of chicken. Aunty consented to get one for us - we wondered where. She did so, cooked it, making a nice lot of soup beside the meat. It was good - so good indeed, that to save any for another meal was not thought of - therefore, all was eaten, and for once in many months those seven stomachs were fully satisfied and very uncomfortable. Shortly after the filling was completed, what seemed a just punishment for such a violation of Nature's laws, followed. The weaker men lost all they had gained, and the action caused a revulsion to the stronger, who had jeered at the weaker ones only a few minutes prior, and they gave up also; thus, all was lost but the recollections of the feast of folly - the gain being, the experience, that prevented any more hoggish examples.

Tobacco was plenty. The wharf was covered with hogsheads of it and had, for the taking, and many took it, that never used it; others, chewed and smoked to their heart's content, and to the discomfort of others who could neither chew nor smoke, and I was one of that kind.

Finally, we were carried - those who could, walked - to the wharf and placed in the hold of the John C. Leary. We lay like herring across the floor, on cots or mattresses. The vessel had only been cleaned after the unloading of horses to replenish the worn Cavalry, and the horse smell was very distinct and not pleasant to the hundreds of weak and sick mortals in the hold.

Three ships left Wilmington on the same hour - two sister ships, that had brother names - John C. Leary and William Leary and the third was the General Lyon. The two last, went ashore at Hatteras Cape, in a rough storm and blow.

Almost the total number was lost, (including the crew) of fifteen hundred prisoners on the General Lyon, escaped prison to die on the ocean. I never heard of the rescue of one of them. Our vessel would, no doubt, have been one more to add to the horror, had not the officer in command of the vessel (not the Captain, but an Army officer) insisted that we steam beyond Hatteras before morning, by an all night run to avoid the gale that was indicated by the barometer, should break upon us. This was the night of February last, and March first, - bad weather at sea in this season. The other vessels lay to and out, south of Hatteras in supposed safety, but the terrific storm drove them on shore. Many times during that long and fearful night, we did hope to die yet knowing that we were on our way to home; still, the awful sickness added to all our other illness - made death welcome only come quickly!

We reached our goal, Annapolis, on a cold morning in a slight snowfall, practically naked, we were carried from the hold, in the arms of strong men, who wept as children at the condition of their comrades, who had been into the mouth of Hell and returned. Immediately wrapped in warm and soft blankets, carried through lines of hundreds of soldiers, where there was not a dry eye and some low tone imprecations escaped them. Placed upon hand cars, closely wrapped from the sharp of winter air - to us, at least, - as we had no flesh, no blood to speak of, hearts too weak to pulsate with action that would warm up what little we had. Though every man should be happy, he seemed listless and talked but little. From our vessel, with six hundred and eighty prisoners, I was told that a few over two hundred and fifty men were taken out alive, the remainder having died aboard. Some, I knew, died the day we left and before evening. Camp Parole was our destination. Some were to go to the Hospital; others to the Barracks. I was among the latter, by my request. Before entering the Barracks, we had to be born again before passing inspection. Taken from the cars by two men, and handled as gently as though

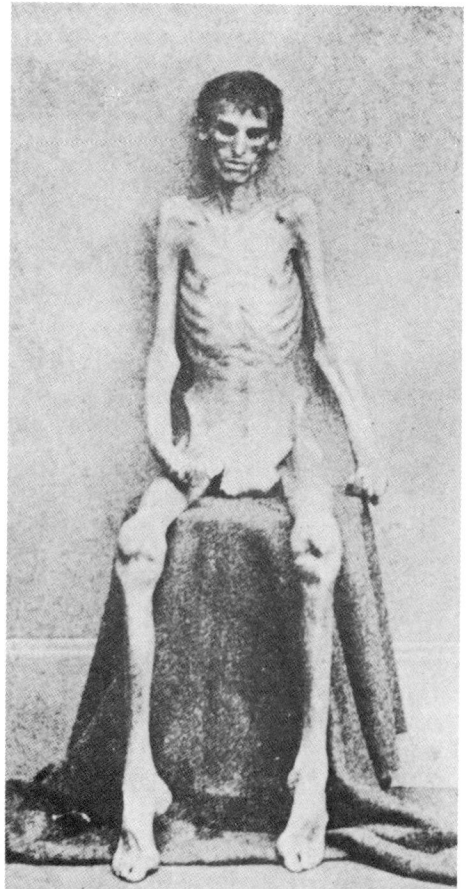
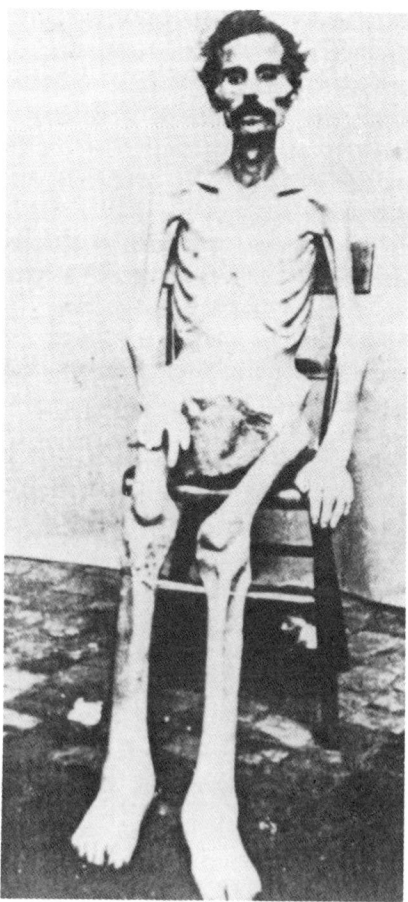

The "living skeletons" of Andersonville. Photographs were taken of the survivors to show the American people what crimes were committed at Andersonville and Florence Prisons.

we were glass, or eggs, as one put it, for fear of breaking something or falling apart.

In an isolated shanty, that had a front and rear door oppisite each other, a large opening on the right as you enter. Between the shanty and a long building, was a ditch, about three feet wide and no bridge. The ditch was filled with water, which was covered with something like tar or oil. I soon learned what it meant. The two attendants, in a jiffy, snatched my rags off, threw them out of the side opening, a man out there was busy at a fire and used a pitchfork to throw our only belongings on the fire. The slaughter was great, our friends cremated! I was whisked out of the shanty across the ditch into a wash or bathroom, or both - rows of long troughs on either side. I was lifted carefully into one, almost too hot, but it felt good to have a warm skin once more; was thoroughly soaped and scrubbed clean. Thus far was good, but now came the "process" of parting with close friends, that had taken possession of the most unexposed parts of our "parchment", and had burrowed a domicile under my cuticle, to raise and family and had, in some instances, sealed up the home entrance, which looked much like a small blister. They were our tormentors prior to our arrival at Annapolis, and had been very close to us for a long time, but now the Government furnished tormentors to torment and destroy them. Really, this process was the most nerve-racking, yet met with, especially to those who were weak already, but, it was a duty and the comrades who performed it, did it as gently as duty would permit.

After some minutes that seemed like months, they had punctured every "cave-dweller" from his premises, pressed the virus out, washed thoroughly the wounds made, then plumped me into cold water at once, thoroughly rubbed me down, applied ointment to the wounds made by puncturing, quickly passed me through a door into a woolen undershirt and drawers and socks. Now reaction set in and I felt that I might try and live, though pretty nearly exhausted. Into another room and a pair of pants that were meant for a man a foot and a half longer and three times broader than I; shoes, the same, but they were not put on, as my feet were not to be fitted by any Army shoe; a blouse followed, a coat also, (both misfits,) and a cap too small, resembling a pint cut on a four quart measure - but they made it fit by splitting down the back seam. Of course, I looked soldierly; but not able to carry my frame, much less the clothes. My comrades carried me into another room, a haversack, canteen, blanket and an overcoat were added to my "requisition". The overcoat was intended for a six footer of about two hundred and fifty pounds, arms like flails, skirts beyond my heels; however, they were mine as my Uncle Samuel said that I must be properly clothed. With my accumulated wealth of covering, etc., I was carried to my place in the barracks, was put to bed, clothes ditto.

Now, after all the precaution to leave behind me a "biting" reminder of the past eleven months about, I supposed that never, never again should I be the point of attack of a "grayback" or a "bluebelly", unless the former was armed with rifle and ball and my condition did not indicate very early resumption of hostilities in the field, but I soon learned that "graybacks" and rootbacks, were not the whole thing, as another "Richmond" was in the field, another strain of the insect was hailed in Camp, the bluebellies were just as persistent and prolific. I stood it a week (because obliged to obey Uncle's orders) and then started for a visit to some friends in Baltimore. Before leaving Camp Parole,

I wish to mention a few things which I noted and heard, notwithstanding that every move made was by the aid of one or two comrades about camp, as I could not walk, or stand alone.

Among the thousands that came to Camp Parole, many were sought by friends who had come from their home, north, east, and west. Many were longingly looked for through Camp and Hospital and not found, being among the dead in the prison Cemetery swamp or the depths of the Atlantic. The pathetic, earnest, searching look in every face in Barrack or Hospital, of fathers, mothers, and relatives, hoping to find their dear one yet alive. A sad, pale-faced mother, in deep black, with a look that indicated her distress at not finding her only boy, asking of men who had been imprisoned, if they did not know her boy, and could give tidings of him! The reply as softly as possible, "no, ma'am, I did not know him," seemed to wither her heart, as she sat down and wept, as only a mother can in such distress.

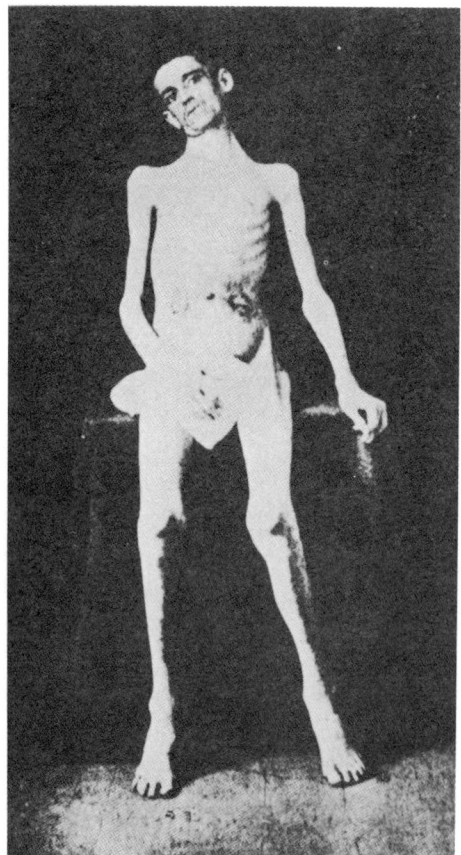

For those who defend Wirz and the Confederacy by claiming that the South could not feed her own soldiers along with the thousands of Federal prisoners, the question must be asked; Were there any Rebel guards found at Andersonville in this condition?

Another lady, moving among the men, keenly noting every one to discover her flaxen-haired boy, the idol of her heart, being a widow, also, by the war - and childless, if her boy was not found among the living - she having having heard that he was among those that came to Camp Parole. She had almost spent her last dollar to reach him and nurse him to health, or take him home, if alive, and his corpse if need be. To every man, she spoke kindly and keenly scanned their faces with a hopeful look that indicated she still thought to find him - a long search, and thus far had been futile, hoping against hope and about to give up the sad search, when she passed a bed nearing the end, gave not much heed to the occupant. With tears coursing down her cheeks and her chest heaving with convulsed sobs, she simply caressed the hand of the soldier who closely clasped it and looking up into her face, said "Mother, Oh, Mother, do you not know me?" Peering strangely at him, she was about to tell him he was wrong, thinking him delirious, when she was arrested by a mark on his temple she well knew. The greeting was one that would melt the strongest heart. She was in time to greet him and comfort him in his passage to Eternity in a day after. She was assisted to transportation and all the expenses home, cost of burial - that none could wish better. The Governor of her State cared for her and all her expenses. That great, generous War Governor of Massachusetts "Andrews"!

A father had come on to find what had become of three stalwart boys that had given up the New Hampshire farm for the native, inborn patriotism to protect the Flag and Country from the curse of division. Hearing from some source that his boys might be among the released, he came on to meet them at the Camp. After a long search, he learned from a comrade of his boys, that one had died in Salisbury, N. C., the other two, he had seen at Wilmington after release and thought they might or would reach Camp. After some time, he found one in the Hospital - only just out of danger from the typhoid fever; the other came into Camp a day later from Charleston, S. C. also ill with fever. He was over-joyed, though not sure that he would take either home alive, but sent the cheerful news home to the waiting, anxious mother and relatives. He settled down, and nursed his boys through the worst and took them home. Though, a man over seventy years, he was as boyish as any boy in his continuous efforts to cheer up the sick ones, who doubtless would have died, had he not been with them - as hope had practically fled from both, because of the weakness, fever had left them in. His playful actions and joyful talks of what mother and sisters would do when they saw them, kept the doleful thoughts from their minds.

These were a few of the many hundreds of cases of the search for loved ones, ending in joy, or most pitiable grief at results. Page upon page could be written of such pathetic scenes, as they crowd upon memory, when once the train of reflection starts, and with the recollections come unbidden tears from eyes that were used to harrowing sights, and the heart throbs again for the moment that quailed not at the cannons' havoc, the "ping" of the Minnie, the sight of the dead and dying on the field or carnage, or the hellish threats of Wirz and his compatriots. Among all the scenes that men who offered their lives at Country's call, were asked or compelled to pass through, from enlistment to death or imprisonment, death or release in Hospital or Camp, there was shown the true temperament of the man. Many yielding up life heroically, without a murmur; others easily and hopelessly.

Some men under the most distressing circumstances could find the opportunity for a joke, even at death's door. These features were clearly demonstrated in many instances in Andersonville and Florence, where men knew not how soon they would be the subject of dog burial - the man with hope and mirth most dominant in his make-up lived the longest and was calmest when death was at hand. Many died that may have lived longer, but for the hope that died within them, and made them melancholy. It was under the daily sights in these prisons that the "man" or "brute" within, developed. The manly man, under all depressing circumstances, his own illness and suffering, could find it in his heart to aid or comfort, to his ability, and to his own discomfort and hunger, those about him who seemed no worse than he, but unwilling or unable to try and live longer, by an extra effort.

On the other hand, the brute was dominant, he could find it a pleasure to rob his sick or dying comrade of every comfort and curse and abuse him for living so long. From such characters came the "Raiders". The genius of the Yankee, was always at work to take advantage of the watchful "Reb". At Andersonville, when squads of four from each "90" were allowed to go out under guard to get wood, some Yankees had the swapping spirit and if by some means, saved anything from a brass button to a shin plaster from the covetous guard at time of his entry to the prison, or "pasture", he would find some guard that would trade tobacco, or a vegetable of some kind for the trinket or "shinny".

At Florence the trading was easier. The Rebs were quite willing as the Yanks to swap, so that during the months of November, December and January when a certain number of men were detailed from the Camp to cut and carry wood, for the Camp, (not so at Andersonville), it was a daily occurrence for the Yanks to smuggle into Camp, beans, pork, onions, potatoes, - anything to eat! The "cutting" was located east from the stockade, in a swamp of gum and maple. The chopper or wood carrier made his dickers near the cutting; the chopper had a decided advantage as he was out all day, while the carrier had to make his deal while there to get his loads, and was compelled to move along in the gang to which he was assigned and be ready when they were ordered to march. The chopper could leisurely make his deal with the guard at his elbow, as it were; would split a stick in hand, hollow out the halves, pack his trade in it, put it together with split dowels at each end, smear it with dirt and walk into Camp with his cache, as each chopper was allowed to take one stick each day, as an extra ration. Some would hollow out a big stick, chip a groove each side of one end, dowel it together, thus leaving a hole to run in the beans to nearly or quite a half bushel in quantity, plugged up the hole and covered up the sign with dirt. This worked nicely for sometime, when a thrifty, but too strong a Yank, was noticed by an observing Reb, who was amazed at the size of the stick the Yank handled so easily. He wondered how any man could take such a stick so far, being of good size himself, was anxious to try his ability to handle it, and he was not careful and it burst open and "spilled the beans"! The ingenuity of the Yank was exposed and he was placed in the dungeon, under the guns at the east corner of stockade, as well as some of his fellow choppers. Thereafter, all sticks of choppers were tried with an axe, every man searched before passing into Camp - and the trade ceased. This recalls a brutal treatment at Florence upon a man named Wilson, who was a sort of a foreman of the choppers. He had winked at the trading, even aided it in every was possible - slyly - and had done some himself, was caught at it, removed from his "exalted" position, and sent to the "Bastile" above mentioned, which was a small stockade built of logs closely planted, about twelve to twenty feet or two hundred and forty square feet, floored above with logs and planking to hold a cannon and other paraphenalia, for readiness in case of a "break" by the prisoner. Under this, was the "Bastile" with its log door and no daylight, except such as sifted through the slight crevices, banked by earth, six or more feet high, outside (the stockade was banked the same and was the "promenade" of the guards) which made it literally a cellar into which the poor devils seeking escape, trading for food, and were caught, were thrown, to suffer as none can imagine. Wilson was "dungeoned" about the middle of January and could be heard nights, moaning - having had his feet badly frozen and given no treatment, besides being starved. Others were with him, but few of them made a long stay. Their condition had become so low, lacking food to make blood, thin blood, no clothing that had warmth, nothing to give the starved body strength, death came soon. Wilson, from the fact that he had fared better than any of them, his opportunity to get was better, and he was in fairly good condition until shut up in the Bastile, therefore, lasted longer. I never learned whether he died or not.

Another made of "humane" "Natural causes" treatment, was observed one morning, after having heard some awful shrieking and groaning, peeping through the open gate (no crowds were allowed to congregate in the street from the gate, as Lieutenant Barrett had ordered them shot) while passing along, with a couple of comrades to aid me, we saw a man - a Yank, as the guard said - who, for some violation of Barrett's orders had been tied by the thumbs behind, then gradually pulled up to the log plate of the building, at least two feet from the ground, and hung there until his arms turned in the socket at shoulder and he hung straight and limp. I learned that the poor fellow died from the torture. Only a little sooner, perhaps, than he would have died, but, the diabolic method of his taking off. Those, who saw, could only look, and not save or help. Some looked on, dazed; others, wept like children; more, groaned in sympathy; still more, heartily cursed the Confederates softly, some may have prayed, but curses and mutterings drowned all else. Had the wishes become instant facts, the Confederate Cause and its abettors, would long ago have been fighting The Devil for supremacy. But man proposes and God disposes - were it not better so? The end seems to prove it though so many thousands of the land's best blood have perished in the trying out, that gave the world, the greatest, the noblest and intelligent, liberty-loving Nation, On God's footstool.

I have digressed from my start home from Camp Parole, Annapolis, and will take it up and finish before side stepping again. I left Annapolis with a number homeward bound; I stopped off at Baltimore to see a few friends to whom I had written and I was met, seemingly by all of them. I had been paid at Annapolis my commutation for rations I did not get from Uncle Samuel, while in prison, and togged myself out in a civilian suit, minus shoes, as before stated, I was fitted as best my friend, Stang, the Tailor, could, to a man of skin and bone. I viewed myself and concluded that I might, with strong talk convince my friends it was I. After a very pleasant visit among Baltimore friends, who saw to my every want - I was wined, dined and taken everywhere about the City, until worn out nearly and requested them to let me on my way, as I had "blood relation" awaiting me. I passed on to Newark, New Jersey, stopped over to see a good Aunt, who had for months mourned me as dead, as well had my own family - having been written to from Camp Parole by two of my company mates, and another of Company "K" of my Regiment, that I had died at Florence, and they saw me dead - they having been exchanged in December. My letter from Camp Parole to my folks, preceded my funeral only three days, which service had been arranged for the Sunday following my letter. Of course all were very happy, even myself, that I had escaped Burial - no one knew where. A couple of days rest was good for me, and in those two days, had passed the soul of America's greatest martyr, to its Maker, Abraham Lincoln.

I reached home by the same route that I left it. The four years had made little if any change, as the same old stage and driver were at hand at Denville to carry passengers to Powerville and Boonton. While the train men were helping me to the stage, Jake Meslar, the crusty driver, became restive and urged them to hurry up; but when he saw me and was told that it was me, he spoke to me to be sure. I asked him if I had changed so much, that acknowledged, old bachelor - crusty, irritable man broke down and cried, - he was also a "Copperhead Democratic" - but this was too much for him. He became tender as a woman, and wanted to make me comfortable as possible. His only other passengers were three women, Mrs. Philip Wooton, Mrs. Barrett, and the other name has escaped my memory. Everything seemed to indicate a smooth passage, until we had gone only a quarter of a mile. The roads in April, were muddy, rutty and stony. The old thoroughbrace stage, a counterpart of Monte Monk's Wells-Fargo line, racked sideways, endways, and up and down. To a strong person, even if heavy, it was a constant struggle to "keep your seat". I lost my grip on the crutches and with no support, I was dashed head first into the laps of the two first mentioned ladies, who were both of goodly proportions, and ended my "leap" in a much mixed state, at the feet of those passengers. Helpless to rise or unscramble myself, they hailed the driver to stop, and with his help they insisted that I should lie across their laps, while the third lady took my feet for her portion and they were a goodly portion too, being swollen to more than twice natural size - and that was not Cinderella either - and this swelling extended to the knees. I objected to being a burden for them, but objections were useless. They insisted and won, and amid their tears and sobs and comforting service, I lived the five miles drive out. Instead of getting out at their houses, they asked to be driven to the house of my brother, that I should suffer no more changes until from stage to bed.

Somehow, the word of my coming had reached my home town, ahead of the stage and a great crowd had collected at my brother's house. Many comrades who had been discharged and had come home and engaged at their usual occupation. Many others, known by me and some others comparative strangers, were waiting to greet me. Men, women, and children - motive, to see a real Andersonville prisoner. Well, they saw him, as fast

The contrast of war. (Above) Charles Hopkins in late 1865. Beginning to regain his health, Hopkins was persuaded to wear a uniform for this photograph. Notice the weary face and the eyes which had seen the horrors of war and the hells of prison life. Compare it to the photograph (right) taken at the start of the war, showing the young, confident and healthy Charles Hopkins. His world had changed much in four years.

as they could pass in and out of the room. Our former family Doctor objected, but I insisted that it could do me no harm - I won. Dr. John Grimes attended me. My brother sent for my father and family to come from Succasunna to where they had moved after I had left for the Army. The Doctor thought it not proper to move me home at present, as I must have some rest and strength before another move, Physicians of prominence, known to Dr. Grimes came from several quarters - Morristown, Parsippany, Dover and as far away as Pompton, Newark, and Patterson - to "look me over", all concluded that my chances to live were slight, and that my legs must be amputated at the knees in order to have any chance. I asked them what my chances were if no amputation was made. All agreed that there would be none. What were the hopes of life if amputation was made? One in a thousand, maybe eight hundred! I asked again, who should decide - they or I? They differed among themselves, but I said, "Gentleman, I am sole owner and no one to leave behind to care for, and I say no!" I again won and after over two years of a struggle with inside and outside troubles, I began to mend perceptively. So much so, that I could walk alone by use of cane, putting that in discard after a short time. Time had proven that eminent physicians, sometimes err in their decisions; otherwise, I would have been legless, or dead, or both, while now quite enjoy the use of fairly good limbs and feet. This also proves that, hope is a good medicine. Youth, good blood, uncontaminated by dissipation, is also a great aid to recovery in such condition.

    I have visited Andersonville twice, since my sojourn there. Once, as a member of a Commission appointed by Governor Foster M. Voorhees, to erect a monument to the memory of New Jersey soldiers who died there. (Two hundred and thirty eight). The base of this monument and the ashlers were cut from stone known as conglomerate, or "pudding stone" from its particolored character, and the stone was taken from within two miles of Boonton, New Jersey; Hence, New Jersey had something more than the privilege of paying for the monument. The monument proper was of Barre Granite of shaft construction surmounted by a fully equipped private soldier, standing at rest, facing South. This was the first monument erected at Andersonville, and it stands in the Cemetery, among New Jersey's dead. On one face at half its height, is a scroll on which is inscribed,

"DEATH BEFORE DISHONOR!"

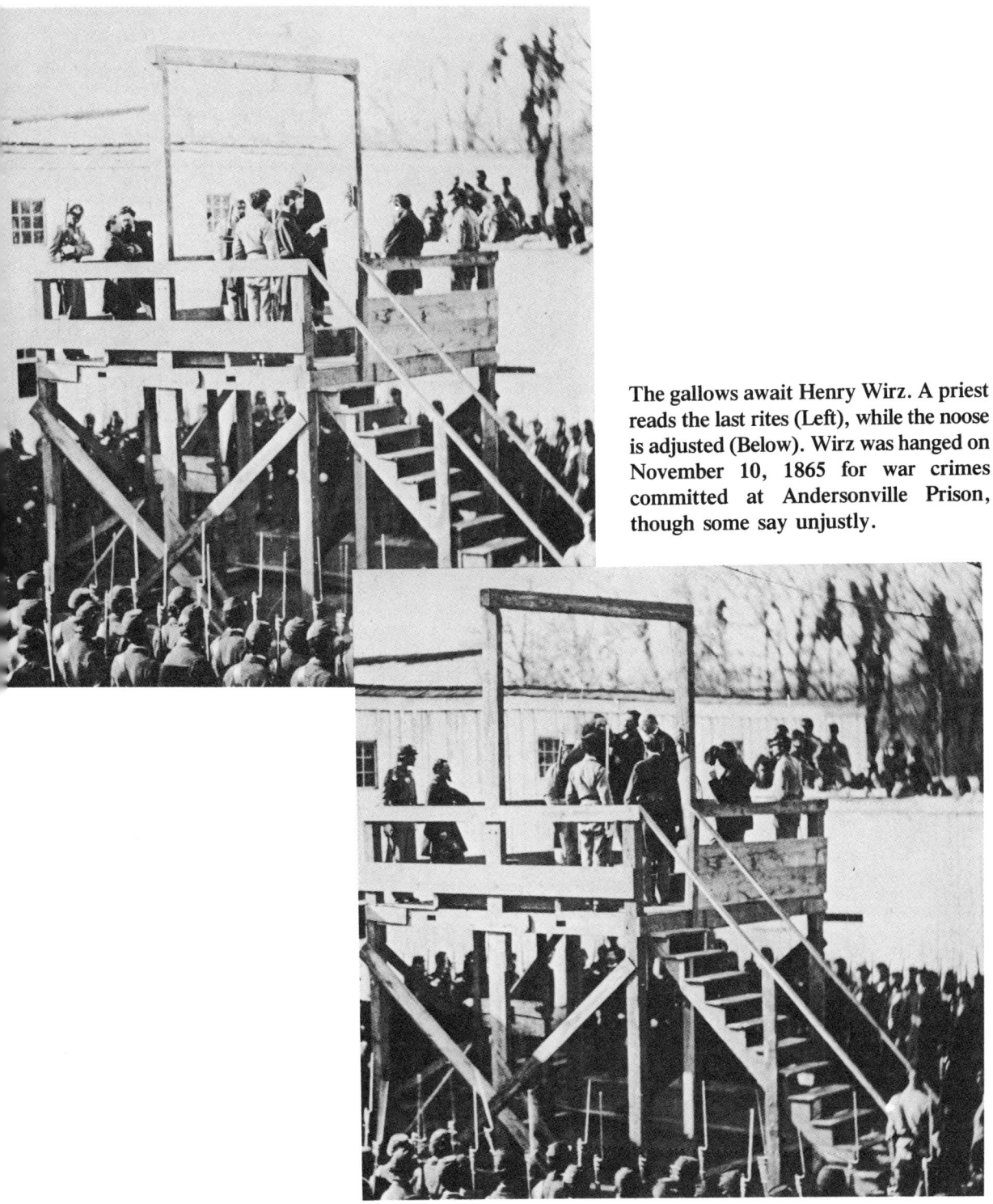

The gallows await Henry Wirz. A priest reads the last rites (Left), while the noose is adjusted (Below). Wirz was hanged on November 10, 1865 for war crimes committed at Andersonville Prison, though some say unjustly.

CHAPTER SIX
THE POST-WAR YEARS

A PORTFOLIO OF ANDERSONVILLE PHOTOGRAPHS TAKEN BY CHARLES F. HOPKINS IN 1899

All captions are written by Charles Hopkins.

W.S. Jackson and Walter A. Young standing where logs were thrown across the stream and within five feet of where the dead line crossed the stream. The water at lower left corner is where men lost their lives while getting water. Being shot down by guards for putting hand on dead line, which was a board strip 4 inches wide on posts 3 feet high.

Two stakes show where the dead house stood outside of south gate. The piece near longest stake just showing above ground is a piece of one of the posts.

Mr. Hopkins standing where he last laid before leaving stockade in 1864.

Capt. R. A. Clark standing on the edge of a tunnel opening from which C.F. Hopkins and 14 others escaped in August 1864.

Where water was dipped at dead line and men shot for placing hand on dead line.

Mayor W.S. Jackson of Belmar standing in the old site of the fire place of Genl. R.B. Winder. Head Quarters, inside of the Star Fort.

Mr. Bailey at Providence Spring, between dead line and Stockade, on west side.

W.S. Jackson sitting near the well at Winders Hd. Qrs. in Star Fort.

South west corner post of stockade, looking north east, Stockade House in distance.

Monument in course of erection, Mr. Jackson and Young in foreground. Group to the left are colored citizens. The row of head stones are sample of all in the cemetery.

Pvt. Charles Hopkins rescuing wounded Sgt. Richard Donnelly from the Confederate onslaught in this sketch taken from *Deeds of Valor from Records in the Archives of the United States Government*, edited by W. F. Beyer and O. F. Keydel, 1907, published by the Perrien-Keydel Company, Detroit, MI. It was for this action that Charles Hopkins was awarded the Medal of Honor.

Charles F. Hopkins circa 1890.

The following account is from Deeds of Valor.

DISTINGUISHED CONDUCT IN ACTION

Charles F. Hopkins touches briefly upon his rescue of a wounded comrade in his description on the action at Gaines Mills, Va., but he was reported and highly praised for this act.

"Our regiment, the First New Jersey Volunteers, was ordered from the south side of the Chickahominy River to support Fitz John Porter, who was attacked at that place, by 'Stonewall' Jackson and Longstreet, determined to crush our right wing. We reached the field about 1 P.M., and were sent in to relieve the Fourteenth Regulars. The First Michigan's right was turned, and they were swept from the field for a short time. This left an opening by which the Fourth New York Volunteers were taken prisoner, only about ninety escaping, our regiment being compelled to retire its right. A similar movement was taking place on the left, leaving our company in the apex of the angle, thus made.

"The order to retire, keeping up the fire, was given by our captain. Not hearing the order, or unconscious of the dangerous position, the company did not retire promptly, and the enemy poured a terrific fire on us from every point but our immediate rear, and even that was not exempt until we reached a point parallel with the line of battle.

"A comrade and myself were laggards in retiring, but were keeping up the fire. Having been twice wounded, I was looking for shelter to cover by backward movement, and, while moving from one place to another among the bushes, came across Sergeant Richard Donnelly of our company, who was badly wounded in the right leg. I told him I would take him out, and we could both chance the awful fire from all quarters. I got him on my back, and through that gauntlet of flame and bullets, made my way to the rear in safety.

"I was badly wounded in the head twenty minutes after leaving him, and was left for dead on the field, but recovered, and was taken prisoner the next morning, being released five hours later with a large number of wounded who were able to walk."

Two of Hopkins' proudest achievements: the markers to Generals Isaac Stevens and Philip Kearny at Chantilly, Virginia and the equestrian statue on Philip Kearny's grave at Arlington National Cemetery.

Charles Hopkins stands proudly in front of *his* monument to General Philip Kearny.

Newspaper clippings about the removal ceremonies of Gen. Philip Kearny's remains. (Above) Also a response card to Charles Hopkins for attendance to the ceremony (Left).

Charles Hopkins can be seen at the far right of this newspaper photograph of the workers removing General Kearny's coffin from the vault at Trinity Church Cemetery, New York City. Charles Hopkins was president of the commission in charge of the removal and also was an eyewitness to the identification of the general's remains when the coffin was opened for inspection.

General Kearny's body after being placed on a caisson is paraded down Broadway with much ceremony.

A PORTFOLIO OF PHOTOGRAPHS TAKEN BY CHARLES HOPKINS IN 1912 OF THE GENERAL PHILIP KEARNY REINTERMENT CEREMONIES AT ARLINGTON NATIONAL CEMETERY

All captions are written by Charles Hopkins.

President Taft and staff.

Head of Column. Capt. Lindsey 15th Cavalry.

Order of Procession; Band 15th Cavalry.

A Troop, 15th Cavalry, 1st Platoon.

B Troop, 15th Cavalry, 1st Platoon.

2nd Platoon, B Troop, 15th Cavalry.

D Troop, 15th Cavalry, 1st Platoon.

2nd Platoon, D Troop, 15th Cavalry.

Kearny's body on caisson and Detachment, 3rd Field Artillery.

Saluting Detachment D. Battery 3rd Field Artillery.

Saluting Party. 3rd Field Artillery and flag at half mast.

The unveiling of the Kearny statue at Arlington National Cemetery, November 11, 1914. President Woodrow Wilson and New Jersey Governor James Fielder along with dignitaries and the survivors of Kearny's New Jersey Brigade. Including Charles Hopkins (foreground), John Watts Kearny (behind Hopkins), Thomas Kearny (behind Wilson), and Gen. Kearny's great-granddaughters.

This article was taken from the National Tribune on November 19, 1914.

President Hopkins Delivers the Monument

Comrade Charles F. Hopkins, President of the Commission, presided. The battery fired the National Salute, the band played "The Star-Spangled Banner" with everybody rising and saluting, Rev. Dr. John Van Schaick delivered the invocation, and then President Hopkins, taking the stand, said:

"Mr. President, Gov. Fielder, Ladies and Gentlemen and my Comrades: Today is our second visit to this sacred and beautiful God's acre to do honor to the hero of four wars, two in which he served under the eagles of France, two under our own glorious flag, in all he distinguished himself for valor and military genius, and gave his life for his country at Chantilly, but a few miles from where we now stand.

"Today will be the closing scene of 12 years of devoted and untiring effort on the part of the men that loved, admired and never forgot their old commander, and revere his name and memory. The movement to make safe for all the future and prestige of that magnificent soldier. Phil Kearny, originated in the ranks of his old First New Jersey Brigade, who, thru the Kearny Commission, appointed by the Governor of New Jersey (now the President of the United States), have accomplished their work; not without shadows and moments of depression, as well as sunshine and times of exultation, but not to be denied in their efforts, they bring their offering today, as proof of the efficiency of their work.

"Many of our comrades deeply interested in the outcome have fallen asleep on the wayside in the past 12 years; twice has the great conqueror visited the original committee from the brigade, and twice the Kearny Commission has felt his touch; yet, with deep sorrow for those gone, just a little in advance, we today rejoice and are happy to know that we have carried out their great desire; that our beloved Kearny should sleep among his comrades, in this beautiful spot, and among the heroes of the civil war, and that his resting place be marked by a suitable memorial, worthy of the man and his brilliant achievements. This memorial has an added distinction, in the fact that, thru the kindness of the War Department of this great Nation, New Jersey has been allowed to place the first equestrian work in this cemetery.

"I wish to state that the genius designer and sculptor of this work about to be given to public view, is a man too modest to publicly announce his work as complete, rather desiring that his work speak for him, and we believe it will be emphatically granted by all that the work of Edward C. Potter is well done, and that the stone work and statue as completed reflects much credit upon Messrs. Potter and Edwards.

"Gov. Fielder, on behalf of Kearny's First New Jersey Brigade, in fact, every soldier that knew Gen. Phil Kearny, we wish to express thru you, the Chief Magistrate of the State of New Jersey, their grateful thanks to the State of New Jersey for the generosity that has made possible the removal of the remains of Maj.-Gen. Philip Kearny from Trinity Church yard, in New York City, to this place, and the erection of an appropriate memorial to his memory.

"The Commission assigned by the Governor of New Jesey to perform this work desire to say that they have been given every assistance possible by the State, thru the Legislature, the Governor and every department in which we came in touch, the greatest courtesy has been granted us, and we most cordially thank every one of those gentlemen, thru you.

"I now place in your charge, on behalf of the Commission, the complete work, in which we have a pardonable pride, when we say it will be found a realistic combination of horse and rider, and a striking resemblance of the man and a credit alike to the sculptor, and the State of New Jersey."

The Kearny statue before its shipment to Arlington National Cemetery.

Reunion badges and ribbons from Charles Hopkins' Veteran organization, Kearny's First New Jersey Brigade Society.

(Left) At the monument dedication ceremony at Chantilly, Virginia, Lucy Kearny Hill recites the poem *Kearny at Seven Pines*, while Charles Hopkins reads along (Far Left). Kearny's descendants, including the General's son, John Watts Kearny, gather around the monument (Below).

In 1915, Charles Hopkins read an account of General Philip Kearny's death and learned that the bullet which killed the General had been given to the Kearny family. Hopkins wrote to Agnes Kearny Upshur, the widow of the General, and inquired if she still had in her possession the bullet that killed her husband.

The following year, Agnes Kearny Upshur presented the fatal bullet to Charles Hopkins for his caring.

Dear Mr. Hopkins-

Washington D.C.
January 6th 1916

It is so long a time since we have had any communications. I hope you are well and I send you good wishes for the New Year. I have been opening boxes which have been stored away for years, containing old relics, many connected with the Civil War. I found the fatal bullet which killed Gen. Kearny. At once I thought you would like to have it, perhaps some of those devoted soldiers so I write to ask you if I may send it to you?

Of course I cannot in my old age keep stored away those things which years ago, I would not give to any person, and I would love to think of this in "the keeping of some soldier."

Sincerely yours

A. Upshur.

The fatal bullet that killed General Philip Kearny.

Dear Mr. Hopkins,

As you say "strange things happen." It is a strange thing that after 53 years I forgotten where abouts, the bullet, that killed General Kearny should come into your possession. If you succeed in establishing its identity by signing of statements the relic will be most interesting and unusual. It cannot fail, in years to come, if carefully preserved, to appeal to the imagination of future generations, just as we now look upon the personal belongings of the great dead of our early history. It is gratifying to know that the relic has come into hands that will hold it in reverence.

It was very pleasant to hear from you again, as I used to when you were engaged in the work of securing at Arlington, a fitting resting place for the remains of General Kearny. The whole family feels grateful for your untiring labor in carrying to a successful and impressive conclusion the whole affair.

I will be glad to learn what further progress you make in the certification of the bullet. I beg of you to present to Mrs. Hopkins and to your daughter my kindest regards and you yourself believe me.

Yours most sincere
John Watts Kearny

In 1987, Thomas Hopkins, the grandson of Charles Hopkins, presented the bullet to Mr. William B. Styple of Kearny, New Jersey.

Taken from *The World,* December 21, 1927

His Citation for Gallantry Under Fire 65 Years Ago Finally Arrives

It begins to look as if the Government is never going to let Charles F. Hopkins, Civil War veteran of Boonton, N.J., forget that back in December, 1892, Congress awarded to him the Congressional Medal of Honor "for distinguished gallantry under fire" at Gaines Mills, Va. June 27, 1862.

Yesterday Mr. Hopkins received a citation and award of certificate from the War Department in documentary proof that to him had been awarded the Congressional Medal of Honor sixty-five years ago. That seems a long time to wait for a citation, but Mr. Hopkins never was one to keep pestering the Government for a recognition of something he had done as a matter of course. In fact, so loath was Mr. Hopkins to ask for anything like that, that he did not receive the medal until thirty years after it had been awarded to him.

The act of valor for which Mr. Hopkins was honored was carrying a wounded comrade more than a mile under fire to a safe place, although he was twice wounded himself. Hopkins was a Corporal, and the man he saved was Sergt. Richard Donnelly, father of the present Mayor of Trenton, N.J. Hopkins never would apply to Congress for his medal. Sergt. Donelly, since dead, finally took matters into his own hands, and at the time of President Cleveland's inauguration, in 1892, went to Washington and explained that Hopkins never would get the medal if Congress waited for him to apply for it in person. The medal was accordingly sent to Hopkins, July 27, 1892.

Hopkins will be eighty-six next May. Jan. 7 he and his wife, whom he married soon after he was mustered out, will celebrate their sixty-first wedding anniversary.

62 YEARS LATE!—
Charles F. Hopkins showing wife the hero medal awarded him for Civil War service. He received it only a few days ago.

No. 201

MEDAL OF HONOR CERTIFICATE

ISSUED UNDER THE PROVISIONS OF THE ACT OF CONGRESS APPROVED APRIL 27, 1916.

To whom it may concern:

This is to Certify, That Charles F. Hopkins was enrolled on the tenth day of June, 1861, to serve three years, and was discharged on the twenty-first day of April, 1865, by reason of being a paroled prisoner of war while holding the grade of Private, in Company I, First Regiment of New Jersey Infantry Volunteers; that a medal of honor was awarded to him on the second day of July, 1892, for distinguished conduct in action at the battle of Gaines Mills, Va. June 27, 1862, when he voluntarily carried a wounded comrade under heavy fire, to a place of safety, and though twice wounded in the act he continued in action until again severely wounded; that his name was entered and recorded on the Army and Navy Medal of Honor Roll on the second day of June, 1916, as authorized under the provisions of the Act of Congress approved April 27, 1916, and that he is entitled to receive the special pension granted by that Act.

Given at the War Department, Washington, D. C., this fourth day of October, 1916.

By authority of the Secretary of War:

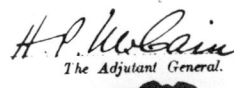
The Adjutant General.

Charles Hopkins' Medal of Honor Certificate. Along with the two medals awarded to Corporal Hopkins for bravery at Gaines's Mill, Va. Both are Medals of Honor, the one on the left being the original and the other a later type.

Mr. and Mrs. Charles F. Hopkins

Charles Hopkins with his children, circa 1931.

Among Charles Hopkins' papers there was found a simple speech written for the Memorial Day gatherings in the various cemeteries in the Boonton, N.J. area.

Boonton, N.J. May 31st 1920

Again we are called upon to observe the day that is set aside for honoring the dead, that died for the cause that welded this Nation as one, and fought to save from desecration, the flag that bespeaks Liberty to all who claim its protection.

Fifty-five years have passed since the rattle of musketry, and the roar of cannon have become quiet in the war to save a Nation, that made it possible to become the real Arbiter of the greatest War in the history since the birth of man.

The veteran of 1865 is answering "here" to the last rollcall by the thousands annually, and a few years will complete the list. Then, the most unique body of men will have passed into history without perpetuation. The Grand Army of the Republic name dies with the death of its last member. The new splendid body of young men will take up the work and finish as has the G.A.R.

Beautiful Memorial Day service is fitting in all communities and it should be sacredly observed for honoring the dead that gave their all to save a Nation whole. The successful Civil War made the World War a success so far as this country was concerned. Honor your dead, and you honor yourself.

The New Jersey monument at Andersonville National Cemetery.

Newspaper clippings about the final reunion of Kearny's New Jersey Brigade on September 25, 1925. (Below) Charles Hopkins stands far right in this photograph of the remaining survivors of Kearny's Brigade.

The following article is from the New York World.

"We who are about to die salute you."

Sixteen white heads nodded cheerily. Fifty younger persons swallowed and blinked mistily.

Among them was one especially honored guest - Patrick Tumulty, uncle of the secretary to President Wilson. He was one of fourteen cavalrymen to capture Sitting Bull; he helped to bury Custer where he lay beside the river where the Indians had shot him down. He fought with the Irish Brigade of the old 69th at the age of fourteen. Private Tumulty pulled at his goatee.

"I am," he said, "the last of the older Tumultys. And I was the only sensible one of the lot, if I do say so."

Before the dinner, the fifteen of Kearny's men - Private Finnegan and Lehlbach had not arrived - voted to disband the society which had bound them together since 1891.

March "Gaily" to Death

"There were 6,000 of us who fought in the brigade," said Private Hopkins, eighty-three years old and the "baby" of the outfit. "Not many came home from the Wilderness. Six hundred joined the society in 1891. Last year only forty-two came to the dinner. This year less than twenty. All my letters come back marked 'deceased'. I think we ought to disband as a body, instead of decaying separately. We're all close to death. Let's march toward it in a body, the way Kearny used to say "Gaily, boys, gaily.' "

Unanimously they voted to accept death in a group as if it were already present. Then they sat down to dinner. For the last time they pressed their lips to each others ears to share reminiscences, for the last time they rose to give testimony to their love for Phil Kearny, who was killed on the Chantilly battlefield.

After the dinner the last of the brigade formed for their photograph. They walked slowly to the Kearny statue in Military Park. Then a wreath was laid. a Bugle blew "taps"

Private Finnegan and his comrades went home to die.

The following obituary appeared in *The New York Times*, February 15, 1934.

CHARLES F. HOPKINS DIES IN NEW JERSEY
State's Only Survivor of Civil War Holding Congressional Medal of Honor
Once Mayor Of Boonton
Modestly Declined to Apply for the Medal Until Thirty Years After It Was Awarded

Boonton, N.J., Feb. 14 - Charles F. Hopkins, the only surviving Civil War veteran in New Jersey holding the Congressional Medal of Honor, died this afternoon at his home here, 209 Williams Street. He was 91 years old and had been ill since last June with ailments incident to his age. Mrs. Hopkins died in 1931, sixty-four years after their marriage. Four daughters and three sons survive: Mrs. A. Lefferts, Mrs. William Milner, Mrs. Ella Relyes, Mrs. E. A. Fisher, Emmet, Frank and Charles Hopkins. A funeral service will be held here at 3:30 P.M. Saturday in the First Presbyterian Church. Burial will take place in Greenwood Cemetery.

Mr. Hopkins was the last survivor of the first Common Council of Boonton. He had served as Mayor of Boonton and as chief of the Fire Department. In the eighties he sat in the lower house of the State Legislature and for twenty-one years he held the postmastership of Boonton under Republican administrations. He was a former chairman of the County Board of Elections. Several years ago he perfomed his last task of a public nature, the compilation of a list of all the Civil War veterans of Morris County, living or dead.

By an act of Congress of December, 1892, the Congressional Medal of Honor was awarded to Mr. Hopkins "for conspicuous gallantry under fire at Gaines Mills, Va., June 27, 1862." The specific act was performed after he, himself, had been twice wounded. He carried from the field a fellow-soldier with a shattered knee, Sergeant Richard Donnelly, father of a later Mayor of Trenton, N.J.

But owing to his modesty in declining to apply for the medal the hero did not actually receive it until thirty years after the award. In 1892 the man he had saved learned that his rescuer had hesitated to apply for it, and set the wheels in motion that led to its delivery to Mr. Hopkins. And through some clerks' carelessness in the War Department the certificate and citation did not reach him until 1927.

Mr. Hopkins was captured by the Confederates and was confined for a time in Libby prison.

He was a member of General Philip Kearny's brigade and for years after the war he was a leader in the affairs of the Kearny Post of the Grand Army of the Republic in Newark. As secretary of the post at the time of its disbanding in September, 1925, he buried the relics of the organization beneath the statue of the General Kearny in Newark.

The gravestone of Charles and Hetty Hopkins.

Members of Company E, 15th New Jersey Infantry at wreath laying ceremonies at the grave of Charles F. Hopkins in 1988.

This poem was found among Charles Hopkins' papers. It is an excellent example of the outlook on life that Charles Hopkins carried through his many years.

It Isn't The World
It's You

You say the world is gloomy,
    The skies are grim and grey,
The night has lost its quiet,
    you fear the coming day?
The world is what you make it,
    The sky is grey or blue
Just as your soul may paint it;
    It isn't the world--it's you!
Clear up the clouded vision,
    Clean out the foggy mind;
The clouds are always passing,
    and each is silver lined.
The world is what you make it--
    Then make it bright and true,
And when you say it's gloomy,
    It isn't the world--it's you!

CHARLES F. HOPKINS

BIBLIOGRAPHY

Atwater, Dorance. Prisoners Who Died at Andersonville Prison. 1865.

Beyer, W.F. Deeds of Valor from Records in the Archives of the United States Government. Detroit, Michigan, 1907.

Biographical and Genealogical History of Morris County, New Jersey. New York: Lewis Publishing Company, 1899.

Kearny, Philip. Letters from the Peninsula: The Civil War Letters of General Philip Kearny. Edited by William B. Styple. Kearny, New Jersey: Belle Grove Publishing, 1988.

Kearny, Thomas. General Philip Kearny: Battle Soldier of Five Wars. New York: G. P. Putnam's Sons, 1937.

Kellogg, Robert. Life and Death in Rebel Prisons. Hartford, Connecticut: L. Stebbins, 1867.

McElroy, John. Andersonville: The Story of Rebel Military Prisons. Toledo, Ohio: D.R. Locke 1879.